transnational america

Next Wave: New Directions in Women's Studies

A SERIES EDITED BY INDERPAL GREWAL, CAREN KAPLAN,

AND ROBYN WIEGMAN

transnational
america

Feminisms, Diasporas, Neoliberalisms ✶ **Inderpal Grewal**

DUKE UNIVERSITY PRESS ✶ DURHAM & LONDON ✶ 2005

© 2005 Duke University Press

All rights reserved

Printed in the United States of America on acid-free paper ∞

Designed by Rebecca Giménez

Typeset in Scala by Keystone Typesetting, Inc.

Library of Congress Cataloging-in-Publication Data

and republication acknowledgments appear on

the last printed page of this book.

contents

✷

ACKNOWLEDGMENTS
VII

INTRODUCTION Neoliberal Citizenship:
The Governmentality of Rights and Consumer Culture
1

ONE Becoming American: The Novel and the Diaspora
35

TWO Traveling Barbie: Indian Transnationalities and the Global Consumer
80

THREE "Women's Rights as Human Rights": The Transnational
Production of Global Feminist Subjects
121

FOUR Gendering Refugees: New National/Transnational Subjects
158

FIVE Transnational America: Race and
Gender after 9/11
196

NOTES 221

BIBLIOGRAPHY 241

INDEX 267

acknowledgments

✷

Books are never written alone. No lonely author scribbling away undisturbed. No room of one's own but then, that room would make intellectual work very lonely, and not very interesting. Also there would be little at stake in such an endeavor. It is because I have been so fortunate to have many insightful people to talk and think with that I can write. And because there are communities to care about, there is something I care to write about. The hours of writing were all the more precious because they were often difficult to come by and there was so much to write about. My thanks to all those whose inspiring work I heard, read, saw, and listened to all through the years. Some of those I have lost touch with or see only occasionally and some I talk to every day. But they are all remembered and valued.

First of all my thanks to my dear friend and co-author, Caren Kaplan. So much talking, thinking, debating went on all of these years since our first jobs in D.C. This book could not have been written without the discussion and writing and work that went into our writings together and without the important theoretical work on mobility and travel and feminism that she continues to produce. Thanks to Caren also for reading so many versions of this book and for helping to nurture it over the years. My thanks also to Eric Smoodin for reading versions of this book, as well as for friendship and humor that enlivened many a discussion. His work in American history was invaluable to this book, and no one can surpass that fine ability to make chai. I am similarly indebted to Minoo Moallem for so much affection, collegiality, insights, discussion, and all the enjoyable times spent in her company—Minoo's work on gender and Islam and on migration helped me to think through a constellation of ideas about feminism and geopolitics. And Shaheen Bayat's presence made these events memorable: politics in Iran was an inexhaustable topic that never failed to excite us all. Parama Roy's friendship has been an important one—her sharp mind and humor, her careful analyses and readings, her passion for Hindi movies and music, and her dislike of Shahrukh's acting abilities never failed to add zest and enjoyment to our every meeting and conversation. Bharat Trehan's hospitality and humor added to the pleasure of each visit. Robyn Wiegman's passion about feminism and theory and her friendship and support were important, as were Tani Barlow's discussions about the future of women's studies, feminism, and internationalism. Cathy Davidson's friendship, support, and encouragement and her mentorship and her ideas have kept that important interdisciplinary flame alive. Leti Volpp has been a wonderful presence, as have her essays and talks and discussions; the aws community has been so supportive and taught me much about race and gender. The group writing against the war in Berkeley—Jenny Terry, Tina Campt, Paola Bacchetta, Caren, Minoo—all helped to sharpen my thoughts about America and the war. And that widespread feminist, women's studies, and social and cultural theory community would not be complete without Amrita Basu, Avtar Brah, Kum Kum Bhavnani, Lisa Bloom, Carolyn Dinshaw, Carla Freeman, Denise Gokturk, Sandra Gunning, Akhil Gupta, Miranda Joseph, Suad Joseph, Surina Khan, Donald Lowe, Purnima Mankekar, Donald Moore, Mimi Nguyen, Steve Poulos, Jasbir Puar, Erica Rand, Arvind Rajagopal, Priti Ramamurthi, Anupama Rao, Sherene Razack, Lesley Sharp, Ella Shohat, Harleen Singh, Alissa Trotz, Ginette Verstraete. Audiences and enthusiastic colleagues in so many places gave me venues in which to speak and their feedback and responses improved the work: thanks to some super audiences and interlocutors at uw Madison, Wesleyan, Rice, U Arizona, Emory, Duke, nyu, Stanford, uc Berkeley, uc Santa Barbara, uc Davis, uc Riverside, uc San Diego, uc Santa Cruz, Amsterdam, Josai University, U Toronto, ucla, Kyoto Seika University, the University of Washington, Seattle, Smith College, and the uchri research group.

At uc Irvine, some terrific colleagues have taught me a great deal in the time I have been here. My thanks go to Laura Kang, Kavita Philip, Victoria Bernal, Joanna Gislason, David Goldberg, Joan Ariel, John Rowe, Jane Newman, Susan Coutin, Bill Maurer, Tom Boellstorff, Teresa Caldeira, Mei Zhan, Jim Ferguson, Liisa Malkki, Karen Leonard, Dina Al-Kassim, Susan Klein, Joe McKenna, Annette Schlichter, Mark Poster, Susan Jarrett, Jill Robbins, Arturo Arias, Connie Samaras, Yong Soon Kim, Ketu Katrak, Glen Mimura, Philomena Essed, and Linda Vo. Thanks to Dean Karen Lawrence for the time and course releases to finish this manuscript. Thanks to CTI and its members—I learn from them all the time. A very extra and special thanks to Dani McClellan—she was incredible in her editorial help, and her friendship and support. Laura Stiel, who has turned things around in the short time she has been in women's studies, made it possible for me to spend time finishing the work on the manuscript.

In the Bay Area and at San Francisco State, where the bulk of this book took shape, I must thank my Narika friends—we have all gone through so much and done so much since we first met that it's hard to believe I don't live near them all anymore. So thanks to Manuela Albuquerque, Shobha Menon Hiatt, Nina Kabir, Huma Dar, Lalita Subas, Viji Sundaram, Naheed Sheikh, Chic Dabby, and Merula Furtado. Narika was also where I learned so much that went into this book and where I learned that failure was instructive; my experiences there taught me lessons about questions of agency and power that have certainly emerged in this book. I must also thank the energetic and enthusiastic group of women who were amazing as undergraduates and brought out the anthology *Our Feet Walk the Sky*, which had a very early version of one of the book chapters. My thanks to my colleagues at SF State: Minoo Moallem, Deb Cohler, Loretta Stec, Julyana Peard, Jim Quesada, Susan Sung, Myung Mi Kim, Roberto Rivera, as well as so many others. And to my students in the M.A. program who were early listeners and supporters of this project: many became so much more than students and so much a part of my life, in particular Sima Shakhsari, Neha Vora, Jenna Gretsch, Ambra Pirri, Kris Peterson—I have learned so much from them.

In India, Bharat Ponga, Neeta Baxi, Maninder and Minty Grewal, Narinder and Savita Goel, KumKum Sangari, Uma Chakravarty—your hospitality, discussions, and knowledge all were enlightening and made my research possible as I did my usual flying trips to India. The librarians at PAU Extension library in Ludhiana were so helpful. Thanks also to so many aunts and uncles and cousins and their families whose conversations, dinners, and visits made every trip special. It can't be work when it feels like going "back home" to a place so familiar!

I've had the good fortune to have had some superb research assistants: Gillian Harkins, Amy Parsons, and Priya Shah. Their investigative skills and legwork were invaluable, especially when administrative work filled my days.

The readers of this book were simply unsurpassed and I have a large debt to them. They were insightful, helpful, encouraging, careful. All of their ideas helped make this book better in every way. I have nothing but appreciation and thanks for their time and their comments.

My special thanks go to Steve Siebert from Tech Support at Nota Bene. The manuscript could not have got out without his help—Nota Bene was right at the other end of the phone every time and came through unfailingly. I wrote my dissertation with Wordstar a long, long time ago and Nota Bene seems light-years away and so amazing every time I use it.

For Ken Wissoker, I have so much appreciation and thanks. He has been such a supporter all these years—an editor beyond compare in every way. I am so fortunate to have had his support and friendship all these years—we have shared some fabulous and unforgettable times. It is thanks to him and his vision and work that interdisciplinary cultural studies, critical theory, and a combination of area studies and race and gender studies have come to be an important part of academic knowledges. And through these years, Duke University Press's terrific staff have been outstanding; my thanks also to Emily Young, Courtney Berger, Christine Dahlin, Richard Morrison, Fred Kameny, and Erin Hathaway, and also to Alexis Wichowski for preparing the index.

For Jagdip Singh Sekhon, my great thanks and appreciation for sharing his work and his ideas—his devotion to the Sikh community in San Francisco, his extensive pro bono work, his commitment to political ideals were exemplary. The chapter on Sikh women refugees could not have been done without him: the information he shared, the files he let me read, and his insights into legal issues about refugee asylum.

To my brother Sukhminder, there are not thanks enough for these years of love and care. His intellectual curiosity about all kinds of topics, his passion about ideas, his observations have all borne fruit here in this book. He carries on single-handedly that venerable South Asian tradition of argumentation and interruption and provocation—there is nothing like that in academia. And he gives inspiration by his passion for politics as well as the courage to live as he does. He is one of few in my family who read all that I write—that in itself deserves my admiration. And where would our debates be without my other siblings and their partners and my nieces and nephews. In addition, I want to thank so many other family members who have been supportive and understanding. In particular, my wonderful aunt, Gurnam (a courageous feminist in all but name), and Walter and Cynthia Jessel.

And last but not least, this book is for Alfred, Kirin, and Sonal. All I do is for you and because of you. There are not words enough to express thanks so I hope I show it every day in different ways.

introduction

✳

This is a book about the production of middle-class Asian Indian and American subjects in the 1990s. As I seek to understand the changing relationship between politics, culture, and the market, my interest lies in the connections between feminism, new social movements, consumer culture, citizenship, and knowledge formation. In particular, this book focuses on the subjects and identities that grew out of the knowledges produced by feminisms, nationalisms of various sorts, forms of governmentality and disciplinary power, and consumer culture. I approach this set of issues by analyzing the circulations and travels of South Asian Indians between India and the United States, probing how gendered knowledge formations produced nationally and transnationally created identity and subjectivity at the end of the twentieth century. Through these circulations, I explore how gender, ethnicity, and consumer identity became entangled within both national and transnational formations. Within this entanglement, biopolitics and geopolitics came together along with disciplinary and governmental technologies to create neoliberal subjects. It is in this dissemination of neoliberalism, along with its assemblage of disciplinary power and governmental technologies, that America played a role, as the signifier of both an imperial nation-state and its practices, which could not be limited to the institutions of the state but circulated within what came to be called a "global civil society." The production of knowledges resulting in "global" process and "globalization" as a problem (or solution) by feminists and other scholars also forms part of the argument of this book, as it seeks to direct attention to how cosmopolitan knowledges came to be crucial in this interconnectedness that was (and is) called "globalization."

Rather than see the United States solely as an imperialist nation-state, I understand what is called "America" as a nationalist discourse that produced many kinds of agency and diverse subjects. America functioned as a discourse of neoliberalism making possible struggles for rights through consumerist practices and imaginaries that came to be used both inside and outside the territorial boundaries of the United States. American national identity worked, in a Foucauldian manner, as a mechanism that combined biopower with apparatuses of governmentality to produce discourses and practices of freedom and choice—yet these discourses and practices had older imperial histories and newer disciplinary formations that were also recuperated in new ways. This imperialism not only was a search for markets (though this aspect was also present) but provided the technologies—the strategies, the rationalities, and the subjectivities—contained within networks of deterritorialized and reterritorialized power. America was important to so many across the world because its power enabled the American nation-state to disseminate the promise of democratic citizenship and belonging through consumer practices as well as disciplinary technologies. The biopolitical aspect of neoliberalism was combined with geopolitics in creating America as a powerful nation-state and American national identity as both paradigmatic and exceptional.

To further elaborate on these claims, there are three main theoretical issues that I will address in some depth in the rest of this introduction. The first, about America and migration, examines the question of what America has meant transnationally to immigrants to the United States as well as to those who live outside the United States. I suggest here a theoretical and disciplinary issue: that America cannot be studied only within the territories of the United States and that postcolonial studies provides some useful ways of examining the relation between imperialism and culture. As a superpower, America produced subjects outside its territorial boundaries through

its ability to disseminate neoliberal technologies through multiple channels. Although the meanings of America cannot be the same everywhere, these meanings have genealogies that need to be contextualized historically. The relevance of America was not solely in the subjects it produced within the United States but in its ability to create networks of knowledge and power, cosmopolitan and "global," that traversed and rearticulated national boundaries. Consequently, even studies of diasporas in the United States must engage with historical studies of the relation between diasporas and the regions to which diasporas are connected, and thus we need an examination of transnational connections linked to diasporas.

The second issue is that of empire and power. Here my interest lies in the conjunction of geopolitics and biopolitics in relation to the production of gendered and racialized bodies and subjects. I describe what I call "transnational connectivities" within which subjects, technologies, and ethical practices were created through transnational networks and connections of many different types and within which the "global" and the "universal" were created as linked and dominant concepts. Appropriation of neoliberal discourses was only possible for particular subjects gendered, classed, and racialized in specific connectivities within which knowledge moved and could be accessed.

The third topic is feminism. While all along my concern has been how gendered subjects were produced in relation to race, class, caste, and other social formations, I want to also examine specific kinds of feminisms that were powerful enough to move along transnational connectivities. My particular focus here is the use of the concept of "choice" as a central ethical framework for feminist as well as neoliberal consumer practices and the imbrication of feminism with consumer culture. The conjunction of biopolitics and geopolitics has historically been made in the modern period through the production of gendered bodies that are differentiated from each other through territorial belonging within which race, class, religion, and nationality become meaningful. The problem therefore lies in what possibilities feminism might have within the neoliberalism in which it is taking shape at different sites and how it produces subjectivities linked to historical genealogies of feminist critique. Thus the question of cosmopolitan knowledges, feminist and progressive, is one that is important in the transnational making of knowledge producers (including academicians and activists or those who combine the two realms of work), who cannot escape neoliberal conditions of possibility but can, as changing, contingent subjects, not be incapacitated by this neoliberalism.

By examining different kinds of transnational movements—of migrants of varied classes, of goods such as Mattel's Barbie or the novel in English, of "global" feminists and asylum seekers, of ideas of cosmopolitanism and human rights—I will probe the connection between postcolonial knowledge production, the subjects produced by older and newer social movements, American nationalism, and the work of the market in producing these transnational connectivities as the social through technologies and rationalities of power.

MIGRATION, CITIZENSHIP, AND THE AMERICAN DREAM
✷

In August 2001, holders of H-1B visas in Silicon Valley worried about the downturn in the computer industry and possible layoffs. Some discussed moving to Germany, where there were possibilities of receiving five-year work permits known as "green cards." Others resisted the idea, after hearing about overt anti-immigrant violence, the need to learn German, and the temporary status for immigrants. They considered Germany a less attractive destination than the United States. After all, tech workers everywhere had heard about Silicon Valley and Bill Gates, and they believed that America was a better place for immigrants. As one Indian holder of an H-1B visa said to a reporter for the *San Jose Mercury News*, "I do not know anybody who would prefer to go to another place after living here . . . The American Dream is strong—have you ever heard of a German Dream?"[1]

The discourse of the American dream was clearly well known to this person. How did information about the American dream circulate around the world? What did this idea of an American dream mean to a newly arrived, middle-class, male migrant from India? To this man, it signified a nation as a place—specifically a California city—where racism was less visible than in Germany, where he could earn a living like other Indians who had come to the United States, where he would be allowed to stay more than the five years that he would be allowed in Germany, where he could speak the language he spoke in his workplace in metropolitan India, and

where he could afford to buy a house and consumer goods that he had
learned about from advertisements, movies from Hollywood and Bombay
cinema, cable TV, and returning and visiting migrants. The "American
dream" was a search for a future in which the desire for consumption, for
liberal citizenship, and for work came together to produce a specific subject
of migration. Although this H-1B visa holder may not have called himself an
American, he certainly participated in the discourse of the American dream
while simultaneously seeing himself as an Indian national. Was his participation in the dream any different from that of people who entered the
United States as immigrants or who became citizens? What was the role of
the American dream within American nationalism and in the world at the
end of the twentieth century and the beginning of the twenty-first?[2] In what
ways did Indian nationalism and race, gender, and ethnicity come to matter
to this migrant? To answer these questions, I will examine how Americanness in the 1990s was mediated among South Asians (specifically Indians)
in the United States and in India, and the networks of knowledge and
communication that produced information about America and what it
meant to participate in the American dream.

The Indian H-1B visa holder's ability to participate in the American
dream was made possible by the expansion of "high tech" jobs enabling the
United States to import workers from other parts of the world, mainly
India, China, and Taiwan.[3] These importations occurred because migrant
workers cost less to corporations, since they could be paid lower wages than
their domestically based counterparts, requiring no pensions or long-term
training or commitment. In understanding such migrations, we need also
to probe why certain groups of people rather than others came to constitute
these workers. Indian holders of H-1B visas represented a group able to
come to the United States because of a number of transnational discourses
in which English-speaking, middle- and upper-class Indian immigrants
were seen as highly desirable "tech workers" (more recently, this group of
Indians has been seen as appropriate for outsourcing work of all kinds).
These workers were hired by "body shops," which were employment firms
set up to import tech workers for computer firms in the United States. Body
shop owners, mostly males of Indian descent, used their contacts in India
to find candidates to bring to the United States. Central New Jersey, home

to one of the largest Indian communities in the United States, had a high proportion of these employment agencies, creating professional networks that tapped knowledge of and connections to India to bring workers, sometimes called "computer coolies,"[4] to the United States.[5] Similar body shops with connections to South Asia existed in Silicon Valley as well. Body shops were also connected, in the United States, to those Indian students and professionals who came to the United States after the immigration laws were changed in 1965, and who became seminal in the computer and information technology industry. This earlier group of migrants retained ties to India through family, caste and class, schooling, and professional networks that they continued to draw upon. It is these histories, produced out of socioeconomic and cultural formations in both India and the United States, that created some diasporas at the end of the century.

Transnational movements of people were made possible by earlier migrants who became cultural and, in this case, economic mediators, paying the visa and travel fees to import workers, but often also exploiting the workers as well. While Manuel Castells's work on the informational economy and on "network society" discusses the importance of information as a commodity, the idea of information in his work remains bound to the notion of knowledge production within information technology, rather than all the different kinds of information that made capitalism and information technology possible. In fact, professionalized networks were not simply professional.[6] Rather, as in the example of body shops, we see that culture, gender, class, nationality, race, and other factors also enabled the formation and maintenance of these networks. For instance, although the body shop owners, mostly males, were linked to their Indian counterparts, they also used their knowledge of educational systems, the Indian and immigration bureaucracies, family and kinship ties, and the Indian-American community to select and import workers.

Furthermore, information about America reached prospective migrants not only from a globalized media, or through professional and educational connections, but also from contact and communication with family members and neighbors who migrated in earlier periods. The Indian communities in New Jersey, Chicago, and Silicon Valley, to name a few urban centers where Indians formed a presence in the United States, were sites that gave newer immigrants the support they needed and also mediated

and materialized new articulations of the American dream. They translated
the dream in its ethnic and multicultural version, creating new discourses
of success in "America," and thus made it possible to be immigrants,
Indians, and ethnic and American subjects at the same time.

These multiple subjects emerged because the American dream, by the
end of the twentieth century, linked itself to American discourses of multiculturalism and diversity through proliferating target markets and diverse
lifestyles. As social movements created new identities in the United States,
marketing practices were designed to understand these communities and
to diversify and differentiate them to sell more and different products.
While in the early part of the century, a corporatized consumer culture
targeted and constructed an American white middle class, thus relegating
to the margins all those who could not or did not see themselves within this
group,[7] the new consumer culture produced gendered and racially marginalized subjects also as consumers.[8]

Yet these social movements suggest that the American dream and the
power of consumer cultures did not mean the end of economic inequalities
generated by racial and gendered subordination in the United States. Along
with discourses of immigrant mobility, the American dream was a discourse
of both whiteness and racism, in which a white identity coexisted in an unstable and changing relationship with heterogeneous notions of being American,[9] within as well as outside the United States. America, at the end of the
twentieth century and the beginning of the twenty-first, came to connote both
whiteness and multiculturalism within the framework of an American excep-
tionalism in which neoliberal discourses provide the possibility of multiple
and changing national affiliations. The slippages in meaning of white and
middle-class, within which whiteness connoted not only Anglo-America but a
more heterogeneous group that passed as "white," were regulated by a discourse of the liberal democratic state and a consumer citizenship seemingly
unbound from territories and races and classes which formed the American
dream and which created and enabled new American subjects in diverse sites.

The subject of this American dream, sometimes a territorially bounded
subject of the U.S. nation-state, sometimes a "global" consumer, or an
immigrant subject of other national diasporas, or a national of a distant
country, suggested that national subjects coexisted, for some groups and
persons, with other national belongings as well. Americanness as a concept

shifted by location and place and historical context, as well as factors such as race, gender, class, nationality, and religion, producing different kinds of subjects. This shifting and changing national subject could be, as with immigrants, transnational, moving across nations and national boundaries to produce American identities imbricated within a consumer citizenship that exceeded the bounds of the nation to become transnational. While the American dream has been an essential aspect of consumer culture in twentieth-century America, producing the "American way of life" as a primary component of nationalism formed through a conceptualization of liberal democracy,[10] it came to signify a variety of affiliative practices of belonging on the part of many migrants within the United States by the end of the century.

These affiliative practices enabled the formation of subjects of displacement and of national belonging by enabling them to become provisionally attached to new identities and nation-states and thus to cross nation-state borders. Thus the power of American nationalism was visible in its ability to produce provisional national subjects out of immigrants and refugees. That is, I suggest that becoming "American" had both a hegemonic and a heterogeneous meaning articulated within and through forms of transnational consumption and struggles for rights. Americanness was produced transnationally by cultural, political, and economic practices, so that becoming American did not always or necessarily connote full participation or belonging to a nation-state. However, the process of identification as "becoming American" coexisted, in some conflictual and non-conflictual ways, with multiple other allegiances to other nationalisms, identities, and networks. As identities are always in process rather than fully formed or stable, this "becoming American" could be understood as changeable, contingent, and historical. In addition, since nationalisms were much less territorially bound than at earlier times and connections to multiple institutions were made through technologies that sped up and intensified transnational connections, these allegiances intersected to produce transnational subjects as subjects of a nation-state. For instance, these multiple allegiances enabled America as nation to be imagined within the United States and outside it by migrants and refugees, such as those from India, who were living in the United States as well as by people living in India.

Rather than being only a symbol of "freedom" and democratic rights,

"America" was a sign of imperial power that used disciplinary as well as governmental technologies within transnational consumer culture. The conjunction of rights discourses and consumer culture was a central aspect of the connection between liberalism and neoliberalism: that is, groups and individuals who believed that they were disenfranchised used consumer culture's technologies, processes, and subjectivities to attain their goals. These practices were inextricable from articulations of civil society and democratic rights as these were being defined and redefined by the state, in the "international arena," and by divergent and subordinate communities within and across national boundaries. However, the geopolitical discourse of powerful sections of the United States state deployed (and still does) America as a sign of freedom to promote new forms of asymmetrical internationalism, corporate power, and white nationalism. These meanings were also disseminated in the marketing of "global" brands and the creation of "global" consumers. Consumption practices, which were part of the imaginary community formed by "American" nationalism through discourses of the "American way of life," were conveyed through transnational media advertising as a dominant white lifestyle of power and plenty as well as a multicultural and "global" one. These lifestyles were incorporated in partial and particular ways by ethnic groups in the United States, and then by cosmopolitans and others in countries such as India. Transnational practices incorporated struggles for liberal democratic rights as they inserted themselves into consumer culture.

Imaginaries of "America" were divergent and various, and this conjunction of consumer cultures and democratic rights cultures traveled to many regions outside the United States as well. For instance, while it is often believed that immigrants learn about "America" after they come to the country, yet transnational media and corporations and geopolitics ensured that many people all around the world have their own ideas about America. To understand what America meant outside the United States, I examine how the term circulated in India within the phase of economic liberalization occurring in the late 1980s and 1990s. I also examine what "America" meant in the United States to ethnic communities such as those formed by immigrants and refugees who had to learn to narrate themselves into the U.S. state and nation. This latter process was not simple, and concepts such as "assimilation" and "acculturation" into American or hyphenated-

American subjects did not adequately describe immigrant or migrant subjectivity within transnationality.[11] The production of state subjects, ethnic subjects, multicultural subjects, and transnational subjects were processes full of conflict and contradiction, as diasporas, nationalisms, "global" feminisms, and multinational corporations—to name just a few of the key formations through which what is called "global" is being understood in academic work as well as outside it—worked within and against the powerful narratives of the United States nation and state. Rather than simply produce national subjects or citizens, these processes caused the emergence of heterogeneous subjects who created identities in relation to the nation-state as well as to new kinds of internationalisms. These internationalisms did not eliminate nationalism but enabled certain kinds of nationalisms to be mystified and others to constitute primary aspects of an identity.

Given these contingent and shifting affiliations made possible within transnational connectivities, what can be made of the nature of citizenship at the end of the twentieth century? Within liberal political theory, rights, rather than consumption, have been the cornerstone of citizenship. T. H. Marshall and John Rawls considered that equal rights with others implied full citizenship.[12] However, if citizenship is not to be defined through access to rights within a territorially bound nation-state, then how are we to understand this concept? Political theorists pushed to understand the concept in many ways—as something produced by birth, as the responsibility of participation in civil society, as offering access to rights, as territorial belonging, as participation in military service, or even as the freedom to move within a territory. These varied definitions of citizenship also testify to the belief among scholars that we cannot do without this concept. While it is clear that being a citizen for some people at some time may only be part of an identity, for others it may become a matter of great urgency. Sometimes citizenship is linked to nationalism and sometimes it is not. Privileges of citizenship are extended unevenly—to women,[13] minority religious groups, and racial and sexual minorities. For instance, Susan Moller Okin critiqued the lack of rights for women, Carole Pateman's "sexual contract" theory argued that the division between public and private prevented women from accessing rights, and Zillah Eisenstein critiqued the masculine norm of citizenship.[14] These privileges of citizenship are also different from one nation to another.

In addition, the question of identity and citizenship, historically linked as

it is within western theories of the nation-state to questions of rights from a
territorially bound state,[15] became even more urgent by the end of the
twentieth century, given the increasing number of persons, many of them
women and children, who were not citizens of any state, or who saw their
identity as connected not to one state but rather to transnational communities, whether these were state-defined, national, or defined by some other
group or collective. The binary of mobility and immobility did not remain
useful to define the question of belonging, since transnational connectivities suggest that mobility of persons no longer remains the salient issue
but rather that moving discourses recast notions of settled and unsettled
subjectivity as well. Struggles for rights and citizenship even in the United
States resulted not only from social movements concerned with the oppression of and discrimination against persons based on their gender, sexuality,
class, or race, but also from those who were dislocated or displaced, as were
migrants and immigrants or refugees. In a transnational age, with millions
of displaced and migrant subjects, questions of identity and citizenship
became both crucial and vexed, since these subjects questioned the legitimacy of the nation-state while also reinforcing its ability to endow rights.

One result of these debates was the claim not simply of rights from a
nation-state but also of "universal rights" regardless of national citizenship.
This concept of rights as human rights articulated a subject that was both
national and international, thus suggesting that the nation-state was powerful but also insufficient. However, this extra-territorial form of citizenship
was not produced solely by claims of human rights. Consumer culture
produced other transnational identifications and subjects whose desires
and fantasies crossed national borders but also remained tied to national
imaginaries. New social movements that linked themselves to human
rights trafficked with both these subjectivities, creating new identities, desires, and communities that remained national but were also transnational.
Rights claims were also produced and consumed within cultural contexts
as commodities that circulated, producing different subjects in different
locations.

In response to these contexts, political theorists began to address how
new forms of nonessential identity and subjectivity within advanced capitalism enabled a critique of ideas of citizenship or identity based on be-

longing to one nation, state, or even community.[16] Some theorists called for a "radical" democratic citizenship while other claimed new versions of belonging which they call "sexual citizenship," "diasporic citizenship," and "cosmopolitan citizenship."[17] Isin and Wood referred to the impact of new social movements on issues of citizenship as the "new cultural politics" which require us "to imagine a postnational state in which sovereignty is intersecting, multiple and overlapping."[18] They argued that new "global regimes of governance" redefined national belonging and citizenship, so that people came to live with "the tension to which multiple loyalties give rise."[19] While some argued for a multicultural citizenship,[20] albeit one that was territorially bound, others suggested that a "diasporic citizenship" had evolved, transnational and moving away from territorially bound and sedentary versions of citizenship.[21] Aihwa Ong's theorization of "flexible citizenship" was another formulation in which diasporic ideas of multiple belonging were being articulated in relation to transnational movements.[22] Ong's use of "flexible" suggested the ability of some groups to move easily across national boundaries through power within new forms of late capitalism's processes of "flexible accumulation."

Theories of citizenship changed in response to these questions, suggesting that citizenship was no longer perceived to be an exclusionary belonging to one territorially defined nation-state. Scholars such as Isin and Wood argued that citizenship was a "status" rather than an identity; this "status" might not have a legal or juridical basis but could be the subject of legal dispute and struggle.[23] Arguing that citizenship could not be seen as the only identity after the advent of new social movements and forms of globalization and advanced capitalism, or even the primary identity, they explored "claims of a fragmented, decentered subject as well as of shifting group rights and identities without succumbing to either essentialist or constructivist views of identity."[24] Thus they articulated the necessity to understand "sociological issues of belonging, recognition and solidarity" in order to understand political issues of "status, rights and equality," since citizenship was not the only or the primary identity of many persons.[25]

Although Isin and Wood were correct in identifying tension and conflicts as central to issues of identity and citizenship, we need also to remember that tensions of this sort characterized many moments in the past as well. We cannot imagine that people only lived with single loyalties in the past; such a belief might stem more from nostalgia than from historical understandings. The new inequalities of the present led many to create new golden pasts—of the nation, the single identity, the loyalty to place. In some instances, social construction theory also came to have a new temporality—of the time when identities were essential, or even when hybridity was uncontested. Conflicting forms of belonging were also central to modernity rather than being specific to late capitalism. In fact, it was the promise of wholeness for a fragmented self that was at the center of the modern subject and continues to be so.[26] Yet what might be different about the end of the twentieth century was the nature of these tensions and conflicts, the technological and consumerist modes in which citizenship could be imagined, as well as the modernist belief that certain (and not all) group loyalties and loyalties to nation-state were incompatible in ways different from those of the past. What was also different, as this book argues, was the imbrication of changing and contingent nationalist belonging with a transnational consumer culture facilitated by new technologies of communication, production, and consumption.

While questions of citizenship remained important in regard to the techniques of governance created to manage and regulate populations, it was not simply a consumer citizenship that regulated subjects but also consumer nationalisms. Nationalism's ability to move, change, spread across different kinds of boundaries suggests that it remained a powerful imaginary which developed in tandem with changing modes of citizenship and consumer culture. In general, Stuart Hall's theories of identification as "points of temporary attachment" in the process of articulation[27] are a more compelling way to think through the problem of nationalism than the use of what has been called "strategic essentialism."[28] Since identities are always "strategic" we need to examine how "strategic essentialism" addresses either the problem of essentialism or the operations of power upon subjects; furthermore it is not clear what levels of self-consciousness are needed to make essentialism strategic or not and whether assuming a "strategic" consciousness about identity is the only way in which power can be negotiated. Which subject-positions can be invested to produce an identity is a question of power that has to be understood within a force field of regulated subject positions and institutions. Although all identities are formed through strategic essentialism, they are neither stable nor ahistorical. They exist to enact specific kinds of agency through the exercise of power. If subjects are formed through the work of institutions and discourses, then these subjects become identities only through identification with already constituted or newly perceptible identities and in response to technologies of regulatory power. Thus we need to focus on new assemblages of power to examine the impact of the market on the identities produced by new social movements. Doing so involves an examination therefore of regimes of governmentality and disciplinary power, connected to older regulatory institutions, which were carried within transnational connectivities to enable the production of neoliberal subjects.

TRANSNATIONAL CONNECTIVITIES AND THE "GLOBAL"

★

In September 2001, the United States began to introduce new cutbacks in immigration and new forms of surveillance of many immigrants from South Asia, the Middle East, and Africa. The annual number of H-1B visas fell from 195,000 in 2001 to 65,000 in October 2003. In Congress there have been calls to curtail immigration drastically: one bill introduced in 2003 (H.R. 2688) aimed to eliminate the H-1B visa entirely and another would have reduced all immigration into the United States. The number of refugees allowed to enter the country fell by 60 percent from 2001 to 2003, to the lowest number in twenty-five years.[29] Even the bureaucracy of immigration has changed.[30] The Immigration and Naturalization Service (INS) has now been absorbed into the Department of Homeland Security (DHS), which is divided into five "directorates," as they are called, in addition to several other agencies. The directorates are Border and Transportation Security, Emergency Preparedness and Response, Science and Technology, Information Analysis, and Infrastructure Protection and Management.[31] The directorates are all, except for one that is devoted to managing the rest, focused on security and surveillance, increasing by a tremendous amount the U.S. state's pursuit of security and empire. The Bureau of Citizenship and Immigration Services (BCIS), one agency in DHS, covers part of the mandate of the former INS apart from its customs and border security work, which have now become part of the Border and Transportation Security division. The BCIS processes all immigration and asylum claims, and reports directly to the head of the Homeland Security Department. According to the DHS website, the Bureau of Citizenship and Immigration Services "dedicates its full energies to providing efficient immigration services and easing the transition to American citizenship."[32]

The Bush administration believes that this entity will be more efficient than the INS in keeping track of all those who enter the United States, helped by reduced civil liberties for all citizens and non-citizens in the United States and in many other parts of the world where the United States exercises its considerable influence; the discourses of neoliberal market efficiency uneasily combined with those of providing security and the hope of complete surveillance through policing and technology are widespread in the United States. As I argue in chapter 5, increased surveillance, especially of Muslim males, male converts to Islam, and those who "look Muslim" or Middle Eastern at airports within the United States and in communities and streets has become common, showing how racial and gender formations enable the disciplinary and governmental technologies that support neoliberal policies. While the American corporate mantra remains becoming "global," the borders of the United States are being increasingly policed against particular groups of nonwhites; and as has been so often mentioned, the mobility of capital and goods is not matched by the mobility of labor (especially labor that is believed to be "unskilled," which defines the work of so many women and the poor), given the new outsourcing not only of low-wage but also of white-collar and pink-collar work.[33]

The new millennium seems to have, as many in the United States would contend, inaugurated what are called "new" dangers and wars after 9/11, but it is clear that an era of neoliberalism was inaugurated with Margaret Thatcher and Ronald Reagan and the end of the Soviet Union. This book is about the 1990s, when a new phase of neoliberalism brought together market logics with concerns for reducing welfare and poverty, and in the process rearticulated feminist and postcolonial subjects out of longer colonial histories and epistemologies. While neoliberalism has been debated as a reformulation of policy linked to the expansion of markets within globalization, or as a new form of hegemony that has produced a new kind of consensus,[34] it can also be understood in terms of a variety of formations through which states arrogated welfare to the workings of the market or applied market logics to welfare concerns. Nikolas Rose has examined some of these marketization practices in the context of the technologies and programs of "advanced liberalism" within which the marketization of welfare took place.[35] Foucault, in an essay entitled "The Birth of Biopolitics," describes the "neoliberalism" of the Chicago school that came to fruition around the 1960s as seeking "rather to extend the rationality of the market, the schemes of analysis it proposes, and the decision making criteria it suggests to areas that are not exclusively or primarily economic."[36] However, in this process, which grew in the last decades of the twentieth century, the diminution of power of states has been uneven—some states have been much more reduced than others and some states have become even more powerful.

Foucault's concept of governmentality has been taken up by Rose and others to understand the practices and programs of self-regulation and conduct that came to be central to the various and disparate practices that made up neoliberal political rationalities. This book argues that neoliberalism is a marketization not just of welfare but of an array of social movements; feminist discourses, previously marginal to neoliberal technologies, became incorporated within them by the end of the twentieth century. Consequently, technologies of feminist empowerment and pleasure that were promoted by late capitalist consumer culture became yoked to the promise of new discourses of modern female and feminist subjectivity and citizenship and the removal of violence and poverty for female populations in what were called "developing countries." Empowerment, self-esteem, and self-help through spiritual and new age movements, exercise and health club attendance, and talk shows and books on the topic, along with new manifestations of cosmopolitanisms, became key to dominant feminist practices in the United States. The segmentation of consumer markets producing a multiplicity of lifestyles—feminist, multicultural, ethnic—was linked to the multiplicity of rights-based identity movements that proliferated through the 1990s. Thus lifestyles of empowerment were created through the struggles that were waged around new social movements. Feminist, diasporic, cosmopolitan, and postcolonial subjectivities were made possible through practices of self-regulation promoted through the technologies of consumer culture and its related programs. The privatization of welfare through nongovernmental organizations (NGOs), the production of cosmopolitan postcolonial subjects, and the creation of differentiated identities through the segmentation of consumer groups were connected to the self-creation and regulation of individuals through nationalist discourses and state policies and relations with other states, and it is here that we find the link between biopolitics and geopolitics. Caren Kaplan and I have already argued for greater consideration of geopolitics in the histories of feminist and women's movements that arose within colonial discourses in the United States and Europe.[37] While Michael Dillon argues that geopolitics and biopolitics come together in the figure of the terrorist, it can be argued that the question of women has had a long history within the modern conceptualization of national rivalries, wars, and colonial relations.[38] When James Mill in the early nineteenth century supported British colonialism by suggesting that the civilizational superiority of Britain can be seen in the way that it "exalts" its women, unlike those countries such as India where women are "degraded," we see early signs of the use of "the status of women" as a link between geopolitics and biopolitics.[39] For example, participation in "saving" Afghani women from the Taliban was a project taken up in the 1990s not only by many individuals and organizations but also by fashion magazines such as *Elle* and organizations such as the Feminist Majority Foundation.[40] Discourses of individuality yoked freedom to participation in consumer culture and associated political freedoms with self-improvement; biopolitics produced populations seen as "free" compared to populations in the "third world" that were seen as victims of patriarchal cultures. Consumer culture provided the modalities through which national and international belongings could be imagined, and resistant identities recognized. Thus at the end of the twentieth century, neoliberalism enabled the marketization of social movements through the link between biopolitics and geopolitics. Here geopolitics could be understood not only as a matter of state politics and claims of territories but also as a mode of regulation in which discourses of territoriality, space, and nationalism produced forms of subjectivity by differentiating between populations and the needs and welfare of what were seen to be very different and contrasting populations.

In conceptualizing biopolitics, Foucault theorized that the object of government was not the individual body but the social body. When this social body was seen as a population, there emerged ways of understanding, managing, and regulating that were focused on the goal of welfare of the population. Foucault saw that modern regimes of governance created population as the problem to be addressed by a whole new way of conceptualizing the social body as needing to be managed through apparatuses of security. New apparatuses and knowledges enabled this new way of conceptualizing power as government, and this power became, as Foucault says, "pre-eminent." This power was "pre-eminent" because it contained within it a moral and ethical rationale that has been used for power within geopolitics. Yet if we bring in the question of geopolitics in relation to biopolitics, it is difficult to see one kind of power as "pre-eminent" over disciplinary or sovereign power; rather, as Foucault also said, we see that there exists an assemblage of different forms of power that work together: "We need to see things not in terms of the replacement of a society of sovereignty by a disciplinary society and the subsequent replacement of a disciplinary society by a society of government; in reality one has a triangle, sovereignty-discipline-government, which has as its primary target the population and as its essential mechanism the apparatuses of security."[41]

Although Foucault's focus on population makes this juxtaposition important, it also means that the two forms of power cannot always be demarcated spatially (for example, governmentality as a mode of power in the West and disciplinary power as operating in the "developing world") or temporally, and that one power may enable a second form of power to come into existence. We also seek an understanding of how populations are judged in relation to each other—differences are produced between populations on the basis of territory, culture, gender, race, nation—and technologies of governance are devised, applied, adjudicated in relation to these differences. For instance, infant mortality is understood not only in terms of a population as a whole but rather in relation to the difference in mortality between different nation-states, communities, genders, races. Population control policies, in response to governmental mechanisms, were devised to target subaltern groups in Asia and Africa, for the most part, and a host of disciplinary modes of power were used to enforce these policies. Mechanisms of governance of populations are also connected to questions of how nations, peoples, and cultures are demarcated in relation to space and territoriality. Thus geopolitics is not simply a matter of the international conflicts between nation-states but rather must be understood not simply, as Gearóid Ó Tuathail has suggested, in terms of what might be seen as "geo-power" (that is, the "ensemble of technologies or power concerned with the governmental production and management of territorial space") but also in terms of how these technologies produce subjects of these territories and the means to regulate them. Neoliberalism produces its own geopolitics in terms of how market logics could be linked to social concerns for differently located, gendered, and racialized populations.

A general problem for a critique of neoliberalism is that it might lead to a utopian search for the pure, uncommodified self or a modernist longing for the uncontaminated Other. In taking on the problem of the relationship between new social movements and neoliberal politics, my goal is consistent with the argument of Wendy Larner: that neoliberalism can be interrupted by fracturing its assumed coherence by means of a "post-social politics" consisting of "critical responses and interventions" produced by the struggle between social movements and the new right.[42] Thus the question of resistance in this book is to be understood in a Foucauldian way, as encompassing the myriad and multiple ways in which neoliberal technologies produced all kinds of agency, and an understanding that agency based on identities arising from movements that were feminist, or antiracist, for example, moved in all kinds of directions and mechanisms that did not remain pure of their conditions of possibility, but created contradictions, tensions, and struggles. Neoliberalism thus could not prevent possibilities for contradiction to its discourses and practices, so that its traffic with social movements that both used its programs and opposed them was complex and uneven.

In all debates on neoliberalism, the nature of the state at the end of the twentieth century has been a key topic. Some scholars have asked questions about the general demise of all states while others have focused on the imperial and colonial state. As I have stated above, this book argues that no universal claim can be made about the nature of some entity generalized as "the state," since states and their powers have some commonalities but many differences as well; the production of knowledge of a general, universal entity called the "state" needs to be critiqued. While some states became more powerful through neoliberal policies, others became less so. It seems that the states whose powers were reduced were also those where the welfare of the population was marketized to a greater extent than in the more advanced liberal democracies; what is crucial is also where marketization processes were managed and by whom. In general, a focus on governmentality may enable an examination of powers outside those of the state and thus can be taken as a reduction of the powers of the state. However, it is difficult to see how governmental powers exist without a continuity with state practices or outside the "triangle," as Foucault called it, of sovereign and disciplinary power. Governmentality could also suggest, alternatively, an increase in the powers of those states which could offer or control marketization processes in other states, since it may also imply the circulation of state power in many directions.

In this formulation, Foucault's theorization of governmentality has been used to argue that state power is overtaken by a biopolitical power that cannot be thought of as emanating from the state.[43] What is, however, a problem is that Foucault's theories assumed a singularity to the state based on the histories of European liberal states and did not include the question of biopolitics within the relation between uneven, dependent, or colonial states, as scholars have pointed out.[44] All of his theorizations of the state are based on examples from Europe and the advent of modernity in Europe. Questions of the relations between states—between states that are discrepantly modern or were in relations of dependency—were not within his purview. Thus in addressing these considerations, the question of geopolitics must engage with biopolitical technologies, especially in examining the effects of neoliberalism in various nation-states. When this is done, even the separation of the three modes of power needs to be questioned, since it would be difficult to see how the three rely upon or morph into each other at different points within states where the welfare of populations has only sporadically been the rationale of the state and states cannot be seen to be liberal. Achille Mbembe's work has taken on this problematic in relation to the nature of the biopolitical in nonliberal states.[45] At the same time, it cannot be said that neoliberalism did not have a geopolitical context in the same way as did liberalism, since the differential application of these neoliberal programs created new kinds of subjects that became differentiated by class, race, and gender.

At the end of the century, the issue of state power also revolved around the question of the United States and empire. While many scholars have examined the history of American imperialism and the nature of the imperial "American century,"[46] others have argued that the deterritorialization of power at the end of the century was such that we cannot think of any state as remaining powerful. The main exponent of the theorization of deterritorialized power and governance was the book *Empire*, in which American imperialism was said to have been replaced by a new sovereignty produced by decentralized power. *Empire* claims that the new power is global—it extends throughout the world, it is new, it will be challenged by a new "multitude" with the "creative forces . . . capable of autonomously constructing a counter empire"[47]—and that the United States is not a global power in the ways that European powers formerly were:

> Many locate the ultimate authority that rules over the processes of globalization and the new world order in the United States. Proponents praise the United States as the world leader and sole superpower, and detractors denounce it as an imperialist oppressor. Both these views rest on the assumption that the United States has simply donned the mantle of global power that the European nations have now let fall. . . . Our basic hypothesis, however, that a new imperial form of sovereignty has emerged, contradicts both these views. The United States does not, and indeed no nation-state can today, form the center of an imperialist project. Imperialism is over. No nation will be world leader in the way modern European nations were.[48]

In this era of the American empire and renewed American nationalism, it is difficult to agree with many of these ideas about the end of American imperialism and thus about the nature of this singular, global sovereignty even while we see some evidence of the decentralization of forms of regulatory power that produce the social. However, in contradiction to *Empire*, this book will argue that in the decentralization, new centers developed, and deterritorialization was accompanied by reterritorialization; thus, America remained an undiminished source of both decentralized and centralized power through the neoliberal regimes, technologies, and rationalities that I describe in this book, and many of the inequalities generated by an earlier era of colonization were important to understanding the trajectories along which new centers emerged.[49] The United States remained a hegemon, and its source of power was its ability to generate forms of regulation across particular connectivities that emerged as independent as well as to recuperate the historicized inequalities generated by earlier phases of imperialism.

Again, totalizing theories of power like those set forth in *Empire* misread the concept of network as simply about deterritorialization and diffusion rather than about recreating nodes of power within the network as it spreads in particular directions. Moreover, the United States, in collaboration with other powerful nation-states, still is able to destroy or change the boundaries of other nation-states through a variety of forms of power—cultural, economic, military. It can also produce liberal nationalisms based on rights that become deterritorialized and reterritorialized; we cannot assume that the only effect of deterritorialized power would be the multitude that would rise up against empire, since this multitude's "global" spread is as much a result of cosmopolitan discourses of power as the earlier formations that the book critiques.

If we see *Empire* as a commentary on "globalization," in a way that sutures some critiques of regulatory power to an older Marxist understanding of capital, then this sort of knowledge-formation represents a specific Euro-American cosmopolitan idea of the "global." In contradiction to *Empire*, this book argues that the "global" is not and never was quite global, but that there certainly was a will to globalization that was both profoundly cosmopolitan as well as imperialist, since "global" capitalism did not constitute the totality of economic or social relations that were existent or possible.[50] As Ulf Hannerz has said of the term "globalization": "Many such processes and relationships obviously do not at all extend across the world. The term 'transnational' is in a way more humble, and often a more adequate label for phenomena which can be of variable scale and distribution."[51] In following Hannerz, this book argues that the "global," by the last decade of the twentieth century, was a powerful imaginary produced through knowledges moving along specific transnational connectivities, as I call them, and that these transnational connectivities, a few of which I examine in this book, constituted a web of connections that moved along historicized trajectories.

I will argue that rather than the term globalization, it is more useful to think about the heterogeneous and multiple transnational connectivities that produced various meanings of the term "global." Conceiving of globalization as an object of knowledge involved discursive practices emanating from and producing a cosmopolitan will to power in which so many different kinds of subjects participated. Thus rather than use this term, I hope to trace the trajectories and histories of knowledges that produced discourses of the "global" as that which was believed to be pervasive, all-encompassing. As a cognate of "universal," the "global" became a means to suggest that there was one sole hegemonic mode of power that existed in all places, that was imperial and pervasive simply because it was deterritorialized. The necessity of disaggregating the diverse and uneven phenomena that make up what has been called globalization, and the need to show their genealogies in earlier periods, as well as the incomplete dissemination of global processes, leads me therefore to understand terms such as "global" and "universal" as regimes of truth that traveled transnationally within powerful knowledge connectivities.

As I have said, Ulf Hannerz's term "transnational connections" comes close to describing the myriad connections that characterize the transnational arena; I use the term "connectivities" to suggest the degree and variety of connections that exist. This term suggests, as it does in relation to the internet, that there are strong and weak connectivities, that it is not only the networks, as Manuel Castells calls them,[52] that we need to examine but the discourses that travel through these networks, how some get translated and transcoded, how some are unevenly connected, others strongly connected, and still others incommensurable and untranslatable. Moreover, in recalling the term "collectivities," the term "connectivities" reveals that the transnational connections here produce groups, identities, nationalisms; that the power of many discourses to be understood, translated, used in a variety of sites means that subjects become constituted and connected through these new technologies and rationalities.

The term connectivity itself has come to have multiple meanings. At the simplest level, it refers to accessibility of information technology: whether some people, groups, and communities are able to access information so as to be part of a "global" community and how they access this technology[53] (for example through dial-up service with intermittent or sporadic connection, through twenty-four-hour high-speed lines, or through various kinds of servers), and at what cost. At another level, connectivity refers to the very mode of delivery of digitalized information that one observer sees as the "unbiased transport of packets of information between two end points" and thus simply another utility and commodity like water and electricity.[54] Yet for connectivity to be understood as a commodity suggests the economics of information technologies that are central for access to this new realm of what is seen as deterritorialized power. Thus while the internet is understood as a metaphor and realm of deterritorialized power in which distance and space have been conquered, this technology only connects select groups of people to what is on the web, in selected directions and to particular sites. How these connectivities occur is a matter of the economic, political, and social technologies and their histories. As Vincent Mosco argues, "connectivity does not mean distance is dying. Rather, the architecture of connectivity accentuates the importance of certain nodes in its global networks making particular spaces."[55] Thus rather than a deterritorialization, the metaphor of connectivity suggests that territories and spaces are rearticulated as new centers of power along new and old routes. In addition, connectivity does not imply a complete diffusion of power into the "global" realm; rather it implies that new networks are created within which nodes of power come into existence through relationships created within networks. Thus, Rob Shields suggests, "Networks may be more or less decentralized, but the general notion of connectivity in a net is that each element is interconnected with a multiplicity of other elements. In a network, then, the status of individual elements is determined by their connections. These make some elements into nodal points through which the network itself may be argued to flow onward."[56]

Thus the internet cannot be thought of simply in terms of derritorialization and flows. The conundrum of technological metaphors is that they are always powerful but cannot be used for totalizing theoretical claims. My claims for connectivity as a metaphor, however, provide an argument about its incompleteness, the exclusions produced by it, and thus for a theory in which unevenness, failure, exclusion can be included. This unevenness does not lead to advocating vanguardist resistance but rather foregrounds power relations within different trajectories, translations that go awry, discourses that cannot link agendas as well as powerful connectivities that link, create new nodes, and recuperate the nation and empire.

In particular, my use of connectivity as a metaphor for the links and routes within which cosmopolitan discourses of power constitute the "global" points to the reconstitution of the social that took place at the end of the twentieth century and that built upon older histories of colonialism and modernity. In all of these transnational connectivities, the asymmetries produced by the discourses of difference between the West and the Rest

remained formative, even though there were cosmopolitans, wealthy
classes and groups, and a number of hierarchies in the West, as there were
outside it. These cosmopolitans included those strongly connected to the
"global" economy as a masculine realm of economic activity and to histories
of internationalism, as well as those who were cosmopolitan only in contingent ways or on the margins of the cosmopolitanism that could think of
itself as "global." The strength or weakness of these connectivities could in
part be attributed to histories of colonialism but also to many other forms of
power that were regionally specific or could grow out of other social movements. Thus the West and the non-West, those divisions produced through
European colonialism, were rearticulated continually to inform the inequalities that demarcated the wealthy nations from the "developing" countries, or wealthy cosmopolitans from subalterns. Although the non-West
might not exactly define a world of wealthy Asian countries or incorporate
the history of Japanese imperialism, the cultural manifestations of imperialism still structured the representational division between the so-called
free world and the world believed to be "unfree." The history of modernity,
as of postmodernity, was still informed by histories of colonialism.

Despite these links to colonialism, there seems to be no single logic of
rule; connectivities brought together multiple logics to create assemblages
of rule that governed the demarcation of space. Thus along with the racialized "deathworlds" that Achille Mbembe argues continue to exist,[57] there
were also worlds governed by the ethics of humanitarianism and forms of
sovereignty that enabled the "powers of freedom"[58] as indexes to both the
possibilities of democracy and those histories of European colonization
that claimed the superiority of "western civilization." In addition, the phan-
tasmal visual worlds of nostalgia and of possibilities (of class, nationalism,
global citizenship) created by consumer culture and transnational media
technologies formed new inequalities and recuperated old inequalities to
produce identities and differences. Above all, it was the juxtaposition of
these multiple logics of rule that created new assemblages of power, and the
juxtapositions and assemblages changed with time and place.[59] In addition,
one form of power may morph into another kind: for instance, in my
chapter on refugees, what is revealed is that a legal discourse of human
rights becomes a tool for management of the "refugee problem." Transna-

tional connectivities made these juxtapositions and changes possible. For example, movements of labor, capital, goods, media, and technologies across national boundaries intensified unevenly and differently from region to region, even while business corporations in the United States and elsewhere incorporated terms such as "global" and "diversity" into their lexicon. Nonprofit organizations and activism became inescapably transnational even while their presence made less of a difference to subalterns in a welfare state than to those in a state without a strong welfare apparatus. Images from across the world flashed on TV screens in the slums of third world cities as much as they did in penthouses in New York or Tokyo or Cairo, even if some of these lifestyles might have been absorbed into fantasy and imagination in different ways. Yet transnational connectivities produced these differences through a variety of mechanisms and assemblages of power.

FEMINISMS AT THE TURN OF THE CENTURY: NEOLIBERALISM AND STRUGGLE

✴

A key aspect of this book is the exploration of the conundrum of neoliberalism, consumer culture, and mobility and the related problem of feminist resistance and opposition produced within transnational connectivities of knowledge production. The relationship between gendered identity, feminism, democratic citizenship, and consumer culture became apparent through the writing of this book as crucial aspects of America in its role as a transnational regulatory apparatus of neoliberalism. There are multiple ways to understand this relationship. For instance, one can argue that the forms of civil society that enable democratic citizenship are the new technologies and new media that are controlled by multinational corporations. In this formulation, we can only imagine having group identities, rights, or responsibilities through lifestyles, modes of communication, desires, and fantasies that are part of a consumer culture crossing many boundaries (though not all of them) very easily. On the other hand, one can also see these formations in constant struggle and negotiation, as feminist movements have become so disseminated and so diverse that some movements disaffiliate from the state and others negotiate with it. Feminists as part of the new informational connectivities of knowledge producers also continue to work on self-critique and remain profoundly self-reflexive, and thus feminism continues to proliferate in many modalities and formations. Foucault's concept of governmentality, as modified to address a transnational arena, provides theoretical insight into understanding some of the problems regarding the separation between civil society and state, and thus makes it possible to address feminism as an ethic and a rationality that generated technologies and strategies capable of being understood as governmental and productive through many kinds of agency. Moreover, the concept of governmentality allowed me to understand feminist action and activism not simply as vanguardist but as a form of power through which gendered subjects were produced, specifically in discourses of welfare, through proper and effective management and in resistance to disciplinary technologies; thus it was necessary, when discussing feminist activism, not to write about an a priori female subject (the woman) but to see feminist activism as constructing a variety of gendered subjects that often refused to remain stable.

This book argues that gender, race, class, and nationalism are produced by contemporary cultures in a transnational framework that is linked to earlier histories of colonization. For example, the interarticulation of rights and consumer cultures means that for feminist scholars interested in social movements, it is important to understand how gender and sex are constructed through what we know as culture, and also how in modernity consumer culture itself produces these categories. Historians of consumer culture in the United States have undertaken work along these lines and produced a formidable literature. This field has most clearly revealed to us the relation between nationalism, gender, and consumer culture, clearing the ground for much theorization of America as a sign of neoliberal consumer culture through concepts such as "the American way of living" and "lifestyle" in the twentieth century, concepts which have moved across many transnational connectivities.

The separation of identity issues and consumer culture as a knowledge formation follows on T. H. Marshall's concept of liberal democracy as an arena separate from the market. If work along these lines is undertaken, as in some work on popular culture, consumer culture is often seen solely as a strategy of resistance in the production of identity. Yet these identity practices cannot be seen as totalizing resistance formations. It is only by examining the production and circulation of consumer culture and consumer goods within the context of biopolitics and geopolitics that we can see how identity politics operate at the complex nexus of political economy, national imaginaries, and related mobilizations of desire and individuality within liberal and neoliberal politics. These circulations, productions, and consumptions cannot be understood as a demarcated "local" realm of action, but rather as effective ways to regulate the local and the international. By utilizing a transnational approach, we can examine the interarticulation of consumption and identity formation as caught up within the movements of people, goods, and ideas across national boundaries, and the ways in which nationalism produces subjects in difference from other gendered subjects. Thus the production of feminist and female subjects through discourses of freedom and unfreedom within transnational consumer cultures needs to be interrogated, especially with relation to the concept of "choice" that became a key discourse of neoliberal feminism.

The focus of feminist modernity within the United States on the topic of "choice" brings to the forefront the problem of its liberal conditions of production at the end of the twentieth century. Since the concept of choice is essential to participation in democracy as well as to consumer culture, feminism was engaged in a struggle with neoliberalism but also dependent on it for its existence. Certainly, mainstream, second-wave feminism in the United States critiqued the liberal state for creating a division between public and private, but itself built on "choice" as crucial for its struggles against right-wing attacks on reproductive rights. Other ways of conceptualizing progressive feminism, especially ones that focus on international and "global" issues, used the idea of "having choices" as the opposite of "being oppressed." From activism against domestic violence to activism in favor of reproductive rights, the availability of "choice" was increasingly taken as representing feminist agency. Critiques of these approaches from radical and poststructural feminisms were also raised in the 1990s, although the powerful circulation of this concept continued as well.[60] In this book, I explore this feminist liberal subject as it circulates in trajectories that transnationalized governmental technologies.

New social movements take shape through a process of knowledge-production and identity formation. The consumption, production, and regulation of this knowledge is thus important to examine and this book attempts to do so in relation to feminism as one social movement. The pervasiveness of liberal discourses of "choice" within feminism, liberal democracy, and consumer culture suggest that there are connections between these formations that deserve greater scrutiny, especially in the formation of what I have understood as the link between geopolitics and biopolitics. Thus my examination of the novels *Jasmine* and *Mistress of Spices*, of Barbie in India, of the "global" campaigns for women's rights as human rights, suggests means by which gendered subjectivity was produced transnationally through discourses of an unconstrained, unregulated feminist agency, whether through discourses of consumption or by human rights. Consumer culture worked by producing desires and fantasies that could be linked to group as well as to individual identities and were also linked to a consumer citizenship through which liberal equality became possible. This is one way in which we can understand *Elle* magazine's investment in Afghani women and its support of women's rights against the Taliban, as well as its emphasis on beauty and consumer culture as an index of freedom for a post-Taliban Afghanistan.

Yet this link between feminism and consumer culture comes from a longer history in the United States. Margaret Finnegan, in her book *Selling Suffrage*, shows us the many ways in which some groups of women working for suffrage in the late nineteenth century used the tactics and the language of advertising to "sell" the message of suffrage. According to Finnegan, suffragists "compared good voters to comparison shoppers, defined commodity-enhanced lifestyles as a right, spoke in tribute to fashion and mass consumption and emulated the graphic, material and visual cues of modern department stores, advertisers, merchandisers, and magazine publishers."[61] Thus early-twentieth-century feminists in the United States themselves commodified democratic politics by "making the right to vote synonymous with physical possession of the ballot," in the process of which the ballot became a commodity which every woman must have.[62] Nan Ensted argues that women workers in the early twentieth century derived important forms of subjectivity and identity from popular and consumer culture and that the representation of consumption as false consciousness, or of women as the victims of commodity culture, does not bear out in the historical record. As she states, "Consumer culture offered working-class women struggling with extremely difficult material and ideological constraints a new range of representations, symbols, activities, and spaces with which to create class, gender and ethnic identities."[63] Vicki Ruiz argues that consumer culture allowed Mexican-American women to negotiate racialized and gendered inequalities within their communities but also outside them.[64] Within these contexts, the right to consume became an important aspect of the struggle for full citizenship and identity in the United States.[65] Lifestyle, "taste," and fashion become central to producing difference through processes of "branding" in advertising and mass media. These lifestyles created an "American consciousness" in which consumption was linked to democracy and choice.[66]

Within what has been understood as globalization, consumer culture has become a key aspect creating subjectivities at the turn of the century. Arjun Appadurai has called this process the "civilizing work of post industrial society," in which serious labor is put into "producing the conditions of consciousness in which buying can occur."[67] While Appadurai's analysis points to the colonial underpinnings of industrial capitalism under which consumer culture developed, there have been theorizations of consumption that have addressed how the symbolic and specular aspect of consumer culture was linked to a national and imperial identity,[68] and in the case of the United States, to a transnational context[69] as well as to the nation's geographic, economic, and political role as a "superpower."

American consumer capitalism, as Ritzer and others have shown, relies on a discourse of rationalization.[70] What he calls the "McDonaldization" thesis states that the principles of efficiency, calculability, predictability, and control of human beings through material technologies underlie a globalizing consumer culture. Malcolm Waters suggests that within this culture, "political issues and work can equally become items of consumption." The only political system possible within such a cultural formation might be a "liberal-democratic political system where there is a culture of consumption precisely because it offers the possibility of election,"[71] and thus of choice.

Within consumer culture's primary role of providing "choices" through a process of differentiating, providing symbolic capital, or producing identity,[72] feminist agency through mobility and movements plays a large role. The technological aspects of practices of mobility have become foundational to the movements of finance capital, laboring bodies, goods, and

media. These technologies are crucial to consumer culture and its dissemination through transnational connectivities of many kinds—of people,
media, and geopolitics. As Ian Barns has said, technological innovation
itself enables an increasing commodification of social life "because of the
cultural grammar that technological innovation expresses." It's not just the
technologies but also the "deeper cultural transformation" associated with
these technologies that make these technologies so crucial to our identities.[73] My interest in this aspect of consumer culture lies not in the technologies themselves, but in how these technologies are both subject-pro-
ducing and subjectifying. Certainly they produce those gendered mobile
and immobile refugees, migrants, activists, writers, and scholars—those
uneven participants of what Castells has termed "network society" and
Lash and Urry have described as the informational networks crucial to
globalization.[74]

Although many agree that consumer culture can be understood as an
American phenomenon, the imbrication of the political with consumer
culture is not limited to the United States. There is a growing anthropological literature on the relationship between colonialism and consumption in
Africa and Asia.[75] Politicians in India, for instance, also rely on spectacle
and cinematic technologies for electioneering, to the extent that movie stars
have regularly been elected to political office. Consumer culture in many
formerly colonized cultures has developed (or underdeveloped) in ways
that are varied and important through the process of colonization in the last
three centuries. While these forms of consumption have new manifestations, they are also connected to earlier practices of consumption through
the inequalities generated by western colonial expansion. Yet late capitalist
modernity increasingly brings the discourse of consumer culture to more
areas of the world through the self-producing practices of governance enabled by neoliberal democratic regimes. For instance, as my example of
Barbie suggests, the current phase of capitalism in India is producing a
new kind of popular, cosmopolitan feminism that seems to operate differently than the feminism that many have come to associate with women's
movements in India. This feminism constructs women as working professionals at the same time as it commodifies feminism through beauty and
fashion culture. The classes and groups that can become neoliberal femi-

nist subjects through discourses of beauty have some overlap with those subjects produced through older discourses of cosmopolitanism created by colonial histories, visible in the texts that I examine in the first chapter of this book. These subjects, produced by postcolonial cosmopolitanisms that are anti-Eurocentric or anti-American are also different from those subjects produced by discourses of refugee asylum and the state practices and institutions that produce refugees since their utilizations of transnational discourse of America are quite distinct in relation to race, gender, religion, and ethnicity. And finally, after 9/11, as my last chapter suggests, ethnic and racialized and gendered subjects are rearticulated out of older racial and gendered histories into neoliberal practices of self-regulation demanded by keeping secure consumer culture's promises of the American dream.

These questions of subjectivity and identity enable us to understand the interactions between nationalist subjects of many kinds, the practices of nation-states, new social movements, and transnational connectivities of many kinds. For Bharati Mukherjee, as I suggest in chapter 1, to become an American writer required an understanding of Americanness that was linked to hegemonic ideas of nationalism and cosmopolitanism. At the same time, the icon of American white heterosexual femininity, Barbie (the topic of chapter 2), circulated in India only to the extent that economic liberalization policies instituted by the Indian state provided new arenas for work and consumption for middle-class metropolitan Indian women and new transnational nationalisms. In contrast, the female refugee subjects that I discuss in chapter 4 were produced both by powerful discourses of the American nation and by various state institutions in the United States and India as well as by representations of nonwestern women that circulated through many transnational connectivities and created unequal feminist and female subjects. Similarly, the internationalist claims of discourses of "women's rights as human rights," which I discuss in chapter 3, are rooted in a "Western" subjectivity that became universalized through transnational connectivities that produced feminist knowledges. In all of the connectivities, discourses of biopolitics and geopolitics circulated in collaboration to produce modern nationalist subjects of many kinds.

In the process of taking on this tangled topic, through the many years in which I struggled to formulate what resisted a single disciplinary or area approach, my book came to be framed within what Caren Kaplan and I have called a "transnational feminist cultural studies" perspective.[76] It was only by combining a postcolonial perspective with textual literary analysis, social and cultural theory, and feminist and ethnic studies approaches that I could begin to engage with the questions in which I was interested. Since all disciplines respond to needs and agendas in particular historical periods, I do not want to argue for the superiority of one discipline over another, or for one methodology over another. In particular, attacks on cultural studies, ethnic studies, women's studies, or postcolonial studies—all fields that are often identified as interdisciplinary at the present time—seem to me to be produced to defend forms of disciplinarity that are either defensive gate keeping linked to professional networks of power or do not address the changing nature of what are called disciplines at this present time. In this project I use literary analysis, feminist theory, cultural studies, social theory, and what might loosely be called fieldwork to figure out answers to questions that I find compelling and important. Thus my interdisciplinary approach may become more disciplined over time, since disciplines are neither primordial nor ahistorical. However, since this project is also about the formation of particular South Asian Indian and feminist subjects within transnational connectivities, I have found that the division between "area studies" and "U.S. ethnic studies" and divisions between "areas" or "regions" are often not useful. My project does primarily focus on ideas of "America" as they are articulated in the United States and outside it and on a group of people who move between the United States and India. For the most part, I address the subjectivities of middle-class and upper-class Indians, though one chapter does focus on more rural-based groups, in which class is somewhat fuzzy, as refugees. Thus the project is limited to what happens in a postcolonial metropolis that is also diasporic, and it is not a project that is territorially defined by a region outside the United States. However, I am interested in how knowledge about regions and "areas" outside the United States, which have come under the rubric of "area studies" in American academic sites, are produced by scholars whose lives, knowledge production, networks, and travels are inescapably transnational. How these distinct "areas" have been produced by scholars and others who mystify or ignore their own subjectivity forms an important topic that has been discussed well by many but is also often forgotten. I do not mean that all scholars need to write about themselves; however, I do question the extent to which contexts of production of knowledge are ignored in a great deal of scholarship. For instance, many discussions of fieldwork see the field as distinct from where writing or discussions may occur or from the sources of research funding. I hope to propose a messier world, where writing, researching, objects, and subjects of research refuse to remain neatly within the boundaries that discipline them. Thus I examine a number of sites where I found it possible to move, given my own subjectivity and identity, to literary works, nonprofit organizations, state practices, and scholarly undertakings of many kinds. This may make my book too undisciplined for many, but I hope more interesting for others. Above all, I hope to suggest that academic production is neither an "élite" theory that is disconnected from the "real" world of "real" people, material practices, state connections, and the market, nor a theory that is completely co-opted or emptied of critical possibilities. Rather, it is only by critically engaging with established and traditional disciplinary formations, and critiquing all kinds of knowledge productions in different sites that produce regimes of truth and discourses of power that we will begin to untangle the knot of power and knowledge in a transnational framework.

chapter *one*

BECOMING AMERICAN: THE NOVEL

AND THE DIASPORA

✴

Within the United States, the record number of those identifying themselves as "foreign-born" (almost 31.2 million according to the last census)
has created an extremely diverse group of migrants who confound attempts
to theorize what it means to be a citizen.[1] Questions of citizenship have
became vexed as new social movements have produced heterogeneous,
changing, and overlapping subjects. Yet it is not possible to argue that social
movements or transnational formations have been able to prevent nationalism or the formation of national subjects. While some assume that nationalism is linked to a more settled subject and that mobile subjectivity
could be resistant to nationalism,[2] it is clear that nationalism itself has
proved to be protean and mobile, providing identities and affiliations to
mobile as well as settled subjects, and indeed to what have come to be called
"global" and "cosmopolitan" subjectivities as well as to specific and local
ones.[3] Thus while some may argue that the appearance of transnational
movements, subjects, and connections has sapped the power of nationalisms,[4] it could also be claimed that the strength of various nationalisms is
visible within the transnational arena,[5] giving a sense of place to those who
see themselves as displaced. As a consequence of these shifts, the binaries

of placement and displacement, mobility and immobility could not adequately capture the ways in which ideas of place are crucial to those displaced, or in which immobility is central to creating mobile subjects.

Within transnational connectivities, in which the flows of goods, capital, labor, and knowledges revealed continuities and discontinuities with older colonial formations, the subjects that could be termed "diasporic," "hyphenated," or migrant were produced through three discourses of identity which were sometimes distinct and sometimes in combination with each other. The first was the discourse of the universal or global subject; the second, that of the national or local subject as separate and distinct and different; and the third, the hyphenated, hybrid subject straddling the first two formations. While the first two subjects were sometimes thought to be quite different from each other, they were linked as subjects of western modernity.[6] The universal or global subject, usually believed to be stateless, outside of culture, or "international," was presumed to exist in a world without borders or even one that would be better without borders,[7] while the national subject was believed to rely on borders around states or communities to produce an identity. The third subject, understood in relation to mobile subjects of various kinds, was sometimes seen as the hybrid that offered resistance to the nation-state or sometimes was assimilable to it. The histories of the overlap between the third kind of subject and the first two at various times and places have become important issues for scholarly debate since the hybrid subject was believed to be sometimes opposed to the other two subjects and sometimes in collusion with them. Thus within modernity's binary opposition of the universal or global as stateless and nomadic[8] and the national subject as settled and placed within the boundaries of the nation-state, the nationalism of the former as well as its location within a nation-state became an important issue.

Given the intensifications of transnational movements of capital, goods, media, and labor, in which those who stayed in one place were just as much transformed by transnational formations as those who moved, instead of focusing on the mobility and immobility of people as the key to identity formation at the end of the twentieth century, I focus on transnational connectivities as the means through which subjects and identities were created. Connectivities enabled communication across boundaries and borders through articulations and translations of discourses that circulated

within networks. Subjects were constituted as discursive nodes within uneven and heterogeneous transnational processes. Comprising histories of
various kinds, of new and old forms of globalization, transnational connectivities enabled multiple nationalisms and identities to coexist as well as to
shift from one to the other. They produced institutions and subjects, places
and identities out of circulating discourses.

In this chapter I will focus on one important mobile subject, the cosmopolitan, and its connections with immigrant, diasporic, and national
subjects. While each of these subjects was produced through various articulations of the global, the local, and the hybrid, cosmopolitan subjects
emerged in relation to specific nationalisms as well as to discourses of
universalism. In the United States, the relationship between South Asian,
Asian-American, and American subjects produced a set of questions that
remained at the heart of issues of gender, race, and nation. This chapter
probes the connection of diasporic, national, hyphenated subjects located
in the United States to the various conceptualizations of cosmopolitanisms
that took root in the scholarship in cultural, literary, feminist, Asian-American, and postcolonial studies. I suggest that given the heterogeneity of the
Asian[9] and South Asian populations in the United States through the
1990s, it is important to examine the various forms of transnational connectivities that enabled these subjects. In these connectivities, discourses of
race, gender, class, caste, and nationalisms all came together to create some
divergent versions of postcolonial cosmopolitanisms.

In using the term "connectivity," my goal is to spatially and temporally
disaggregate the various levels of connections that make up cosmopolitan
subjects. If our understanding of transnational movements is merely spatialized, it will be impossible to examine why some subjects are formed and
not others, and why some connectivities were more powerful than others. I
argue in this chapter, therefore, that transnational connectivities and their
histories lead us to rethink the relationships of migrants to the state, the
nation, and the international. By doing so, I examine why for many migrants from India, the term "cosmopolitan" is useful to describe some
versions of postcoloniality that were expressed within literary and aesthetic
cultural productions.

The term "cosmopolitan" became important in the last decade within
scholarly debates on the politics and identities of displacement and pro-

voked a number of key questions: Did awareness of being part of transnational processes make one a cosmopolitan? Could all immigrants be seen
as cosmopolitans?[10] What were the connections between diasporic and
immigrant subjects and what relation did these subjects have to cosmopolitanism? What were the terms generated by the institutions of the nation-
state and which terms were especially connected to the transnationalization
of economic, social, and cultural formations?[11]

Instead of suggesting that only mobile subjects could be cosmopolitan, I
want to suggest that cosmopolitanism depended on participation within
various discourses of the global, national, and international that moved
across transnational connectivities and enabled subjects to cross borders or
claim to transcend them. Thus cosmopolitanism depended on the particular connectivities possible at a given time and place and the transmission of
these discourses. Furthermore, while some subjects may have been constituted by these connectivities, others participated in them intermittently
or in unstable ways. Consequently, rather than focus on the cosmopolitan
as a stable or homogeneous subject, I want to instead address the discursive
practices that produced ideas of universality and the global and that enabled
the formation of uneven and unstable cosmopolitan subjects. In particular,
I focus on the production through transnational connectivities of what can
be called "postcolonial cosmopolitanism" and a feminist version of this as a
condition for the emergence of South Asians as liberal, multicultural, or
American subjects in the United States. Thus I argue that while some
versions of cosmopolitanism can be understood only in terms of "western"
subjects,[12] histories of colonization and of transnational connectivities have
produced postcolonial,[13] feminist, and national as well as racialized and
ethnic versions. In this formation of subjectivity, histories of trade and the
movements of goods and ideas remained key, as the globalization of consumer culture enabled the production of differences of many kinds.

In the three texts that I examine in this chapter, all written by authors
who reside in the United States, cosmopolitan discourses appeared in diverse versions. One author, Bharati Mukherjee, saw herself as a nationalist;
another, Chitra Divakaruni, articulated a multiculturalist position; and the
third, Amitav Ghosh, sought an anti-colonial cosmopolitanism. Whereas
these three authors might all be called Asian-American, since they live and
work in the United States, or diasporic, given that they all emigrated from

India after the changing of immigration laws in 1965, it is not clear that
these identities were claimed by these authors or that their works suggested any common identification at all. Bharati Mukherjee, for one, rejected the label of "Indian-American" writer in favor of an American and Bengali nationalist identity.[14] All three authors participated in cosmopolitan networks of knowledge production while also articulating quite divergent identities and discourses of nationalism, Indian, Bengali, and American.

The three texts produced quite distinct postcolonial cosmopolitanisms which incorporated an explicit and articulated relationship to nationalisms on the basis of their own class formation and from the histories of a colonized subjectivity that was privileged yet subordinate to the West. To Ghosh, for instance, a valorization of mobility was central to the production of a liberal, colonized subject produced not in relation to one state but to a broadly conceived global or international arena of anti-colonial struggle and solidarity. In his text, *In an Antique Land*,[15] Ghosh recuperated this cosmopolitan subject to reconstruct and critique Indian history and knowledges produced under British colonial conditions as well as to suggest anticolonial cosmopolitanism as a possible solution to divisive nationalisms. The second subject, the national subject, could be seen in *Jasmine*, a novel by Bharati Mukherjee published in 1989, just three years before *Antique Land*.[16] Mukherjee reconstituted the national subject in this novel as well as in her own practices of identification, claiming that she was an American of Bengali origin. Mukherjee's cosmopolitanism coexisted easily with her belief in the nation-state as the guarantor of rights and privileges as well as with a stable ethnic identity that was not seen as conflicted with her American identity; her work was clearly not anti-colonial or even written in response to the continued power of the West within late-twentieth-century globalizations. Consumable in the United States and India within a genre of Asian immigrant women's writing that rapidly became popular by the end of the twentieth century, and participating in the transnational production of works that depicted Asian "traditions" as unmodern, this text was able to create connectivities that articulated knowledges about women within transnational and cosmopolitan, feminist and literary circuits. The third text, Chitra Bannerjee Divakaruni's *The Mistress of Spices* (1997),[17] also participated in this transnational circulation of knowledges of Asian women, but it did so to exoticize and romanticize the notion of "tradition," incorporating it within a belief in a liberal multicultural state in the United States as well as in India. Here the colonial constructions of the division between traditional and modern were exoticized rather than denigrated as they were in Mukherjee's text. Multiculturalism was the universal and desirable global condition.

All three texts have genealogies that connect them to an earlier phase of globalization engendered by British colonial policies in India in the nineteenth century, and this history provided the precondition for the authors' participation in the cosmopolitanism of the late twentieth century. All three writers have the background of a particular social formation, the Bengali, English-educated middle class created by British colonization in India during the nineteenth century.[18] The British policy of providing an "English" education to Indians, as articulated in Thomas Macaulay's "Minute on Education" (1835), was initiated to produce a middle class which might function in the British government as an intermediary between the colonial state and the Indian population.[19] Well versed in British literature and in the English language, this group emerged in Bengal in particular as a vocal entity, which became active in nationalist and anti-colonial politics and produced famous writers and poets. It came to constitute an élite through knowledge of and contact with the West.[20] Although many other groups of Indians came to be influenced by an English education, each group had a particular history and genealogy; the Bengali middle classes were important targets of English education. However, it can be argued that the entire class of English-educated Indians came to have a colonial cosmopolitanism that inserted its members into circuits of knowledge about Britain and India that were not previously open to them. This cosmopolitanism, although quite different from the postcolonial cosmopolitanism of the 1990s, was nevertheless a condition of possibility for that later articulation. All three authors are also what Salman Rushdie called "midnight's children" in his novel of that name (1981): that is, they were born just before or after Indian independence, a generation wrestling with the legacy of colonialism and the problems of decolonization.[21] As such, all were brought up with a British colonial education and the Indian state's attempts to decolonize it. There is a considerable literature on this group that tells us about its relation to British colonialism, its postcoloniality, its public culture, its educational systems, and, in the case of Bengal, its relation to Bengali nationalism.[22] Much less has been written about its internationalism or its later

diasporic formations, so that for my purposes what is important is how the three authors that I analyze participated in transnational connectivities that are linked to these earlier histories of colonialism but that also create new national subjects in locations outside India and Bengal.

Within postcolonial cosmopolitanisms, the publication and circulation of literary works, especially those written in English as are the three texts under discussion, were made possible by the globalization of the publishing industry and the ability of texts to circulate across national boundaries.[23] Which texts circulated depended not only on the language in which they were written but also on histories of literacy, of publishing and trade, as well as on the kinds of narratives that enabled readers to consume texts in different ways in various locations.[24] These connectivities of representational practices and of knowledge production, I will show, have long histories that resulted in specific formations during the 1990s. These works also participated not solely in diasporic but also in transnational networks of knowledge production that encompassed India and the United States, anti-colonial nationalisms and American nationalisms, global feminisms and postcolonial networks. Nineteenth-century English education in India created a class which was able to move into the West with a facility that was not possible for others in India not well versed in this education.[25]

Within transnational connectivities, literary and aesthetic productions by these subjects participated in the circulation of knowledges about India and, in the case of two of the novels I discuss, about the United States. Although novels were a small part of these circulating knowledges, given the presence of music, movies, academic texts, and informal networks, they were nevertheless key to the production of aesthetic and political value among dominant classes. These texts were both products and producers of these knowledges, and their transnational publication and readership as well as their use of English enabled the circulation of a range of knowledges about India and its diasporas. Though the anti-colonial nationalism and cosmopolitanism of Amitav Ghosh was in marked contrast to the American and Bengali nationalism of Bharati Mukherjee, both of their texts expressed a cosmopolitanism that circulated in different connectivities—Ghosh's within networks of anti-colonial histories and Mukherjee's in neo-liberal nationalist discourses. However, their work participated in the production of a "literature" which by means of its aesthetic qualities disseminated images of India and the West. Within this work, late-twentieth-century cosmopolitanism can be seen not merely as a "discrepant" version[26] or a liberal goal for a transnationalized civil society but also as a class-, gender-, and racially specific network of discursive practices circulating within transnational connectivities.

THEORIZING COSMOPOLITANS

✳

The cosmopolitanism of the last decade of the twentieth century was a legacy of two subjects: the liberal subject as a possessor of rights and the subject of international trade. While the liberal subject evolved from the nineteenth-century idea of "the world citizen" as a form of belonging to the world and a subject of rights on a global scale, the subject of international trade was the product of global economic exchange and trade that began many centuries ago[27] and gained renewed force and dissemination through its late capitalist incarnation of consumer culture. These two ideas became key aspects of cosmopolitanism so that one could not exist without the other. Quite often, however, the interlinked nature of these processes has been mystified so that the connectivities between the two become invisible. This mystification has been as important in producing cosmopolitan subjects as it was in earlier centuries. Whereas in earlier formations, it was mostly Europeans who could be cosmopolitan, by the end of the twentieth century forms of globalized consumption and trade produced postcolonial cosmopolitans among formerly colonized and non-European Others through relations of power with the West and histories of colonialism.[28]

If the fundamental cosmopolitan position in the West has been that political participation is a human right of the first order, then the fullest extension of this argument leads to a claim of a transnational political participation and to the eclipse of national citizenship. Scholars have traced the cosmopolitan idea to the Stoics, and then in the modern period to Rousseau, Kant, and Marx. As one scholar, William Barbieri, describes the dominant meaning of the term, cosmopolitanism "militates against the intrinsically territorial idea of sovereignty and thus is ultimately impractical . . . Its individualistic logic leads ultimately to the reduction of national differences, to a sort of overall human homogeneity and conceivably to the destruction of the cultural diversity that many take to be an essential human good."[29] Barbieri's claim, that cosmopolitanism was at odds with national sovereignty, was common in nineteenth- and twentieth-century European thought. However, this very claim of non-affiliation to a state became a mode of nomadic power that used colonial and racial privilege to cross national boundaries. As Caren Kaplan has argued, this nomadism cannot be seen as a loss of privilege but as an assertion of power. This nomadism, Kaplan explains, has allowed cosmopolitanism to be associated with the representation of Europeans as "world citizens," that is, as those who are able to wander and travel at will, to become "native" in "foreign" lands while retaining their identity and power as Europeans.[30]

As a consequence of this mode of power, we can see that for the cosmopolitan "world citizen," the project of European civilization and the end of cosmopolitanism has been to produce a notion of the "universal" that could erase differences. However, the strategies and epistemes of imperialism also produced racial and gender differences, so that the work of hegemonic knowledges was to identify differences through the "comparative" mode of knowledge production. This project became a powerful idea through the nineteenth century and into the twentieth, and an important mode of organizing knowledge about the world. In this form of cosmopolitanism, the universal and the global become collapsed so that both sameness and difference are produced as temporal and spatial categories. Johannes Fabian has theorized this production of temporal difference through the concept of "coevalness" and the time lag produced within colonial hierarchies.[31]

The debate on cosmopolitanism regarding the affiliation between nomadism, nationalism, and cosmopolitanism has led to some new theorizations of the concept. For example, Bruce Robbins argues that rather than operate as an "ideal of detachment, actually existing cosmopolitanism is a reality of (re)attachment, multiple attachment, or attachment at a distance."[32] Robbins and Pheng Cheah follow James Clifford's important theorization of "discrepant cosmopolitanisms,"[33] leading Cheah to articulate cosmopolitanism as "a variety of actually existing practical stances."[34] In his consideration of cosmopolitanism, Cheah observes that the opposition between cosmopolitanism and nationalism has always been "unstable."[35] As

Caren Kaplan has argued, cosmopolitanism demarcates center from periphery and erases possibilities of imagining distance in less binary and more complicated ways within transnational cultural production.[36]

Despite this clear link to nationalism, late-twentieth-century cosmopolitanism presumed the insufficiency of the nation-state and its necessary transcendence in favor of international regimes or of nomadic and global subjects and universal knowledges. Although nineteenth-century European cosmopolitanism, articulated as the condition of being a "citizen of the world," presumed that national affiliations were easily ignored, its power lay in the ability of its subjects to believe that nationalism could easily be forgotten even while it was the standpoint, through imperialism, from which cosmopolitanism could be articulated. Furthermore, even the form of internationalism that became hegemonic assumed its conflation with cosmopolitanism.

By the end of the twentieth century, the cosmopolitan position saw the nation as insufficient and also often, for some nationalisms, as dangerous, and saw a "global" or "world" citizenship as being in opposition to the work of a mobile capitalism.[37] Thus, for instance, international human rights instruments came to be understood as the only protection for displaced or resisting subjects to some nations. Yet both internationalism and cosmopolitanism often mystified national belonging and the nation-state even while nationalisms produced gendered, raced, or classed standpoints that could operate within and through discourses of cosmopolitanism. For instance, Tim Brennan argues that cosmopolitanism gives space to the nationalism that it disavows. Yet one cannot simply decry cosmopolitanism, as Brennan does, for being a mode of postcolonial globalization that leaves out the socialists, the nationalists, and those who are, as he calls them, "incommensurable" to the global. Since neither nationalists nor socialists can be understood without the global networks in which they are produced, it is important to see nationalism or socialism as being supported by many transnational processes within what might be called the "global." Furthermore, Brennan's search for the authentic subaltern underlies his view of cosmopolitanism both as "selling out" and as a form of homogenization into a corrupt American popular culture. In Brennan's account, writers who write in English and who participate in the global publishing industry are the postcolonial cosmopolitans with a false consciousness that allies

them with colonial power structures. Although Brennan's charge about
postcolonial cosmopolitans as élites is not without some merit, his account
relies on an idea of subjects as homogeneous and whole, unchanging and
static, as well as without histories. Why some postcolonial subjects could
more easily participate in cosmopolitan circuits of knowledge is a question
that needs to be answered with some attention to specific historical formations. Élites also need to be analyzed and examined historically, especially if
class is understood as a dynamic formation. Furthermore, élite positions
include many varied classes, genders, races, and sexualities which participate in the transnational productions of knowledge about cultures and
nations. Thus it seems important to trace the genealogy of various cosmopolitan knowledges that produce these subjects and their changing relation to colonial and postcolonial formations.

To a certain extent, the question of class needs to be understood in
relation to historical changes in ideas of place and nation. How ideas and
discourses circulated and were articulated in particular places through cosmopolitan or nationalist or international subjects requires a historical analysis. As Amitav Ghosh argued in his essay "The March of the Novel through
History: The Testimony of my Grandfather's Bookcase," on the development of "world" and "international" literature and its institutions, cosmopolitanism was as much about placement as about displacement.[38] The
circulation of texts, particularly novels, canonized by institutions such as the
Nobel Prize across what came to be understood, within an evolving cosmopolitan discourse, as an "international" arena, enabled the production in
the second half of the twentieth century of a new discourse of cosmopolitanism as a form of belonging that placed through the articulation of displacement. The international novel, Ghosh argues, produced cosmopolitans in
all kinds of sites, distinguished by their access to the texts, mainly novels,
that institutions of "world literature" like the Nobel Prize identified as
"literature." Not only did this cosmopolitanism produce the sense of place
nurtured by the novel form, as Ghosh has noted, but it also inserted persons
across the world into the consumption of literary texts as a source of aesthetic and artistic value, which in turn gave readers and buyers a new cultural
capital. For instance, that Rabindranath Tagore, the Bengali writer, won the
Nobel Prize for literature in 1913 meant that subsequent generations of
Bengalis (and Indians) were inserted into the world of "international" litera-

ture in new ways. Ghosh's understanding of the subjects of a literature that is international begins from this position. One can speculate that Ghosh's grandfather's collection of Nobel Prize–winning literature received its inspiration from Tagore's Nobel Prize, and thus that Ghosh's participation in the production and consumption of these novels within the international literary world became possible through this familial and colonial history.

In his essay, Ghosh describes a postcolonial cosmopolitanism as a condition made possible by the circulation and articulation in India of a genre such as the novel.[39] The novel, according to Ghosh, has been "international" for over a century, and within it forms of intertextuality between the novels in Russian, Spanish, English, and French developed as a result. Ghosh points out that institutions like the Nobel Prize for literature brought together many writers from different nations within one bookshelf and created cosmopolitan readers as well as writers. However, rather than argue that the cosmopolitanism transcended location or place to become a version of the "international" that is understood to be nomadic and placeless, Ghosh argues that the genre of the novel, as it circulated within India through the institution of the Nobel award, was about producing a particular sense of place and laying claim to it. Thus for Ghosh, the growth of the Bengali middle class, educated in English, with access to a set of books sanctioned as "great literature" by the institution of the Nobel Prize, produced a cosmopolitanism that was nationalist in its allegiance to place (of belonging to Calcutta and Bengal and India in the case of Tagore), but was also produced in relation to a somewhat different idea of internationalism from that of the "world citizen."

To extend Ghosh's analysis, it can be argued that this notion of internationalism was created by the ability to participate, from a colonized position subservient to the West but privileged among those colonized, in the idea of an "international" aesthetic that could cross national boundaries as national literatures. The literary cognate to the "world citizen" of nineteenth-century cosmopolitanism was Goethe's concept of "world literature," which he defined as a "common world literature transcending national limits" which was to be produced because, according to Goethe writing in the nineteenth century, "nowadays, national literature doesn't mean much: the age of world literature is beginning."[40] No doubt Goethe's idea was produced by the circulation of a body of writing deemed "literature" within European culture, in which it was possible to compare, judge, and combine rather than see cultural productions as incommensurable, and which led to

what Vinay Dharwadkar calls "the internationalization of literature."[41] This
idea was later institutionalized through institutions such as the Nobel Prize
for literature, created by Alfred Nobel through the funding from his invention, patenting, and manufacturing of dynamite. The Nobel Prize was (and
is, to this day) a sign of "international literature," of the western idea of the
"literary" as "universal," that is, of a common aesthetic that could be found
by means of comparison across the world through its ability to be national
as well as "international." Whereas Nobel's will stipulated that the prize for
literature be given to works with an "idealistic tendency," during the first
half of the twentieth century these awards, for the most part, were mainly
given to European writers of many different genres and philosophies. Tagore's prize in 1913 was the first to a writer from Asia, facilitated by his ability
to translate his own work into English. While the notion that one winner
could be judged out of the many different aesthetics and ideas of the "literary" is itself a European aesthetic, as Christopher Prendergast points out,
Tagore's prize was a choice that resonated in political ways.[42] It made Tagore into an "Indian" and a "Bengali" writer as it gave value, within an
international arena, to the voice of a growing English-educated Indian élite
as well as to the notion of a literature with a national identity.

Yet it is noticeable that in Ghosh's account, this cosmopolitan internationalism is gendered as a masculine articulation, since Ghosh's grandfather's bookcase found its reader in Ghosh himself rather than any of his
female relatives. The cosmopolitan world of connections remained one of
connections between males, maintained and produced patriarchally by the
"grandfather's bookcase" as a legacy to the grandson, Ghosh. The legacy
was, in Ghosh's account, crucial to his sense of himself as an author who
could be read in many parts of the world and to his insertion into a world
that could move him away from the site of reading and the bookcase to
other national cultures described in the books that he read as a child, to an
international discourse of literature and literariness. However, there were
soon women writers from India creating a female version of this literature
in English that could cross borders; Sarojini Naidu comes to mind, as does
Toru Dutt.

With new technologies of connection between South Asia and the
United States, and greater interest in reading multicultural and postcolonial writers in the West, late-twentieth-century writers such as Mukherjee

and Ghosh gained audiences in both India and the United States. Technologies that enabled transnational connectivities circulated knowledge with greater facility and intensity than in the past. Amitav Ghosh's works, for instance, are co-published by Indian and U.S.-based publishers, so that they reach multiple markets and audiences almost at the same time. His writings about the histories of precolonial, postcolonial, and colonial South Asia produced a cosmopolitanism that moved across time and place, creating knowledges that could circulate across South Asia and its diasporas as well as to other audiences. Written in English, historical and erudite, his work gained appeal across scholarly and literate audiences. Ghosh's writings identify him as a writer about British colonization and Indian nationalism rather than as a writer about the immigrant experience, although it is clear that living in the West has not only informed his politics through an interest in borders and crossings but also expanded the audience for his writings. However, his work on border crossings and migration does not address the immigrant experiences in the United States as a movement from repression to freedom, but rather as a problem created by colonial powers that drew and redrew boundaries to alter national affiliation, thus creating migrant communities cut off from earlier homes.[43] His research and emphasis on histories of South Asia and his postcolonial cosmopolitanism lead Ghosh to write against the West, though from the cosmopolitan subjectivity of the writer of literature, instead of probing the complexity of living within it. Within his writings, travel and migration do not constitute movements from East to West, but rather from one part of the East to another part of it. Thus these are not diasporas in the way that these have been understood in recent years through examinations of communities of migration in the West, but rather forced migrations within Asia and Africa or migrations intrinsic to movements of trade. Yet these migrations constituted the dominant form of migration in the twentieth century, while smaller migrations to the West created some problematic narratives, as I will discuss below.

AMITAV GHOSH'S POSTCOLONIAL COSMOPOLITANISM

*

Analyses of diasporas and colonialism in the 1980s and 1990s came to be connected through the work of theorists such as Edward Said, Homi

Bhabha, and Stuart Hall.[44] However, Ghosh's text *In an Antique Land* took this link in another direction: that of examining the redrawing of national borders by colonial regimes that created diasporas. Furthermore, rather than examine diasporas created by such movements in the West, and thus the movements of migrants from East to West which were the primary focus of the theoretical formulations, he writes about a much more pervasive form of displacement from one part of the non-West to another. While Ghosh's text suggested the concept of "imaginative recovery" which Stuart Hall claimed was one way in which an "imaginary coherence" could be created out of the "experience of dispersal and fragmentation which is the history of all enforced diasporas,"[45] it is possible to understand Amitav Ghosh's important work not as a strategy of diasporic identification but rather as an anti-colonial political project. Hall constituted the Caribbean as a site where displacement created the aporia of recovery and where the European and American representational regimes led to new hybrid and syncretic formations. The Caribbean diaspora was produced as a specific formation created from within itself, as well as from resistance to Europe and America. However, Africa appeared in this diaspora theory only as a marker of an aporia rather than as a site of anti-colonial resistances and social movements. "Africa" for many diasporic subjects living in Europe or North America remained in the past once again, while diasporas and the West were seen as modern, with syncretic identities, creating a division between "home" and "host" that became foundational to diaspora studies.

While theories of migration focused on movements from a "home" country to a "host" country as a process of assimilation and acculturation from one essential identity to another, diaspora studies emerged to account for the heterogeneity of many national and cultural formations.[46] Yet some theorizations suggested that diasporas were resistant to a nation-state or to a nation,[47] leading groups to become "alienated or insulated" from their "host society."[48] For the most part, while the nationalism of a diaspora was seen as disentangled from that of a "host" nation, or the homogeneity of the diasporic group was disaggregated by gender, sexuality, or class, the binary of diaspora and "host" culture created an unproblematized "host" nation whose homogeneity was unquestioned.[49] In addition, the consequence of this binary led to yet another binary of diaspora and "home" or origin through which, quite often, the site that was said to be the "origin" became temporally non-coeval. However, one could argue that if Africa or Asia were not to remain within the logic of non-coevalness or of "origin" narratives that could never be recovered, then their syncretism also needed to be acknowledged along with the means by which anti-colonial nationalisms became transnational movements through the twentieth century. Ghosh's articulation of a long nonwestern history of cosmopolitanism brought to crisis the ways in which diaspora theories produced new continental divides between the "old world" and the "new."

Instead of the break with the past that diaspora theories suggested, Ghosh's text produced continuities of many kinds, especially of the pre-colonial past with the transnational present. In fact, the text argued for a cosmopolitanism that he suggested was not western in its origin but rather a product of Indian Ocean trading practices of the tenth and eleventh centuries. His work created a golden past not of the nation, but of cosmo-politan connections between groups divided by religion and yet unified through trade. By formulating the *histories* of itineraries and routes as a way to understand cultural connections, *In an Antique Land* mapped the Indian Ocean and the spice trade in the way that Paul Gilroy's work *The Black Atlantic* mapped the slave trade.[50] Ghosh's work can also be seen as a powerful corrective to the delinking by Gilroy's work of the Atlantic from the Indian Ocean. Yet unlike Gilroy's *Atlantic,* within which Africa was subsumed in favor of the cultural productions of those created in the New World, Ghosh's work sought to produce a new map of the Old World as the world without Europe. Moving away from the contest between a "West" and the "non-West," the text created a world where the West was either nonexistent or irrelevant and where the focus was the relationship between two "nonwestern" regions. The book proposed a new field whose history and geography could be examined from medieval times to the present in the service of an idealized, non-Eurocentric, postcolonial cosmopolitanism. More importantly, its difference from the theorizations of Western cosmo-politanism lay in its refusal to produce universal claims and knowledges, its willingness to keep its project to the historical specificity of tenth- and eleventh-century Indian Ocean trading practices. Yet as we shall see, Eu-rope and the New World could not be erased, and Ghosh's text, in its romanticizing of the Old World, cannot escape its origins in postcolonial and national knowledges produced within contexts and histories of cosmo-politanism produced by the "West" that the text hoped to disavow. Like the

European cosmopolitanism that Ghosh hopes to discredit, this text too argues that nationalism and cosmopolitanism are opposed to each other. In particular, "the premodern" as the past without Europe becomes the focus of this postcolonial cosmopolitan imaginary that can capture the seductive power of postcolonial history for a past purified of colonialism's taint. It is perhaps this imaginary that has come to have an international appeal in the worlding of the literature of postcoloniality.[51]

In proposing a new cartography, Ghosh presented a postcolonial reversal of European cosmopolitanism, arguing that the nationalisms and internationalisms of the nineteenth and twentieth centuries could not be seen as positive versions of cosmopolitanism. Rather, the text represented the so-called cosmopolitanism of modern Europe as a version inferior to that produced by the tenth- and eleventh-century spice trade of the Indian Ocean. Jonathan Ree pointed out this aspect of Ghosh's project, stating that readers could get, from the "beautiful" reconstruction of the life of a twelfth-century Jewish merchant, a glimpse of premodern cultural and geographic difference as an experience "innocent" of any ideas of national character or identity.[52] Ree's terms "innocent" and "beautiful" captured the nostalgia for a non-national perspective on cosmopolitanism that pervades Ghosh's text. Interspersing his self-reflexive ethnography of contemporary rural Egypt, where he traveled for fieldwork, with the story of Bomma, the Indian slave of Jewish traders in the twelfth-century Indian Ocean spice trade, Ghosh contrasted past and present, the non-cosmopolitans and nationalists in the present with the cosmopolitan traders of the past. The narrative cuts back and forth in time and space between Egypt, Mangalore, and Princeton, in the transnational pursuit of knowledges to help bring the eleventh-century Indian Ocean trading culture to life.

In contrast to modern capitalism's roots in the "Black Atlantic" and the horrors of the Atlantic slave trade, the text suggested, somewhat problematically and romantically, that the pre-European spice trade circuit was much more benign; Ghosh narrated an alternative history of slavery to contrast it to the Atlantic slave trade. He presented the medieval spice route as a corrective to the idea that the first explorers were Europeans, the first global economy the European one, and the first cosmopolitanism that produced by Western Europe. The Eurocentric history of travel was thus shown to have erased the world that existed before, in which the global economy linked the Mediterranean and the Indian Ocean. Accounts that had been erased include those of the cosmopolitan cities of the Indian Ocean. In Cairo's section of Fustat, the text states, the merchandise came from as far afield as East Africa, southern Europe, the western Sahara, India, China, and Indonesia, and Fustat itself was the conjuncture of some of the most important trade routes in the known world and the nucleus of one of the richest and most cosmopolitan cities of the world (38). The Jewish traders of Fustat, according to the text, "traveled regularly between three continents and their travels and breadth of experience and education seem astonishing even today, on a planet thought to be newly shrunken" (55). Ghosh revealed that the traders counted among them scholars, doctors, and philosophers. The counterparts to Cairo on the Indian coast were the towns of Mangalore and Calicut, places that attracted visitors because of their wealth and their position as gateways to the largest spice-producing areas of the world.

In Ghosh's text, the medieval cosmopolitan community of the spice trade was contrasted to the religious and cultural nationalisms of contemporary Egypt and the imperial power of colonial Europe that nurtured these nationalisms. European colonialism, for instance, was described as "that unquenchable demonic thirst that has raged ever since, for almost five hundred years, over the Indian ocean, the Arabian sea and the Persian Gulf" (288). According to the text, such was this demonic thirst that it swallowed even the Jews who became European, forgetting their Arab past, and helped denude the Geniza of its documents by thievery and trickery. This same thirst destroyed the spice trade of the Indian Ocean, changing the relation of Egypt to India while also subordinating these cosmopolitan places within another hierarchy. The Portuguese, who demanded that its Hindu ruler expel all Muslims, destroyed Calicut's cosmopolitanism. *Antique Land* attributed the tolerance of all religions in the spice trade to the demands of trade, as well as to the pacifism of some of the Indian communities participating in the trade. All this was destroyed by the European entry into the spice trade, and by the violence and aggression of the Europeans.

Not only were European trade and colonial aggression antithetical to cosmopolitanism, but other nationalisms surfacing in the context of European colonization were also represented as destroying the cosmopolitanism of the Egyptian and Indian past. The gulf between Egypt and India in the past and the present was visible, according to the text, in the ignorance among the villages of Nashawy and Lataifa about Indian and Hindu customs. This ignorance, in the narrative, was attributed to the destruction of the spice trade and its routes by the European colonizers, as well as to the nationalisms that taught ethnocentrism. Histories that needed to be remembered were erased, according to this account, and this work, like all Ghosh's other works, relied on historiography as a political project. Despite the presence of words, customs, and beliefs that Ghosh found in Egypt, which enabled him to connect Egypt to India, the villagers were ignorant of India and looked toward the West rather than to India for constructing their identity. For instance, one policeman who questioned Ghosh's presence in Egypt could not imagine that there was any religious identity beyond Muslim, Christian, or Jew.

The village men and boys who questioned Ghosh about customs in India were astonished that men and women there were not circumcised and that most people did not believe in Islam. This religious nationalism as it articulated with state nationalism frightened Ghosh, because it recalled other nationalisms in India that were not so benign. In particular, questions about whether Ghosh himself was circumcised reminded him of religious nationalisms in South Asia, in particular the history of the Partition of 1947. In both Punjab and Bengal, Muslim and Hindu males were differentiated and identified by whether they were circumcised or not and thus either killed or let go. Death or deliverance on different sides of the religious divide depended on just this bodily identification. In Nashawy, therefore, innocent questions about India and astonishment that men and women are not circumcised became intolerable and a source of terror. Even if Ghosh saw these questions as innocent, the book suggests that the innocence was frightening and painful because it signaled an ignorance that translated into a loss of cosmopolitanism, in contrast to the religious pluralism and tolerance practiced in medieval times in the context of the spice trade. The presence of water-pump technology from India, one modern example of the ancient link between India and Egypt, could not shake Ghosh's sorrow at the loss of connection. Thus in this account, the West had destroyed cosmopolitanism instead of nurturing it. Implicit here is a claim that the origins of cosmopolitanism could be located outside Europe.

Moreover, according to Ghosh's text, there were those who were not so innocent of difference but downright intolerant of it. These were subjects of colonialism and its product, modern nationalisms, which were based on forgetting the connections of the past. The imam in Nashawy, for instance, berated Ghosh for not working to change Hindu traditions which he called "savage" (235), "primitive and backward." He asks Ghosh, "You've been to Europe; you've seen how advanced they are. Now tell me: have you ever seen them burning their dead?" (235). Ghosh used the narratives of Indian nationalism to respond to the imam's Egyptian nationalism. Ghosh's response reinforced his belief that nationalisms had divided people who were earlier connected. Thus, instead of being cosmopolitans, both he and the imam had become travelers in the West and were thus living within the West's representational histories. He understood the imam's citation of the West as a participation in western knowledges that produced conflicts instead of cooperation: "We were both travelling, he and I: we were travelling in West. The only difference was that I had actually been there, in person" (236). The argument displayed the difference between the imam and Ghosh on the one hand and their ancestors who participated in the Indian Ocean trade on the other, and Ghosh bemoaned the loss of "the centuries of dialogue that had linked us" (236). Ghosh blamed the loss on the impact of western colonization and its civilizational hierarchies that placed India and Egypt on the "ladder of Development." The incident suggested to the narrator that he was a "witness to the extermination of a world of accommodations" that he "had believed to be still alive and in some tiny measure still retrievable" (237). It is this "dialogue," the "world of accommodations," that defined cosmopolitanism, as a different form of mobility than modern travel within which coevalness was not possible. In colonial contexts, both Ghosh and the imam had become travelers, one mobile and one immobile, in a hierarchy within which they were equally subordinate to Europe.

The subtitle of this work says that it is "History in the Guise of a Traveller's Tale." It would be more accurate to call it a postcolonial history that attempts to move travel away from its western origins to another time and place, in fact a utopian time and place. Vinay Lal has suggested that this sort of recuperation is a daring act of historiography.[53] However, though it is certainly a wonderfully daring history that builds on transnational and anticolonial affiliations between Egypt and India, this history itself is guided by colonial narratives of migration and trade and the forms of travel, which, as Ghosh implicitly acknowledges, are the only way to reach histories of connection between Egypt and India. For instance, the definition of cosmopolitanism as a "world of accommodations" was itself the ideal of cosmopolitanism that had been articulated in the West for many centuries, and as many scholars have pointed out, it resulted from the link between trade and cosmopolitanism in the West in the early modern period. Ghosh's narrative of a lost cosmopolitanism created the same connection between trade and cosmopolitanism that had been central to western constructions of cosmopolitanism, since the trading communities of Jews in Europe were considered cosmopolitans who could not belong to any nation.

Yet it cannot be said that Ghosh's cosmopolitanism was the same articulation as the "world citizen" of nineteenth-century cosmopolitan western travelers or even the new formulations of this position in recent works such as *Empire*.[54] The postcolonial aporia of this history lies in the problem that Ghosh's historical connection was only possible through Europe and, of course, "America" as the repository of the documents that made this history possible. The Eurocentric perspective of the production of the "premodern" and the "precolonial" has been critiqued by Kathleen Biddick, for instance, who also takes to task the "neo-orientalism" of those who search for the "real" precolonial in European archives.[55] Yet even when an archive's source is not Europe, the archive is often housed in Europe and North America, and these locations produce their own erasures. For example, although Ghosh cited the work of Professor Goitein for bringing the history of medieval trade to life, Goitein's opus bore the title *A Mediterranean Society*, not a title referring to the society of the Indian Ocean.[56] To a scholar such as Goitein, it was Egypt's relation to the Mediterranean that was of interest rather than its relation to India.

It is not only the problem of the archive as it was interpreted or dispersed that revealed the difficulty of reclaiming medieval history as postcolonial cosmopolitanism, but also the construction of gender and class in Ghosh's text. How do we understand the increasingly mobile lives of the poor late-twentieth-century villagers who leave Egypt to work in Iraq or the Gulf, or those like Ghosh himself who travel, or the imam whom Ghosh calls a traveler in the ideas produced by Europe? Were all these subjects cosmopolitan? Or even if these subjects revealed the "discrepant" cosmopolitanisms that were, as Jim Clifford suggests, characteristic of the end of the twentieth century, surely we need to see how these cosmopolitanisms combine with other subject positions for the scholar, the traveler, and the migrant worker. If the scholar and anthropologist rearticulated cosmopolitanisms, the migrant workers, like Ghosh's friends from Nashawy, were back, if they were lucky, to living in their villages after being expelled from Iraq—their cosmopolitanism was somewhat unstable and uneven. Furthermore, how do we differentiate these cosmopolitanisms from those of the Europeans in the nineteenth and twentieth centuries? If Ghosh's text suggested that the Europeans did not practice the cosmopolitanism of the medieval traders in the Indian Ocean, then how are we to understand the cosmopolitanism of colonial trade or the "world traveling" of nineteenth-century English travelers like Isabelle Eberhardt, both of which were western articulations?

Certainly, one way to resolve this issue is to argue that what Ghosh's medieval history and colonial nomadism had in common, unlike the villagers from Nashawy, was ease of travel, the power to cross oceans and borders without impediment. Colonial cosmopolitanism may not have had the "dialogue" between Egyptians and Indians, or cared to have a dialogue with any but other imperial powers, but Ghosh's medieval traders were powerful and wealthy, though they were not Europeans. Yet the texts reveal a problem in relying on mobility as a standpoint for cosmopolitanism. In the story of Bomma, the Indian slave, Ghosh summoned the fissures in the cosmopolitan narrative, as we learn that the slave was paid very little, spoke against his master, and resisted the power of the wealthy traders. The "Slave of MS H.6," though the impetus of the book, remains somewhat shadowy, so that the historical narrative recreates much more of the life of the masters than that of the slave. The text is at pains to show that subalterns are not easily visible in archives.

While the Slave remained in the shadow and gestured to the power relations that marred the utopian narrative, the fate of Ben Yiju's daughter, as related in the text, suggests other contradictions. According to Ghosh, Ben Yiju, the trader, moved to Mangalore in India from North Africa and married Ashu, a slave whose freedom he granted. When Ben Yiju decided to return to Cairo to see his family, he took his children from the union with Ashu but not Ashu herself. Ghosh explained this event by stating that Ashu's membership in the matrilineal Nair community would have prevented her from accompanying Ben Yiju to Egypt. Yet if Ashu's family is matrilineal, it is not clear how her daughter was able to leave with the father.

Perhaps Ghosh did not delve too far into this contradiction because contra- dictions of this sort would have unraveled the cosmopolitan story valorized in the text. Moreover, the daughter's future provided Ghosh with an even more interesting example of the reach of the spice trade. The daughter married her cousin from Sicily in Fustat, Cairo, bringing together a Nair woman with a Jewish man from across the Mediterranean. Ghosh resolved this failed cosmopolitanism through the narrative of the hybrid spread of cultures in which a new hybridity became a response to Eurocentric histories.

Although these contradictions in the text complicate the utopian narra- tive of precolonial trade, they bring to our attention the kinds of histories that connected subalterns in the past to those of the late twentieth century. In the process of acquiring the facility to cross boundaries, immigrants and refugees became cosmopolitan subjects, but the subjectivities were unsta- ble and often short-lived. Migrants such as Nabeel, one of the villagers from Lataifa, led dangerous and precarious lives in Iraq, as they were unable to transcend or mystify the continuing and developing nationalisms that de- stroyed them. Their cosmopolitanism does not have the long history of Ghosh's own cosmopolitanism. Ghosh's account mentions that Nabeel has "vanished into the anonymity of History" (253), and as Vinay Lal suggests, by so doing he has become the subaltern whose identity will be researched by some historian in the future.[57] As the characters shuttle between na- tionalisms, their cosmopolitanism cannot enable their passage out of pov- erty and their class positions dictated by long histories and national and transnational conditions.

Although Ghosh's text well describes the divisions and inequities of the end of the twentieth century, it creates a golden past of transnational trade. In Ghosh's text, nationalists could not be cosmopolitans, though colonial cosmopolitan travelers could. Certainly, Ghosh's own investments in his Indian identity are visible in the book and in its project to create a history without a European presence. Yet we cannot see this postcolonial cosmo- politanism as a product of the same nationalist project as the intolerant right-wing nationalism that by century's end infected both India and Egypt, which was about creating borders rather than seeking the regional soli- darities and connections of the past.

Trade created the first cosmopolitans, in Ghosh's account, and to a certain extent Ghosh's cosmopolitan hopes for the future were made possible by the trade in knowledges and books. Both nineteenth- and twentieth-century cosmopolitans were connected through a narrative of trade, whether colonial or precolonial, and the relation between trade and national boundaries was both shifting and powerful. Ghosh's narrative inserted the histories of trade into questions of nationalism and belonging that enabled the emergence of cosmopolitan subjects. Many versions of cosmopolitanism ignored this narrative of trade and consumption to produce the subject of rights, whether national or international, as either delinked from economic histories or in opposition to them. Nationalisms as well as internationalisms relied on the transnational movements of finance capital that created the power relations I have identified as cosmopolitanisms, as well as their unstable relation to discrepant modern, national, and postcolonial subjects. Thus movements of goods and finance were integral to transnational connectivities, though it is difficult, in this current phase of globalization, to think of trade as either benign or emptied of colonial power relations.

POSTCOLONIAL FEMINIST COSMOPOLITANISMS

✳

If in Ghosh's world only male subjects could be cosmopolitans, was there a differently gendered version? Cosmopolitanisms, like the nationalisms and internationalisms to which they were linked, were not just patriarchal. Postcolonial feminist scholarship examined how the individuality of European women from the eighteenth century rested on what Gayatri Spivak has called the "worlding" of colonized women.[58] Indeed, feminism and nationalism became mutually constituting discourses in many sites, as feminism and modernity became possible in conjunction with the growth of nationalism and emerging nation-states. Certainly this was the origin of modern feminism in South Asia and India.[59] Yet this link between feminism and modernity suggested the continued strength of the binary of tradition and modernity which became a central trope of modern formations along with the production of the "free" modern woman. Through the nineteenth and twentieth centuries, racial and cultural superiority was embedded in feminist narratives of the rescue of nonwhite women by white

women and men. A dominant narrative within this cosmopolitanism was a
contrast between the Asian and African women shown as victims of static tradition and culture and the modernity of European women within a European culture marked by mobility and speed. Similar representations endure to this day and remain integral discourses within new global feminisms circulating across transnational circuits. Western modernity, by depicting the intrepid western nineteenth-century woman as "world traveler" and savior of her less civilized "sisters," produced the white, female subject who could be the nationalist and the internationalist, unlike the "third world" woman who could never escape her culture.[60] This difference enabled white subjects to see themselves as modern compared to their "traditional" sisters and to constitute themselves as modern and free, liberal subjects. The late-twentieth-century western version of this subject was the one that could be identified as the "global feminist," one who rearticulated colonial tropes of women victimized by nonwestern "traditions" within transnational feminist connectivities of knowledges about "international" contexts.[61] However, global feminism was not a homogeneous formation emerging from the West; rather, global feminism's tropes were produced within transnational connectivities of knowledge production by many different subjects whose participation in cosmopolitan knowledges was diverse, uneven, and unstable. Global feminism has thus come to formulate a transnational governmentality that brought together geopolitics and biopolitics in which the construction of the free self occurred by means of the embodied, unfree "third world" female subject.[62]

While the trope of the rescue of brown women by white men and women was certainly not the discourse of all postcolonial feminisms, feminist discourses circulating across transnational connectivities remained tied to the binary of tradition and modernity as the central metaphor for understanding progress and development and constituting feminist modernity. Even though feminist and nonfeminist authors and scholars wrote against it and with it and subverted it, the trope remained a hegemonic way of representing women, especially across North-South national boundaries. The problem created by this binary constituted the struggles of postcolonial feminists especially within transnational contexts as they articulated their own and related agendas at various sites. Postcolonial feminist cosmopolitanism was connected to global feminisms based in the United States but was produced in relation to many other agendas and hegemonic formations. This postcolonial feminist cosmopolitanism rearticulated and subverted the modernity-tradition binary, but was still unable to constitute itself without it in transnational connectivities.

Even as feminism produced its own version of cosmopolitanism, other social movements based on race and sexuality in the United States created new versions as well. Social identities altered participation in cosmopolitan discourses in diverse times and ways. Whereas earlier paradigms of acculturation and assimilation turned immigrants racialized as "Asians" into Americans, newer paradigms of ethnicity, multiculturalism, and diasporas rendered this immigrant subject as a heterogeneous one, as Lisa Lowe has argued.[63] Yet the heterogeneity of this subject included a form of cosmopolitanism that accompanied some very changing and plural ways of becoming American, for instance, bringing together multiculturalism and cosmopolitanism through new discursive practices. In the 1990s American narratives of immigration produced specific raced, gendered, and sexualized subjects able to negotiate transnational contexts in cosmopolitan terms, although this was not so for every immigrant at every time and place.

While mobility was valorized within the construction of some diasporic cosmopolitanisms, it was often believed that the hyphenated American subject was constituted through opposition to the nation-state and through forms of cultural citizenship[64] rather than through discourses of mobility. The dominant way to discuss these formations was to see them solely as resistant or oppositional to the nation and state. If other narratives appeared, it was only in relation to how an "intersectional" analysis necessarily complicated and extended a thesis of a pure resistance.

Yet through the end of the twentieth century, racialized and heteronormative immigration policies created new problems for the production of knowledge. The term "Asian-American," for instance, could not be sustained as a term for a unified subject of resistance given the histories and new demographics of migrations from Asia by century's end. These dramatic changes are illustrated very clearly in relation to the knowledges about migrants from South Asia. For instance, within academic scholarship and research in the United States, the history of South Asian migration to the United States was not given much attention in the 1970s and 1980s.[65] The reasons for this omission were many, but I will focus on some key aspects of this migration to suggest the connection between twentieth-century cosmopolitanisms and Asian-American subjects. South Asians were left out of academic Asian-American studies, which emerged as a key site for the production of knowledges about Asian America, because migrants from South Asia, mainly Punjabi farmers, remained few in number given that they could not bring their families to the United States. In 1890 there were 202 "East Indians" in California, where most immigrants from India lived. By 1950 the number was 815, a decline from a high of 1,948 in 1910. Many had married Mexican women, since no women from India were allowed to enter the United States, which further confused the question of the immigrants' Asianness. Karen Leonard's fine study of the Punjabi Mexican population in California reveals the difficult conditions under which its members lived and raised their families.[66] Some claimed a Caucasian identity in order to be allowed to stay in the United States, as did Bhagat Singh Thind when his claim for naturalization was turned down by the U.S. Supreme Court in an opinion by Justice Sutherland in 1923.[67]

Moreover, Asian-American studies, created in the wake of student strikes in California universities in the 1960s and 1970s, at first focused heavily on history and sociology, with literature added somewhat later.[68] Given that these were the main disciplines from which scholars came to create Asian-American studies, this direction was not surprising. The emphasis on literary studies also contributed to erasing South Asians from this new discipline, though Ron Takaki did include their histories within his groundbreaking historical work.[69] For the most part, with some exceptions, South Asian migrants were from rural farming communities in North India (mainly Punjab) with minimal literacy and limited or nonexistent English skills. There were also students who came to the United States in the first half of the twentieth century, but they were few in number and did not articulate a separate Asian-American identity. Their experiences were also quite different from those of the working-class migrants who ended up doing agricultural work in the West.[70] It was only when upper-caste South Asian migrants educated in English literature, who were able to migrate after 1965, came to the United States in larger numbers that a so-called Indian-American literature was produced which focused on the experiences of migrants in North America and gained the attention of a reading public in the United States and of scholars of literature. Until the 1980s the only well-known authors of Indian or South Asian descent were based in India or in England, V. S. Naipaul, R. K. Narayan, and Salman Rushdie being the most prominent. Bharati Mukherjee was one of the first writers of South Asian descent to gain a wider audience among the North American reading public when her first novel was published in 1972, followed by a number of writers who wrote about the immigrant experience in the United States and North America as well as about South Asia.[71] Of the descendants of the early migrants, Kartar Dhillon had short stories and pieces printed in the anthology *Making Waves* (Beacon Press, 1989).[72] However, while Mukherjee is widely known as a writer about the South Asian immigrant experience, Dhillon is known only to a small number of scholars and others interested in the early history of migrants from South Asia to the United States.

If Mukherjee has been a pioneer in writing about the experience of Indians in North America, one of the reasons for her success at the end of the century was that she was able to articulate the trope of the Asian woman within the context of a liberal idea of America. The two texts that I discuss in the remainder of this chapter, *The Mistress of Spices* and *Jasmine*, reveal different relations to this trope. While the first book created a hybrid between tradition and modernity through the resurgence of the "ancient" wisdom of women, combining cultural feminism with a valorized nomadology, the second validated the trope, creating a clear division, temporally and spatially, between an India that represented tradition and an America that represented modernity.

The consumption of narratives of distance and alterity has a long history in the West in relation to knowledges produced by European colonization, but American race and gender politics produced a specific version.[73] The immigrant novel written by or about the "Asian" and "Asian-American" woman constituted a particular genre whose production, marketing, and regulation revealed a great deal about the transnational circulation of knowledges of nation, race, and gender. By the end of the twentieth century, this genre brought together a number of discourses in which a gendered and immigrant subject was made visible both through racial difference and through origin in the Asian "third world." Although there were many works from other immigrant groups that shared some aspects of the Asian-American woman's narrative, specifically those of immigrants from the

Middle East, the particular representations of Asian women in the United

States, deriving from Orientalist depictions and American imperial projects in Asia, produced a discourse for Asian-American women which was
unique. These cultural productions, which included novels, poetry, screen-
plays, painting, photography, film, and video as well as other works, were
executed in a context in which social movements constructed identity politics based on race and gender. Whether the works were claimed as "feminist" or not, they did not escape the binaries that were shared by feminists
and nonfeminists alike as they represented the lives of women in and from
Asia.

The features that characterized the genre of the Asian immigrant woman's novel could be seen in the discourses within these writings but also in
their conditions of circulation and production. Whereas the male migrant
from Asia was constructed in the first half of the twentieth century, as in
Carlos Bulosan's work, through the tension between exclusion from America and hope in its liberal ideas, the female migrant was construed, at the
end of the twentieth century, through the process of migration as a movement from incarceration within a patriarchal culture to freedom within
American liberal civil society.[74] The migrant herself moved from being a
victim to having more "choices" in her life in America. This movement was
also set up as the tension between tradition and modernity and the process
of a woman's escape from one to the other. The interruption of this process
or the failure to complete this movement often constituted the tragic aspects of these narratives. Many of these works were framed in the binary
oppositions between the United States as first world site of freedom and
"Asia" as third world site of repression, though one important interruption
of this paradigm was the Japanese-American narratives of the internment
and its aftermath.

Although these narratives emerged from a history of European colonialism in Asia and Africa, they remain important as discourses of modern
feminism in the West as it constructs feminist subjectivities. The discourse
of migration to the first world suggested that freedom and "choices" were
not available in Asia. This discourse valorized movement and mobility over
staying in one place,[75] and indeed reveals that the constitutive *movement* of
feminist modernity in the United States, even at the end of the twentieth
century, was from the repression of "tradition" to the freedom of modernity

as "choice." A number of other binary divisions then were mapped onto this division and articulated through it. Sometimes, the difference was characterized as movement from sexual and reproductive oppression to freedom articulated in terms of the formation of sexual identity,[76] or a class division or a generational division, as in the writings of Amy Tan.[77] In these works the space of home as the private space became racially, culturally, or linguistically demarcated from the space of the public or market. Resistance to racism was often featured as a negotiation with participation in the public realm rather than with the binary itself.

Gendered narratives and their subjects were also formulated through the discourses of exclusion and inclusion within America. For instance, Gish Jen's *Typical American* constructed resistance to racism as resistance to assimilation, to "becoming American."[78] Here the term "American" signifies the American dream. The immigrant search for success was shown as a search for participation in consumer culture—to buy a house, to have a car and all the objects that the dream promised. Yet becoming American was also a dream not fully open to Asian immigrants, since they were unable to participate in public life and the public sphere because of racism against Asians. Even private participation in the national game of baseball is treated ironically in Jen's novel, for it is suggested that the search for America and consumer culture leads to dishonesty, loss of family, and loss of cultural values. However, by the end of the 1990s, with countries in East Asia and Southeast Asia emerging as leading participants in consumer culture, this narrative changed in many ways.[79]

In other works, participation in this public realm became a rejection of what was said to be a "traditional" or inadequate nationalism through claiming a more "progressive" nationalism believed to be marked by choice. Opposition to this so-called tradition was often figured as a rebellion against one's "culture." For most female characters in these productions, embrace of modernity and "choice" was a vexed process, possible only within a loss of a homogenized "culture" of origin that was figured as "tradition." Although there are many texts that work against these divisions and many that recuperate them, these divisions constituted the dominant tropes through which Asian immigrant women were depicted and with which Asian women writers had to contend.

However, what has been particular to the narratives produced in the

United States was that the movement from "tradition" to "modernity" was figured also within the discourse of "choice" as a central element of a liberal democratic agenda for which the United States and America became both model and context. Choice here was not only the act through which freedom could be understood as central to the subject of modern American as well as of liberal feminism, but also an important aspect of neoliberal consumer culture's imbrication within the liberalism of democratic "choice" figured as "freedom." The particular "freedom" of "America" thus became the ability to have the "choices" denied to those in "traditional" societies and "cultures."

Although some of these cultural productions were not explicitly marketed as "feminist," the discourses within these works were closely connected to liberal feminisms in which the movement from tradition to modernity signified a woman's move from repression and exploitation to freedom. Thus quite often it was not globalization or military repression or lack of resources or state policies that were used as an explanation for the continued subordination of women in the so-called third world, but rather the power of "tradition."

Yet in addition to being pervasive in cosmopolitan representational practices in the West, binary divisions were rearticulated within transnational feminist movements as well as in the networks of knowledges produced transnationally about Asian women. These discourses enabled the connectivities that allowed many cultural productions to circulate around the world. The genre of Asian immigrant women's writing, framed as it was around this narrative, circulated these discourses within literary markets in many regions of the world.

BHARATI MUKHERJEE'S MULTIPLE NATIONALISMS
✴

While texts such as Maxine Hong Kingston's *The Woman Warrior*[80] and Amy Tan's *The Joy Luck Club* can be seen as classic examples of the genre of Asian immigrant women's writing, I want to now turn to another text in which this genre came to full expression. *Jasmine*, written by Bharati Mukherjee and published in the United States in 1989, is widely read and studied as a major work by an Indian woman writer in the United States.[81] The first-person narrative of a Hindu girl living in Punjab, India, whose family has been displaced after the partition of India and Pakistan in 1947, the novel describes her struggles within India, how she reaches the United States, and her life in the United States. An anomaly among other young women, Jasmine is dissatisfied with her life and struggling against the miserable existence that is revealed as the lot of all women in Punjab. After her husband is killed by Sikh "terrorists," she enters the United States without documents. Raped soon after by one of the white men who are paid agents facilitating border crossings by undocumented migrants, she is rescued by a Quaker lady, who trains her to be a childcare provider and maid. She falls in love with Taylor, the father of the child she was hired to care for in Manhattan, then leaves him to live in Iowa with a paraplegic, adopts a young Vietnamese boy, and is finally reconciled with Taylor at the end of the novel.

Within this trajectory of migration, the narrative frame of the novel remains the journey from oppression and misery and conflict (religious, for the most part) in India to a closure of "hope" as the protagonist becomes an American in the United States. Along the way, struggles and conflicts in India are presented, very problematically, as the struggle of the learned and kind "cultured" Hindu family of Jasmine against the rapacious, violent, evil, and fanatical Muslims and Sikhs of Punjab. Relying on the Indian state's repressive discourse during the 1980s and 1990s, of the "terrorist" as a Muslim or Sikh, Mukherjee's narrative endorses first the Indian state's hegemonic discourse of law and order and security, and then the discourse of American nationalism as providing freedom through migration.[82] Women in Punjab, where the Indian state's counterinsurgent practices were used to repress all rights of the population during the 1980s and 1990s, were shown as completely oppressed by their parents and husbands and cultures, except for Jasmine, who felt "American" from the very beginning, even though she had never visited or lived in the United States. In this narrative, it is not any state that was responsible for poverty and violence, but rather some communities and cultures that are seen as essentially violent, and a lack of individuality on the part of women of the culture, and their allegiance to their tradition, exacerbated the violence.

Within this narrative, America becomes the locus for Jasmine's emergence as an individual with desires and "choices." Here we see the link between biopolitics and geopolitics in that security and care are believed to be impossible in Punjab because of the inherent violence attributed to its populations, but in America safety, security, and "ordinary" life are possible. In articulating the dominant discourse of American consumer culture as one that creates individuality and provides choices, *Jasmine* suggests that freedom as a form of empowerment comes from participating in the dominant power structure of the nation-state. This text suggests that it is the responsibility of immigrants to become part of the American "melting pot" rather than produce a separate hyphenated identity. As Mukherjee says about her own move to the United States from Canada: "I became a citizen by choice, not by simple accident of birth."[83]

But is the United States really a better place for immigrants? Immigration to Canada and the United States has had different patterns, since after 1965 the United States focused on selectively bringing professionals to the country. As a result, Indian immigrants in the United States have been mostly middle or upper class, rather than working class as they are in Canada. A large number of Indian immigrants in Canada were also from Punjab, rather than from across India, and were not élites, as they were in the United States. The general acceptance of South Asians in the United States, which was not forthcoming for many other immigrants who faced racism daily, may have to do with the professional status of many South Asians in the United States, unlike South Asian immigrants in Canada. Educated in British schools in postcolonial India, and often invested in Indian nationalism, immigrants to the United States were cosmopolitan subjects who could more easily become American. By contrast, the Canadian state more explicitly endorsed a national discourse of multiculturalism, which the United States began to incorporate only in the 1990s.

The notion in *Jasmine* of what constitutes the "ordinary" relies on a neoliberal idea of "freedom" and "choice," the key terms through which a modern individual can be constituted, and on America's neoliberal ability to realize every individual's potential through the choices that it offers. The presentation of the third world as a combat zone, in contrast to the peace of "ordinary" life in middle-class white Manhattan, remains centrally within a liberal American discourse of migration as providing freedom to its populations. In Mukherjee's text, the gendered subject before migration was alienated from a problematic and oppressive Indian culture which she hoped to leave to become "free." Even though a heteronormative discourse of the nation is recuperated in the narratives of migration, Jasmine's mobility enables her to realize her potential. Driven out of India by sectarian violence (which is seen as uniquely "Indian"), she is described as uniquely American because she is so adventurous and so mobile, unlike the other women around her in Punjab. Scornful of living away from white Americans in what are seen as stifling South Asian ghettos, she prefers to live with a white couple in Manhattan as a nanny. Miraculously all white men fall in love with her, and she possesses an ability to obliterate racism with the taste of the curry she makes for them. She then becomes the rescuer of other victimized Asians, and in doing so becomes the liberal imperial subject whose power is expressed through the mode of rescue she performs for other Asians; she expresses the humanitarianism that is part of the subjectivity of cosmopolitans in the West. Thus she adopts a Vietnamese refugee boy, even while showing contempt for other Asians and South Asians.

The novel suggests that successful migration to America is possible for those lone adventurers, individualists, risk takers who were "Americans at heart" wherever they lived. This narrative ignores the histories of race, class, religion, nationality, sexuality, and gender that have enabled participation for migrants within particular transnational connectivities.[84] For someone from the middle or upper classes in India, with an English education and many benefits from élite educational systems in India and the United States, migration could indeed be a matter of selective melting into America, while, as with Mukherjee, retaining a strong identification as a Bengali or Brahmin. Without such privileges, migration has always been a story of difficult and weaker transnational connectivities, and of the power relations within South Asian communities. Over a century of migration from Punjab was made possible through community networks, intensely connected groups of relatives, neighbors, and villagers who provided support, money, information, and the means to travel. These transnational connectivities made migration possible and continued to create and draw new migrants. In *Jasmine* these networks are represented as only virulent and abusive.

Mukherjee sees migration as a process of self-invention and transformation; in her novels as well as in her conversations and interviews she offers herself as an example of one who negotiated the "no-man's land": from "the country of my past" to the "continent of my present."[85] It is this biopolitical project of empowerment through identification with the American nation that is so important in her book, although her own trajectory of identification seemed to move from one regional, caste, and ethnic identity to American citizenship, rather than from one national identity to another. While Mukherjee is on record as saying that she wants to be called an American rather than an Asian-American, her claims to an Indian national identity are not so clear. Thus when speaking of her past, she has identified herself as being from Calcutta, being Bengali, or being Hindu and upper-caste rather than Indian. In one interview she called herself an American writer of "Bengali origin."[86] She recollected that her childhood was spent as part of a dominant powerful group in Calcutta, where she remembered living among a "homogeneously Hindu, Bengali-speaking and middle-class population."[87] This observation revealed Mukherjee's investments in a hegemonic discourse of law and order of the state, since Calcutta after mid-century was riven by caste conflicts, Hindu-Muslim riots, migration from impoverished rural areas, and an extremely diverse population that was always in uneasy negotiation with the dominant Bengali Hindu community. By the late 1960s, the Naxalite movement in Bengal had become, especially in Calcutta, an urban guerrilla movement, which exacerbated class divisions and created considerable class conflicts. Many intellectuals from the left supported the movement in an effort to fight the poverty that was not being ameliorated by the state. This privilege of not recognizing the many different groups who lived in the Calcutta of the 1950s reveals that for Mukherjee, it was the dominant discourse that was to be endorsed, whether it was a national or an ethnic or caste identity. Paradoxically, however, although she argued for an America that accepted all kinds of migrants, she argued that the terms of acceptance were participation in the dominant culture of the American nation.

As a consequence of these political beliefs, Mukherjee's novel endorses American nationalism as a neoliberal political vision of democracy in which ethnic identities are produced and racism overcome through choice and individual will and acts. Even though the protagonist in *Jasmine* encounters many kinds of violence in the United States, the country offers her something that India cannot, which is the choice to reinvent herself. As Mukherjee has said, immigrants have a privilege: "of not only inventing your biography, but also deciding for yourself . . . *choosing* your homeland."[88] It is this liberal America, where identity could be a choice, which forms the core of Mukherjee's American nation. In the United States, according to Mukherjee, immigrants are able to change their identities, whereas in India identities remained frozen. Yet this American nation which provided choices could only be affirmed through its difference from India, that place where there were believed to be no choices, especially for women; Mukherjee's technologies of self-making supported a geopolitics constituted through national difference. Even in Mukherjee's autobiographical narratives, there is a vast divide between India and the United States, so that unlike in the Old World, life in the New World is believed to be full of "scary improvisations and heady explorations."[89] Thus in *Jasmine*, India is characteristically "traditional" and unchanging, while everything in the United States was speedy and modern. The representation of modernity located its center and origin in the West, and this modernity became normative to a cosmopolitanism that could only see a third world as abnormal and outside the "ordinary." *Jasmine* offers difference without a historicized understanding of inequality. The novel's lack of any specificities regarding the lives of South Asian women in a particular period, or of the complexities of the history of modern South Asia, allows the discourse of tradition and modernity to replace the complex histories of postcolonial India as well as the problematics of historiography.

In defending herself against charges of misrepresenting India, Mukherjee claimed that she wrote fiction and not "pure and exclusive sociology," so that she did not write about what India was like but rather about how "one person inhabits the world."[90] However, Mukherjee's ways of "inhabiting" the world are precisely the issue, revealing how the biopolitics of the Self endorsed problematic nationalisms even within liberal critiques of racism. While assailing Sikh or Muslim nationalisms as producing violent patriarchal formations, Mukherjee's text values American nationalism as the path to a liberal democracy. In doing so, *Jasmine* recuperates the Indian and U.S. state's discourse of the Sikhs and Muslims as "terrorists" and thus the postcolonial state's violent enforcement of "law and order" as well as the geopolitics of terrorism as the key to connections and differentiations between states and nations.

In another transnational context, *Jasmine* rewrote the histories of migration of Indians to the United States. Its discourse of the Sikhs as violent displaced an older history of Sikhs from Punjab as the first South Asian migrants who formed, in San Francisco for instance, an important front in the struggle for Indian independence in the 1930s and 1940s. They formed the majority among the first South Asians to come to the United States. By erasing these histories in favor of the repressive discourse of law and order produced by the postcolonial Indian state, and by relying on the problematic geopolitical discourse of the "terrorist" that recuperated violent raciologies, Mukherjee's text remains within the Indian state's nationalist politics in India at the end of the twentieth century.

In a short essay for the magazine *Mother Jones*, Mukherjee wrote that her "rejection of hyphenation" was not "race treachery" but rather "a demand that America deliver the promises of its dream to all its citizens equally." Mukherjee argued that "America" was a "myth of democracy and equal opportunity to live by" and "an ideal goal to reach."[91] Although she did not gloss what she meant by "myth of democracy," it is clear from her comments that she called herself American because she hoped that a set of migrants who were diverse in race, language, and nationality could live the liberal dream in America. Thus, she stated, "our nation is unique in human history in that the founding idea of 'America' was in opposition to the tenet that a nation is a collection of like-looking, like-speaking, like-worshiping people. . . . America's pioneering European ancestors gave up the easy homogeneity of their native countries for a new version of utopia."[92] This narrative of America posited diversity as a founding notion rather than as a discourse negotiated through a struggle for civil rights, or as a notion which became central to the transnational movements of capital and goods. Yet in Mukherjee's narrative, the making of a "new American culture" could not be done, as she stated, on the basis of a multiculturalism grounded in race. According to Mukherjee, this multiculturalism, because of its "emphasis on race- and ethnicity-based group identity led to a lack of respect for individual differences within each group, and to the vilification of those individuals who placed the good of the nation above the interests of their racial or ethnic community."[93] In this account, diversity was fine but a racial group identity was not. The only diversities that were possible here were those of varied nationalisms and of the narrative of national origins. Thus racism was to be opposed through a quest for inclusion within the nation that disavowed formation of group identities or identity politics.

It is ironic that although Mukherjee rejected a hyphenated identity, she came to be identified as an Asian-American writer and a writer of "multi-cultural" America, revealing that identity could not simply be seen as a matter of individual will or choice. Furthermore, since she wrote about the immigrant experience, her work was (and is) given a great deal of attention within the academic field of Asian-American literature. Since Asian-American women's writing was also structured around the movement from tradition to modernity, and thus within the discourses that depicted Asian and Asian-American women in the West, it was understandable that she could be identified in this way. Marketed both as an immigrant novel and as a multicultural novel, *Jasmine* was consumed through the discourses of the tradition-modernity binary. For instance, the copy on the cover of the paperback edition of *Jasmine* signaled to this discourse of migration with a quote from the *Baltimore Sun*: "Poignant . . . heart rending . . . The story of the transformation of an Indian village girl, whose grandmother wants to marry her off at 11, into an American woman who finally thinks for herself."[94]

Jasmine has had a large and popular readership. Not surprisingly, it became one of the most widely read novels written by a South Asian writer living in the United States, receiving very favorable reviews in the popular press. Although Mukherjee won the National Book Critics Circle Award for her collection *The Middleman and Other Stories*,[95] it was *Jasmine* which was read more widely at one time.[96] A quick survey of readers' reviews on the Amazon.com website, twenty-eight in all, tells us something about the popular response to *Jasmine*. Although these responses do not suggest the totality of responses to the novel, they do confirm that the discourse of the victimized Asian woman and the tradition-modernity binary continues to make the novel intelligible to many readers in the United States, especially those who felt moved enough to post their response to a website. Although a few readers remarked that the plot was "unreal" and far-fetched, most readers were enthralled by the story. Only four of the reviews were negative; the others all admired the novel. Three of the twenty-four read *Jasmine* in connection with academic coursework and all three enjoyed reading it.

Several readers found the narrative about India and the part of the novel set in India to be the most compelling. One reader wrote, "Her story of the plight of a woman in India seems to be real. Women are oppressed and must learn to survive."[97] Another wrote that although a "sense of hope is conveyed" in the novel, "it paints a disturbing picture of traditional India: the caste system, the miserable status of women, the horrors facing a widow, the overall poverty and pervading corruption, the religious wars."[98] A third reader commented, "Learning what it was like when [Jasmine] lived in her country was in fact the best part of the book." The same thought was expressed in another reader's comments: "The only sections of this novel that are worth reading are those that take place in India where Jasmine is a child-bride." If a fascination with "traditional" India and its horrors accounts for much of the interest in the book for some of its admirers, others understood it in terms of universal narratives of "love and hope," "of human struggle in an alien environment." Still others took it as a realist narrative: "it seemed real and plausible," it explored the "American experience," and was a "good story on the transformation of people." One reader wrote that the "story of how a young Indian girl becomes an American is intriguing"; another wrote that the novel showed "a real girl" who was "seeking a new self definition." Even if its recounting of the experience of migration did not make the novel meaningful, its message of self-fulfillment within a culture of self-empowerment did. For readers who responded to this message, the strength of the book was the way it depicted the difficulties of being a woman in an India still constrained by a strong patriarchal tradition and the possibilities for transformation and change by an immigrant who became an American. Only one reader, writing from Calcutta, mentioned that she liked the book because it showed that the immigrant's life was not easy in the United States, contrary to what the reader had heard. It is surprising that none of the other readers, nineteen of whom identified themselves as being from the United States, pointed out that the immigrant experience was shown to be difficult. Although some readers saw it as a "struggle," most thought the Indian sections were more worthy of comment.

Academic criticism pointing out the problematic aspects of Mukherjee's discursive practices was not as kind as these popular reviews of *Jasmine*. Arnold Harrichand Itwaru, a South Asian Canadian poet, noted that "the only escape is flight from India to 'America' and its 'promise,' where interestingly, America-the-good is found—America-the-good as white America." Critics such as Anne Brewster stated that Mukherjee produced a "neonationalism" in opposition to arguments that ethnic migrants produced a difference that opposed imperialisms or nationalisms. Mukherjee's dis-course of assimilation, Brewster argued, was reflected in the adulation that she gained in the United States, and her assimilationist narrative was coun-ter to the transnational and bicultural ties maintained by non-élite immi-grants.[99] While some critics saw *Jasmine* as a narrative of a woman's strength or an immigrant's struggle,[100] or even as the embodiment of the successful immigrant's ability to survive,[101] others critiqued the novel as shallow, as having characters that were "marionettes performing a part" or ideologically suspect.[102] For some critics, Mukherjee's élite cosmopolitan aesthetic was particularly problematic in claiming postcolonial alterity,[103] as was its char-acterization of a homogeneous immigrant experience.[104] Gurleen Grewal, for instance, argued that the novel ignored histories of race and class in the United States, showed the immigrant woman as exotic Other, and valorized the American dream.[105]

The postcolonial scholarship within which such critiques of Mukher-jee's novel appeared focused for the most part on Mukherjee's nationalism rather than on the transnational practices and class and ethnic connec-tivities within which she could become a writer about India and about the Indian immigrant experience in North America. These critiques were im-portant not simply because they examined the politics of a particular writer, but also because they revealed how postcolonial cosmopolitanisms' cir-culating discourses produced a variety of contexts for reading Mukherjee's works. Thus if there were readers who saw the protagonist, Jasmine, as modern in opposition to the "oppressed third world woman," there were others who saw the novel as problematic in its support of American na-tionalism.

COSMOPOLITAN MULTICULTURALISM: CHITRA DIVAKARUNI'S *THE MISTRESS OF SPICES*

✳

Whereas Mukherjee's narratives endorsed the American dream, other writers worked through discourses of tradition and modernity and of na-tionalisms in alternative ways. Moreover, the narratives, even in the United States, have not remained unchanged in the decades since they appeared. In the last two decades of the twentieth century, narratives of "hybridity" and multiculturalism also emerged to challenge discourses of migration as

assimilation. Whereas in some works this hybrid of tradition and modernity was celebrated, in others the celebration contained within it a nostalgia for the non-hybrid past. Meena Alexander's memoir *Fault Lines* was an example of a work depicting the diaspora as hybrid but also as fragmented and unreclaimable.[106] The author's pain and longing for a past that was undiasporic, although full of tensions based on differences of class, gender, sexuality, and religion, pervaded this text and presented diaspora as a site of struggle rather than of resolution or of arrival to freedom. Yet the binary of modernity and tradition remained in this text to reveal the author's struggle against the "home" in which gendered roles became repressive and stultifying. The binary of tradition and modernity still structured the narrative, but in it migration is a movement that produces struggles rather than resolving them as in the assimilationist view of migration.

In Chitra Divakaruni's novel *The Mistress of Spices*[107] the cosmopolitan feminist discourse of the migrant's movement from tradition to modernity remains the structuring mechanism, albeit in a more exoticized version than in Bharati Mukherjee's *Jasmine*, from which it differs greatly. Mukherjee's nationalist cosmopolitan was constructed through the neoliberal biopolitics of choice underlying both liberal democracy and consumer culture; Divakaruni's is more clearly about consumption and the means by which difference could be consumed through an exotic aesthetic. The story of Tilo, a crone-witch who appears in Oakland, California, in the guise of a beautiful young woman, is told through the description and use of spices. Every chapter bears the name of a spice: turmeric, asafetida, fenugreek. The mysterious and fascinating heroine, Tilo, is a sati come to life, one who can resist the colonial discourses of the victimized Indian woman. Tilo is transformed by her initiation through fire and learns from her foremother, the "Old One," another crone-witch, to use spices as magic. The spices are used as magic potions, healing mixtures, and truth serums, and, in the tradition of Kali, to destroy as much as to create. Represented as ancient wisdom based on Hindu mysticism, the information about spices mentions their use in cooking as well as healing. Spices possess magical powers, since they bring lovers together, reconcile to her parents a young woman marrying out of her community, and assist another to leave her abusive husband. Much as Ghosh's narrative created a utopian version of the nonwestern, precolonial spice trade in the Indian Ocean, *The Mistress of Spices* similarly represses the violence of the modern history of spices by enabling them to appear magically in the United States through the cosmopolitan discourse of the "healing powers" of eastern tradition, the feminist politics of empowerment, and the cosmopolitan enjoyment of Indian cuisine.[108]

Published by a major publisher, Anchor Doubleday, *The Mistress of Spices* was reviewed in the *New Yorker*, *People*, the *Los Angeles Times*, and the *San Francisco Chronicle* and made the bestseller lists in the San Francisco area. A mass-market paperback edition at one point was even available at Costco. Given this wide distribution, it can be assumed that the book was read not only by South Asians in the United States but also across a spectrum of the urban middle-class population. Thus it is important to examine the discourses that crossed a number of different market segments and created a wide readership. In this novel, spices are not the signs of violence that they have been in the history of the West, but rather are exoticized as signs of difference and of female knowledges exotic to the West.[109] Gender and national difference create a cultural identity that could be consumed in a cosmopolitan and transnational framework connecting upper-class India and the United States. Divakaruni's narrative was intelligible to a wide variety of readers because of this connection between consumer culture and its search for the exotic, along the way supporting the discourse of a multicultural America by producing ethnic identity through exotic difference.

Furthermore, the cosmopolitanism of this narrative emerged also from its participation in the transnational production of the difference between "modern" and "traditional," especially as this binary was gendered through the articulation of a heteronormative biopolitics produced through discourses of mobility. This narrative of the encounter of "ancient" with the cosmopolitan and the contemporary produced a heroine who relied on "tradition," yet who as an American immigrant was willing to give up the past for a life with her American man. With a prose style that the *New Yorker* termed "pungent," this account of spices produced American ethnic identity by exoticizing difference; this difference was valuable because it proposed to revive and reveal the secrets of ancient cultures within late-twentieth-century consumer culture. The postcolonial cosmopolitan discourse mediated between the worlds of modernity and tradition, and was able to resolve this opposition by embracing a multiculturalism that allowed tradition and modernity to coexist.

This narrative of the ancient and modern, distinct from the division that Ghosh articulated of the precolonial from the colonial, sutures the world of late-twentieth-century cosmopolitan travel and cuisine with American cultural feminism's new transnational spiritualities that enable empowerment through discourses of premodern and nonwestern goddesses. Exotic power is empowerment, and feminism and exoticism are first demarcated and then reconciled. Exotic spices enable women to become feminist subjects by using their magical and healing qualities to fight patriarchal Indian tradition. One customer whose life was changed by the magic of spices is a young woman who flouted the "tradition" of arranged marriage by marrying a Chicano of her own choice. Another customer is neoliberal feminism's stock figure, an Asian woman in an abusive arranged marriage, who is helped by Tilo, through the spices and through information about a women's shelter, to leave for safety. Other examples of these two figures became visible in the 1990s in numerous narratives of South Asian women in the United States, in which the "arranged" marriage was a signifier of tradition denoting the absence of choice. Divakaruni's collection of short stories, *Arranged Marriage*, was organized around this trope.[110] In comparison, marriage for "love" signified passage into America through the discourse of "choice." The story of Tilo, who falls in love with her American named Raven (who passes for white but who we are told is really Native American), finds happy closure through the reconciliation of ancient with modern. Simultaneously, a heterosexual union with Raven is reestablished as the only feminist path by means of which Tilo can bring her healing arts to work in the new world. Although the text raises some tensions between the Orientalized exotic and the construction of multiculturalism, as when Tilo expresses her suspicion that Raven loves her only because she is exotic, this tension is quickly repressed in favor of the romance of modernity and the movement of the immigrant to modernity from tradition. Tilo sheds her old woman guise as well as her beautiful, young femme fatale body and becomes the ordinary woman living and working with Raven to rebuild Oakland after an earthquake. The novel's closure is enabled through the production of America as a site of redemption.

The Mistress of Spices reconciles American multiculturalism with Indian nationalism's own diversity discourse in a transnational link mediated through the figure of the oppressed "third world woman," who is saved not by the western feminist but by the magic of spices and the "ancient" healing arts. However, we are told that the magic works only on those who belong to Tilo's "own kind." Tilo is told to save only her "own kind," and this racialized category includes subjects produced through Indian nationalism's model of "unity in diversity." These subjects include the Kashmiri Muslim taxi driver and the Sikh youth, from communities that in the last two decades of the twentieth century in India produced insurgent nationalisms repressed by the Indian state. All these Indian minorities are said to be in danger of losing their identities in "America," even though the novel itself is testimony to the circulation and consumption of ethnic identity. Just as Indian restaurants and spice shops in every major city in the West provide a cosmopolitan "experience" of India as both nation and ethnicity, *The Mistress of Spices* produces ethnic identity for cosmopolitan consumption in the familiar binary terms of America the modern and India the ancient.

Using the past more as a repository of exoticism, the "spices" in this text produce cosmopolitan subjects through the magical movements of people and goods across borders. Accounts of the labor and hardships that most working-class Indians endure after coming to the United States are erased in favor of a discourse of magical crossings that more strongly characterize the "flexible citizenship" of upper-class Indians.[111] Consumption represses the histories of production and of the circulation of goods, since the spices appear magically in the metropolis; both Tilo and her spices simply appear in Oakland one day. Thus the text represses the inequities and the violence of the spice trade to produce a narrative of racial solidarity among Indian immigrants, Mexican immigrants, Native Americans, and African Americans. However, as with many other narratives of diaspora, India remains exotic and magically different by virtue of being "ancient." Consumer culture and multiculturalism become productively linked.

*

I have argued in this chapter that the "third world" woman as colonial and neocolonial trope remained central to new cosmopolitan subjects in the last decade of the twentieth century, as it was in the nineteenth. Consumed in

feminist internationalism or postcolonial feminist cosmopolitanism, it created national and feminist subjects in both the third world and the first. The
"worlding" of this figure, as Gayatri Spivak called it, created not only the
female individual in the West but also multiple cosmopolitan subjects in
many locations. These subjects could not be said to be oppositional to the
nation or to nationalisms, since new forms of diasporic and cultural nationalisms also emerged.

Within the networks of information linked to trade and consumer culture, cosmopolitans were produced by transnational connectivities within
which particular knowledges about cultures and nations circulated. As such,
divisions based on gender, race, class, caste, religion, and ethnicity were
rearticulated within varied transnational connectivities. By examining a variety of postcolonial cosmopolitanisms, my goal has been to understand how
literary authorship, histories of colonialism, and the politics of migration
came together through an assemblage of discourses to construct feminist
and anticolonial subjects. The "world citizen" emerged as the consumer of
multicultural, immigrant, and postcolonial novels through a neoliberalized
difference in many regions. Cosmopolitan narratives of tradition and modernity, nationalism and internationalism became necessary to the modern
recasting of tradition.

chapter *two*

TRAVELING BARBIE: INDIAN

TRANSNATIONALITIES AND THE

GLOBAL CONSUMER

★

Although some scholars argue that the nation-state is no longer as relevant as it once was within the current phase of globalization, it is impossible to make universal claims.[1] Transnational capital has helped to resuscitate some nation-states while simultaneously reducing the power of others. In addition, nationalism, in its cultural, ethnic, religious, and nation-state manifestations, can neither be ignored nor seen as the localized form of resistance to the global; the local itself is also reconfigured within these processes. In India, the power of the nation-state became more directly imposed on citizens and noncitizens through repression of insurgencies, the rise of right-wing Hindu nationalism supported by the central government which decreased the rights of minorities, and the continued war against Pakistan. At the same time, transnational movements of goods, labor, capital, and ideas in a newly liberalized economy changed the nature of this nationalism. For instance, while the Indian diaspora helped transnationalize cultural and social formations within India, it also supported dominant nationalisms and extended the power of the Indian nation-state.

Within transnational connectivities, consumer culture became the medium through which discourses of race, gender, and class produced nationalism. Consumer citizenship, simultaneously transnational and national, enabled increased levels of connectivities with transnational consumer culture. This version of citizenship, in which liberal democracy could only be imagined or made possible through consumer culture and its focus on choices between alternative goods or through the work of the market, produced liberal subjects in various parts of the world. The movements of goods and capital along with changes in national economies that took place during the last decades of the twentieth century affected all kinds of cultural formations. Feminism was one of these formations that were altered. For when transnational corporations such as Mattel moved to a newly liberalized Indian economy, they became part of an assemblage of interrelated changes in discourses about femininity, gender, race, class, sexuality, and nationalism. In this chapter I examine some of these changes, looking at how Mattel's goods and practices were altered in India and how the company participated in new versions of consumer feminism that took root in India. The discourses of gender, race, and class that moved within transnational connectivities, enabling Mattel to function in India and consumers to buy the Mattel product, are the focus here—yet this is not simply a narrative of the movements of goods and capital from the United States to India. Rather, it is a more complicated narrative that cannot be understood simply in terms of mobility, since it affects gender in the context of middle-class metropolitan masculinity and femininity in both India and its diaspora.

In light of this localization and these transnational formations, when the Mattel Corporation set up plants and began to sell Barbie in India, it did not produce an Indian or South Asian Barbie. Instead, it offered what it saw as a "traditional" Barbie:[2] a white, "American" Barbie, but one who traveled. She had, in one version, blonde hair, the "standard" face with the ideal Euro-American female body, a shiny sari, and a red bindi on her forehead (figure 1). The side panel on the box stated: "Dressing in an all-seasons classic saree [sic] with exotic borders, Barbie is totally at home in India." This reconfiguration of Euro-American fashion discourse used the term "all-seasons" to differentiate the sari from the fashion industry in the West, which is organized around seasonal clothes. At the same time it referenced the rising importance of the fashion and garment industry to India's eco-

1. Barbie in a sari.

nomic and cultural life. The term "exotic" was a reminder of the long history of romanticizing and commodifying difference within cultures of tourism and travel. Furthermore, Barbie in a sari materially evidenced the movements of transnational capital to India. It also suggested that difference, as homogenized national stereotype, and as a marker of race and gender difference, could be recuperated by multinational corporations: that the national and the foreign could exist in this "global" economy. As a white female tourist in an India opening itself to investment from abroad, Barbie, an icon of white, heterosexual American femininity, was able to put on the sari, a signifier of Indianness, and be "at home." An embodiment of the Indian state's policy of economic liberalization and its need for foreign investment, Barbie was ready to enter India.

What cultural and economic changes allowed Barbie to enter India and Mattel to claim that she found herself "at home"? India's process of economic liberalization began in the 1980s with increased incentives for foreign investment and multinationals and a more open market policy. Although some economists believed that economic liberalization was another term for deregulation of markets and the privatization of formerly state-owned businesses, others saw the process as being more about the globalization of the Indian economy and the "shift from the import substituting policy regime to an export promoting one."[3] This shift brought the Indian economy under the structural adjustment measures advocated by such international financial organizations as the World Bank and the International Monetary Fund (IMF) and opened up the economy to foreign investment and competition from abroad.[4] These changes were important in altering the nature of consumption and in producing new consumer subjects in India, as well as in connecting the subjects to patterns of transnationalized consumption, production, and circulation.

If cosmopolitan literary aesthetics depended on histories of transnational connectivities, as I have argued in my last chapter, consumer culture and its corporate products, such as media and global branded goods, relied on producing new transnational consumer subjects based on historicized differences of race, gender, sexuality, and nationalism. Consumer culture circulated transnationally through innumerable networks.[5] As a medium that produced hegemonic ideas of Americanness and the American dream,[6] the forms of consumption that marked twentieth-century consumer culture created new gender relations and cultural contexts in many other nations.[7] Yet Barbie in India is not a narrative of cultural imperialism or of cultural homogenization. For one, the desire for increased transnational connections for the economy on the part of the state and the financial sector occurred alongside Indian nationalism's continued need for consolidation and differentiation through ethnic, national, and religious nationalisms, and gender and sexual hierarchies. While globalization's cultural effects are hotly debated, my research showed little evidence of a homogenized "world culture" as posited by Francis Fukuyama,[8] or evidence that nation-states, as Kenichi Ohamae[9] and Robert Kaplan argue,[10] were losing power. Moreover, as the case of Barbie in India suggests, national affiliations remained relevant to provide identities based on ethnicity, gender, and class in a world in which borders seemed more porous than ever before. While consumption was important for producing identities, it did so in relation to gender, religion, ethnicity, class, and nationalism, rather than by itself.[11] Nationalisms emerged that were not solely based on geographical regions; nationalisms based on religion, ethnicity, culture, and sexuality proliferated as well. Many national borders remained powerful and salient, for cultural identities and also as a means of reorganizing economic and social power structures and hierarchies. These new structures came about through embracing economic liberalization's processes as well as through opposing them. Furthermore, as the example of the Vajpayee government in India reveals, right-wing nationalism trafficked with both financial globalization and virulent religious nationalisms. Thus transnationalism's varied processes, such as the "scapes" of media, finance, and culture that Arjun Appadurai has argued constitute the global arena, are not synchronic but rather consist of multiple discourses that produced collaborations as well as conflicts within transnational connectivities.[12]

I use Barbie as the entry point into understanding the transnationalization of gender through consumer culture and thus to the ways in which multinational corporations participated in altering culture in India through the 1990s. My interest lies in the wider shift in cultural formations (some connected to global consumer culture and others quite diverse) that enabled consumers to buy Barbie toward the end of the decade. Although Barbie has been a topic for feminist writing of many genres, much more scholarly work remains to be done with regard to its international dimensions. Although there are already some references to this area, for instance in the work of Erica Rand, the travels of Barbie around the world need further elucidation.[13] By focusing on the marketing of Barbie in India, and analyzing the discourses produced by Mattel and its subsidiaries, I examine how economic, social, and cultural transnational practices affected the rise of consumer culture in India as it produced segmented markets and consumer groups based on gender and class.

Although consumer responses have been represented in scholarly works through anthropological fieldwork with consumers or though marketing surveys, my methods here are somewhat different, including what some may call fieldwork, archival work on Mattel, and interviews with a range of persons in India, as well as textual analysis. While informants' responses in fieldwork tell us a great deal about how individuals understand their culture, they may not by themselves enable us to understand all the mediations that produce the responses. Thus a wider cultural and historical perspective is often necessary to understand cultural formations and to make sense of informants' responses. I examine how a changing culture endowed a product with meanings that resonated historically and transnationally—that is, across both time and space. By reading narratives such as Mattel's annual reports, analyses in publications such as *Business India*, and conducting interviews with local manufacturers and corporate marketers, I analyze how a multinational corporation was able to sell an American product and icon in a very different cultural context. I examine the demands placed on manufacturing and marketing strategies by changing consumer and cultural responses as they were mediated through the production process. In addition, since my research covers almost a decade, it examines consumer response as it changed in response to shifts in production and marketing over time. This strategy was important: Barbie did not sell as well as expected in its first years in India, and consequently the shifts in marketing strategy become important markers of changes in consumer culture itself as well as in corporate strategy. Mattel's strategic shifts after this initial failure reveal a great deal about the circumstances in which Barbie could be sold. These changes included greater levels of connectivities to transnational consumer culture provided by the participation of diasporic Indians after the Indian state embarked on its plan of economic liberalization.

A number of issues can be raised regarding the connection between transnational consumer culture and economic liberalization in India in the last decade of the twentieth century. One important issue is the segmentation of the consumer, especially the child. I argue that the child as consumer did not previously exist in India in the same highly segmented way that it did in North America, Japan, or Europe, where consumer culture has produced subjects for a longer time. While consumers are active participants in the construction of national, gendered, and classed subjectivities through consumption, these consumer subjects cannot be assumed to have existed in as segmented a way among middle-class Indians before economic liberalization. When Barbie came to India, a segmented, differentiated children's market had not fully taken shape, even though of course children were targeted by products and advertising. Although manufacturers did advertise their goods, advertisements did not reach as many consumers or market segments as they did in countries with a longer

history of participation in globalized consumer culture. Mattel's marketing strategies and the transnational connectivities made with the fashion,
beauty, and garment industries that were directed particularly to what are
called "developing countries" and what is perceived as their large, "passive," "cheap" labor participated in creating new gendered, segmented,
"global" consumer subjects.[14] Thus this chapter also traces the development of children, in particular girls, as "global" consumer subjects during
the 1980s and 1990s through the increasing presence of the gender-
differentiated global beauty and fashion industry.

Consumers are seldom available as a ready and willing market; rather,
the work of consumer culture has been to produce the desires and the
conditions within which buying a product becomes meaningful.[15] Thus if
Barbie was not initially a successful product, then we need to ask why this
was so. Was it a matter of conscious resistance to an American product and
to the presence of an American multinational corporation in India? Was it
that Indians were alert to the ideologies of race and gender that were connoted by the product? What kinds of subjectivities resisted this product and
how these subjectivities changed is thus an important aspect of this book's
project of addressing transnational connectivities.

Resistance to multinationals in India came from different locations and
could not always be presumed to be subversive to dominant formations or
to the presence of all multinationals. Certainly this resistance was not widespread among the population, nor were all those in opposition to multinationals unified in their agendas. The Indian central government's support
of open markets was opposed at many levels by religious fundamentalist
groups such as the RSS (the Rashtriya Swayamsevak Sangh, the Hindu
right-wing party).[16] Whereas left-wing groups opposed these policies because they did not think they would benefit the poor, the right-wing groups
saw them as a "Western" and "American" threat to national sovereignty.[17]
Other kinds of resistance appeared in the obsession with "ethnic" chic, for
instance, or the recuperations of "tradition" by various entities.[18] My analysis of the marketing of Barbie in India reveals both the subversions and
the recuperations that occurred in the formation of consumer subjects in
the 1990s.

If consumer subjects in India did not welcome all the global brand-
name goods that appeared in India during this period, their unwillingness

to buy signaled that they were not as yet subjects of this particular discourse of consumption. We cannot assume a resistance to an "American" product, although this may be the explanation for some part of the response. There is little evidence that opposition to Mattel and Barbie was widespread. The failure of new products on the market does pose many questions; most people do not buy indiscriminately. Why certain products sell and others don't raises important issues of culture, identity, and subjectivity. The cultural work required to create consumer desire for a product is not as simple as producing a marketing plan; rather, the plan contributes to and participates in wider cultural changes within which the product can become meaningful (or not) in ways that often cannot be predicted. Marketers and advertisers are constantly hoping to anticipate the meanings, though they may fail to do so. Barbie's initial "failure" as a product led to marketing attempts that did not by themselves create a successful product. However, these attempts participated in the larger cultural changes that allowed Barbie to become a part of the lives of middle-class Indian girls and to become meaningful to emergent consumer subjects. Thus for Mattel in India, wider cultural changes occurred that led to better sales by the end of the 1990s. Among these changes we can include the greater participation of members of the Indian diaspora in the economic and cultural currents of the 1990s; these occurred in tandem with an impetus for economic liberalization from the Indian government, as well as an intensification of transnational media and finance that became characteristic of late capitalism in the twentieth century.

Diasporic subjects became crucial for many nation-states for a number of reasons and thus became the nexus of a number of discourses. The creation of the Non-Resident Indian (NRI) as a financial category in India was an indicator of this imperative. The need to maintain relations between the South Asian diaspora and its "home" was connected not only to colonial and neocolonial and nationalist imperatives or to diasporic needs to create an Indian identity in response to racisms and ethnocentrisms in Europe and North America, but also to the demands of the International Monetary Fund to open the country to foreign capital. The NRI as a special category was effectively defined first in the Foreign Relations Regulations Act of 1973, which established the category "person of Indian origin." This category included anyone who had ever had an Indian passport, if either parent or any grandparent was an Indian and a permanent resident in undivided India at any time. A wife, though not a husband, of a person of Indian origin could also be an NRI.[19] As far back as 1975, as a consequence of the oil crisis, and even before the economic liberalization programs were launched by the Indian government in the mid-1980s, the Indian government wanted to improve foreign exchange flows by creating the new Foreign Currency (Non-Resident) Accounts scheme. This scheme protected NRI investments against exchange risks and made them repatriable. In 1982–83 the government, with Indira Gandhi as prime minister, announced that NRI deposits of more than a year would have a 2 percent higher interest rate than local deposits of the same maturity, thus privileging diasporic capital.

As part of the process of economic liberalization that occurred in the mid-1980s through Rajiv Gandhi's government, a greater emphasis was placed on generating investments from NRIS, including Overseas Corporate Bodies (OCBS) owned by NRIS. OCBS were companies and partnerships of which 60 percent was owned by individuals of Indian nationality or origin resident outside India. The new policies included giving NRIS tax breaks and incentives to invest in the stock market, easing bureaucratic restrictions on buying real estate and creating manufacturing companies, and increasing the extent of the telecommunication and information technology business.

Though in 1991 the outflows of capital from India became greater, they did not grow much over the 1990s. A report by the Sodhani Committee, commissioned by the Reserve Bank of India, recommended more investment incentives for NRIS, such as repatriation of principal as well as profit in housing and real estate, and several other programs.[20] This financial incorporation of the diaspora coincided with a rapid increase in communication and transportation technologies that enabled those in the diaspora to become involved in India in many ways. Easier and less expensive international telephone calls, faster air travel and the economic means to purchase tickets, the advent of e-mail and access to media on the web, as well as satellite TV, all occurred at the same time as the liberalization of the Indian economy. In fact, the participation of NRIS in the Indian economy at the end of the century could only have come about through the connectivities made possible through the coexistence of Indian economic liberalization policies

and technological changes. This nexus produced economic as well as cultural changes in India. These changes provide a contrast to the cultural and
economic environment that prevailed earlier, when multinational companies could only invest in India in collaboration with Indian companies.
Although global brands were present in India throughout the twentieth
century, first in colonial India when British companies were dominant and
later when multinationals such as Union Carbide and Coca-Cola came to
India after independence, they were not welcomed by the state; certainly,
they were not given the incentives promised in the liberalization policies of
the 1980s and 1990s.[21]

While the Barbie product could only come to India because of the Indian
government's changing policies of economic liberalization in the 1980s, it
began to make inroads into the consumer market only when it could be
understood within a discursive context created by the transnationalization
of the beauty and fashion industry in India as well as the transnational
connectivities produced by diasporic Indians. Without such a context, Mattel was not initially successful when it first opened factories in India in the
mid-1980s. In its search for markets, Mattel participated in making consumers in India into participants within a globalized consumer culture. Yet
the presence of strong nationalisms meant that consumers could be both
national and global, with cosmopolitan, national, class, and gender identities. Middle-class Indians increasingly saw themselves linked transnationally to other countries in many ways. Increased travel enabled affluent and
upper-class Indians to visit relatives and take business or vacation trips to
Southeast Asia, Dubai, Europe, and North America. Goods, images, and
finance moved in all directions, as did migrants, businessmen, traders,
tourists, and travelers. Satellite television brought more images of the
"West" into Indian homes than ever before. The belief that the "West"
consumes and the "non-West" produces thus can be seen to have been
destroyed by the reach of transnational media.

Barbie's presence in India came at a time when the national imaginary
became a transnational imaginary, in which diasporic cultural formations
created new forms of patriarchy under conditions of globalization. Diaspora and "home" were connected in new ways in this new economic climate, such that NRIS were integrated into the political, cultural, and economic practices of the Indian nation-state, and Indians became aware of

their participation in global consumer culture. Thus theorizations of diasporas as resistant to nation-states cannot always be sustained for every
group.[22]

An important aspect of this transnationalism could be understood in
terms of not only the movements of migrant labor and bodies of various
kinds but also the ways in which goods, media, and information were
"transcoded," as Stuart Hall has termed this process of localization, at
different sites, sometimes in terms of nationalism and at other times for
localized agendas related to gender and class hegemonies.[23] However, this
sort of transcoding occurred only in situations where connectivities could
be made and through discursive formations and the genealogies that provide these connectivities. Within India's economic liberalization process,
diasporic lifestyles of South Asian immigrants in the United States became
part of the connectivities that marketed a transnational consumer culture
through ethnic identities. While diaspora culture has been theorized in
many ways, mostly in Europe and North America, as a subcultural resistance to white, Eurocentric culture, it was quite differently incorporated
within India in consumer contexts as a marketing tool to imagine a transnational nation. This nation proposed an identity that connected people
through ties of consumption to "home" as nation-state, while not seeing it
as a necessary or essential place of return. Popular culture echoed these
changes in many versions, most prominently in the many movies produced by Bombay cinema, in which the diasporic young man or woman
was both a part of India and also valued and exotic because of a life lived
outside it.[24]

As a result, the study of migration needs to be rethought in relation to
transnational connectivities produced by consumer culture by the end of
the twentieth century. Transnational theories may not be simply about migrant cultures or the "bicultural" rather than unicultural perspective of the
immigrant.[25] Rather, the perspective may also reflect how, for instance,
lifestyles of those within the nation-state become transnationalized across
many national boundaries, as well as the many kinds of belonging and
identities based on ideas of "origins" or "home." In the wake of economic
liberalization policies, the impact of travel by élites and migrants created a
new Indian transnational imaginary, in which new élites and new subalterns were produced not only in the so-called diaspora but also in India.

Since it was not only élite classes that participated in globalized consumption, given that one important aspect of new subjects of consumption is their highly segmented nature, the identities produced were also segmented while at the same time being nationalist in various ways. Barbie, as it was marketed in India, participated in the gendered segmentation of these new consumer subjects as "global" brands become localized in specific ways.[26]

Since market segmentation in the United States has used gender, race, ethnicity, and multiculturalism to sell products, and since products cross national boundaries, multiculturalism has also become transnationalized through global marketing practices by transnational corporations based in the United States. Within these processes, the value of "diversity" to American multinationals in the late twentieth century was that Asian immigrants could be used as experts in various ways to tap into the Asian market. For instance, Indian NRIS in the United States became valuable as multicultural experts for American multinationals. Multiculturalism, as it was understood in the United States, was no longer solely a claim on civil rights but now a neoliberal corporate project of selling goods to a transnational consumer culture connecting many national identities. Within this project,[27] multiculturalism also circulated as consumer culture in which immigrants created negotiated lifestyles from the "American lifestyle" that was so much a part of capitalist formation in the United States. The impact of market segmentation and the defining of target markets meant that differentiated cultural formations, existing under the sign of multiculturalism, could "travel" to different sites and become used in other localized contexts.

THE GLOBAL/NATIONAL CONSUMER

✳

Consumer subjects, seen by the marketing industry in India as predominantly urban but in North India existing in most towns and cities, depending on class and caste status, were gendered and classed in ways recognizable from colonial and nationalist histories, but also new in many ways. Business magazines articulated these subjects through the term "global consumer" as those able to recognize "global brand names" even if this recognition was incorporated into a unique cultural environment. Marketing agencies mapped the globe in new ways, seeking to expand markets and obtain knowledge about consumption practices. Corporations thus participated in the new transnational governmentalities that produced knowledges about a global population and sought to produce segmented markets from such knowledges.

During the 1990s international surveys created by various marketing agencies examined consumer attitudes globally, categorizing and comparing consumer perceptions by nationality. One survey, undertaken by the Marketing and Research Group, based in India, along with allied groups internationally, surveyed Indian consumers by location in "metro" areas, class (minimum income of 1,500 rupees, or about $30, a month), and age (18–55).[28] The survey showed that while multinational corporations were gaining recognition, national and local brands were seen as either superior or second best. For instance, respondents in India felt that Indian companies were second best in producing blue jeans, cameras, and home electronics but made the best moderately priced cars, chocolates, beer, wine, TV programs, and movies. Global brands clearly functioned as national signifiers—blue jeans for the United States and electronics for Japan—and these symbols were powerful in a world where nationalism and the nation itself often worked as brand names. Surveys conceptualizing "the global consumer" constructed a world of multinationals and global brand names amid what were seen as national behaviors and national cultures. According to this survey, the subject of transnational consumption was a national "Indian consumer," gendered masculine (the pronoun used is "he"), sexuality unclear, who was defined as a "brand loyalist" and "luxury innovator." The survey found that his "consumer confidence" was not high because of the state of the economy and because "money is a problem." "His" political beliefs were seen as quite conservative regarding wealth and poverty but more liberal regarding the environment.

This new profile of the "Indian consumer" suggested a shift from the older version of media marketing, since the consumer recognized global brand names and expressed brand loyalty even if he lacked the ability to purchase the products. The survey reported that the "Indian consumer" was a nationalist but also globally aware, an urban man who would like to work more but often did not get the chance to do so.[29] It is noteworthy that a global consumer identity was not seen as contradictory to that of the national consumer. The survey and others like it created knowledges of populations based on consumption of global and national branded goods rather than on other class or caste formations including ownership of property, family status or connections, or job opportunities, even as these did factor into the ability to consume. The connection between the "global" and the "national" was visibly part of the new transnational arena of consumption that produced new consumer subjects through surveys of this kind.

Mattel needed this global/national consumer to sell its goods. In India, the specificities of the Indian consumers could be understood through the ways in which the national and the global were localized within other hegemonic formations. These specificities also explained why Barbie did not take the Indian market by storm. Arguing for American cultural imperialism might suggest that Barbie would sell very well because it was a prototypically "American" product, or that its reference to a racial privilege of whiteness would have been attractive in India, but this was not the case. Most (or all) locally manufactured dolls had pink or white bodies, so that Barbie's whiteness was not a unique or novel feature;[30] histories of colonialism and racial hierarchies in India that privileged whiteness were not new but had to be resignified. Barbie's racial signification, its body shape, its "American" identity were all distinctive but not sufficient to make the product a success. Initially, its sales were quite unremarkable. In fact, when my relatives and friends in India asked me to describe my research, they parodied my topic by calling it "bhabhi" (the Hindi word for brother's wife, a role that is not seen as powerful in an extended family). The parody indicated some of the complexities of Barbie reception in India, the inability of the product to conquer the market and its struggles for name recognition—all of which were intertwined with the nature of gender, class, and family in India. It was only when Barbie appeared in a sari and advertising practices utilized and participated in creating a transnational consumer culture within India that sales improved. Thus the "Americanness" of Barbie, the "standardness" of its white femininity, had to be mediated by various other factors that were localized, and national as well as transnational.

In fact, Mattel had to rely on specificities of cultural practices in urban India to create successful advertising campaigns that would achieve greater brand-name recognition in India. Thus it was not Americanization, as simple cultural imperialism, but a very mediated notion of America which was used to sell this product as well as its ability to become "Indian." Leslie Sklair has written at length about the centrality of the "American dream" as a lifestyle in the functioning of global capitalism.[31] This notion of "America," though quite different from older notions of the cosmopolitan "west" of colonial modernity created under American cold war imperialism, was also not dissociated from it. American corporations used the imperial power of the United States to create markets by utilizing neo-imperial inequities and practices. Yet by expanding the notion of the "American" lifestyle of consumption to incorporate a heterogeneous and multicultural America of conflicting ethnicities, as well as by building on specificities of particular national or regional markets, transnational corporations like Mattel created new kinds of gendered, age-differentiated, and classed consumers.

The impact of target marketing in the United States also modified the "American lifestyle"[32] as a prototype of consumer culture. In the 1950s lifestyle advertising and target marketing became new forms of consumer culture. By the end of the twentieth century, all kinds of lifestyles and identities became incorporated into advertising. Claudia Dreifus has argued that in the 1960s new radical lifestyles broke up the monolithic American lifestyle and communities, and that cultures based on race, ethnicity, gender, and sexuality were also integrated into consumer culture in new ways.[33] Even the international comprised national lifestyles, and international ad agencies began mapping national behaviors and lifestyles as well. Mattel's international collection of Barbie produced national types, with Jamaican, Japanese, Indian, Swedish, and other versions. Like international beauty pageants, these were national types produced in the context of a beauty and clothing industry that was increasingly transnational.

In addition to the American consumer and the use of national types within American consumer culture, the evolution of the global consumer and global advertising became key aspects of transnational culture. The global consumer, marked by his or her recognition of global brand names, was identified by marketing agencies as a means to expand markets across national boundaries. Marieke de Mooij, in her book *Global Marketing and Advertising: Understanding Cultural Paradoxes*, argues that a global brand may either be associated with the nation from which it originates or be a standard brand name even if the contents change drastically from one country to the next.[34] For instance, respondents to the marketing survey in India that was referred to earlier thought that Indian companies produced the best moderately priced cars, chocolates, beer, wine, TV programs, and movies. Marketing experts thus worked with the concept of national diversity to explain how global brands work in different contexts.

As Danae Clark, Donald Lowe, and other scholars have shown, advertising strategies used identity politics in the United States as they circulated among diasporic subjects to create consumer styles;[35] Robert Bocock has argued that "consumption patterns may be used to maintain and mark out differences between groups, to demarcate boundaries between ethnic groups."[36] In the United States, identity politics have produced strong connections to consumer culture as "market segments" are categorized by ethnic identities as well as other dimensions including race, class, and sexuality. While the analysis of "lifestyle" for advertising purposes marked a new segmentation of consumers into groups,[37] it has also been argued that lifestyle, as Donald Lowe puts it, signals the "new social relations of consumption" that have "overshadowed class as the social relations of production."[38] Yet it is clear that new class formations also resulted out of consumer segmentation. "Ethnic" and "multicultural" were terms that resonated in consumption practices linked to class, as subjects were recast in terms of their purchasing habits within groups and communities. Consequently, "American" subjects were created not only through discourses of citizenship and civil society but also through lifestyle consumption, such as through "buying American,"[39] and thus a contingent participation in discourses of identity linked to consumption.

Since "American" goods and geopolitics circulate across transnational connectivities, they absorbe, utilize, and rework the notion of "American" into particular agendas and strategies within which states and nations play uneven and heterogeneous roles. As various market segments rework and recreate the "American" lifestyle, the emergence of consumers with both national and ethnic specificities indicates a very selective and changing incorporation of Americanness. Immigrant America is important here as a mediator of Americanness that could not be reduced to the cultural imperialism of the United States, since the relation of ethnic formations to the U.S. state's practices was, because of race, gender, sexuality, class, and other factors, often quite uneven and vexed. This selective appropriation and utilization of Americanness as a desirable lifestyle became part of the formation of the distinctive cultural practices of ethnic identity formation. For instance, the U.S.-based NRIS of the segmented South Asian ethnic market participated in the transnational connectivities producing affiliations with both India and America, with the result that the nation-state was both sustained and exceeded.

By using ethnic market segmentation, diasporic consumer styles mediated and modeled the emergence of global consumers in India. Diasporic Indians became signs of a shifting and changing America as they negotiated Indian national practices with the American lifestyle that signified a successful immigrant existence. "American" products like Barbie, which has been marketed as an American icon in the United States, had to "travel" and alter themselves to enter the Indian market. However, retaining some aspect of Americanness was important even as the product was modified to succeed in the Indian market. For instance, Mattel did not create a dark-skinned or brown "Indian" Barbie, but rather a white "American" Barbie wearing Indian clothes. It retained its connections to white supremacy and power and relied on their being attractive to Indian consumers. Given the racial formations within India, where whiteness has been privileged in many ways, and the need to bring wealthy Western (read "white") tourists to India, this strategy produced a discourse of the "multiculturalism" of India and its variety of "ethnic" cultures as a valued aspect of cosmopolitan consumer culture. Different versions of multiculturalism could be the connectors within transnational formations of this kind.

MATTEL AND ITS CORPORATE PRACTICES: CONSTRUCTING DIFFERENCE AND UNIVERSALITY

✳

In 1985 Mattel had affiliates and plants in South Korea, Japan, Hong Kong, the Philippines, Australia, Chile, Venezuela, Puerto Rico, the United Kingdom, France, Spain, Switzerland, and Canada. Through the 1980s and 1990s Mattel became a multinational with factories, offices, and affiliates in Tijuana, Monterrey, Guangdong (China), Jakarta, Japan, Berlin, Budapest, Prague, Kuala Lumpur, and Bombay. A new plant opened in Thailand in

1985 after Mattel applied for an eight-year tax "holiday," a common practice to stimulate investment from the United States and other countries.[40] Mattel closed two plants in the Philippines in 1988 after conflicts with what the corporation called "militant labor unions."[41] Most Barbies sold in the United States through the 1990s were made in China, Malaysia, and Indonesia, with plastics made in Taiwan from oil bought from Saudi Arabia, hair from Japan, and packaging from the United States. Making Barbie is extremely labor-intensive work, requiring at least fifteen separate paint stations and thus an enormous supply of cheap labor. Labor costs were about 35 cents for a Barbie costing about $10 (out of which almost $8 went to shipping, marketing, and wholesale and retail profits; Mattel made about $1 of this amount).[42] Using the services of Asian women paid low wages for assembly line work, Barbie's production was as gendered as its consumption and circulation.[43]

After a period in the mid-1980s during which U.S. sales remained steady while international sales increased by almost 40 percent, sales declined in 1987, necessitating layoffs of 22 percent of the work force in the Mattel headquarters in Hawthorne, California, which meant almost five hundred jobs. The Bombay office opened in 1988, even though at that point sales had declined by 30 percent from their peak, a fact not surprising when the corporate view was, according to the CEO, that "the future of the toy industry lies in international markets."[44] By 1992 Mattel had come out of its slump, with a net sales increase of 25 percent, and by the following year Barbie sales worldwide hit $1 billion. That year Mattel donated $1 million to children's health programs in the United States.

In Mattel's corporate annual reports, the whole world was represented as a market waiting to buy Mattel's products. The annual reports reveal a belief that every child somehow naturally wants these toys and that the desirability of the toys is universal and transparent. Yet, paradoxically, every country is seen as a market in which the conquest of children is the goal. To pursue this children's market, Mattel linked up with Disney, another iconic name in the U.S.-based multinational production of what I call "children's transnational culture," agreeing to manufacture all the Disney brand toys. Awareness of Disney as a nationalist signifier of Americanness has been well documented.[45] After the deal with Disney, Mattel in 1992 called Barbie and Disney its "global power brands."[46]

How did Mattel's annual reports explain what they represented as Barbie's continued power and fascination? Barbie's global marketing practices were linked to America as a symbol of freedom and rights, especially for women. The marketing strategies linked the product to discourses of powerful "Americanness" associated with race, class, and gendered hierarchies. Relying on discourses of American nationalism that linked "choice" to "freedom," Mattel used race, gender, and nationalist discourse to sell its product. This connection was borne out in many subtle and not-so-subtle ways, as in Mattel's claim that when the Berlin Wall fell, Mattel "was the first company to advertise."[47] Yet even while clearly using America as a marketing tool, Mattel universalized the child. Thus the corporate reports claimed that Mattel understood all little girls' fantasies, which were seen as universal: "Mattel has long believed that children's play patterns are the same around the world and that a successful toy has no nationality. The validity of this tenet was proven in Japan last year, where in a test market and subsequent expansion, the traditional Barbie doll was embraced by Japanese girls."[48]

This "embrace" of the "traditional" Barbie purportedly reinforced the company's claims that it could cross all borders, since play and the consumption of toys are universal. But there was no mention of how this universal play was marketed and consumed in various nations, nor of how Barbie as a symbol of Americanness was consumed in these specific sites. One method that Mattel used to produce effective transnational connectivities was to exploit the discourses of feminism, made neoliberal by its association with free trade, entrepreneurship, and capitalism. The complicated baggage of the "American" image of Barbie as white, straight, young, and blonde in the 1990s began to utilize the gendered discourses of freedom and women's rights to make itself relevant to the greater presence of liberal feminism within popular culture in the United States. Moreover, these discourses relied on cold war representations used by the United States to link neoliberal democracy to a "freedom" to consume, which was promoted as quintessentially American. The same discourses invoked feminist themes in supporting women's participation in capitalism, contrasting women in the United States with those from the "third world" and "Other" women,[49] and emphasizing the centrality of "choice" as a goal for liberal feminism. In using these discourses, the universality of gendered divisions as produced by Mattel's discourses of toy consumption was established.

According to Mattel, just as boys needed high-tech action toys such as BraveStarr to develop, girls grew through "imagination" and play with dolls. I do not suggest that such play could never be subversive of gendered stereotypes.[50] Yet the corporate focus on fantasy for girls and action for boys suggested that for Mattel, the imaginary of the play that girls enacted worked in tandem with the symbolic and virtual nature of consumer culture. In a global framework of consumption, as Arjun Appadurai's work suggests, fantasy linked translocal practices connected through the imagination.[51] The transnational imaginary of new nationalism was most easily available through the phantasmic life produced by consumer culture through which the consumer citizen could be constructed. As Ulf Hannerz argues, fantasy and aspiration are constitutive of the "global ecumene" of advertising that is at once diverse and homogenizing.[52] To produce this citizen subject, however, fantasy had to be linked to the nation. As Lauren Berlant and Elizabeth Freeman have pointed out, even for groups subversive of much hegemonic culture, such as Queer Nation, consumer pleasure has become part of activist reformulations of public culture, linking "the utopian pleasures of the commodity with those of the nation."[53] Mattel's use of discourses of "freedom" and "choice" connected fantasy with the nation, Americanness with liberal and neoliberal democracy. Thus Erica Rand points out that Mattel modifies its products to "bring competing definitions of good role model and acceptable fantasy object within its own conception of Barbie and to present its offerings as precisely those that fulfill consumer 'needs.' "[54] The focus on imagination and fantasy used terms and concepts similar to those used by Disney in its theme parks.[55]

What were the consumer fantasies that were put into circulation by Mattel? A consumer feminism was one of these discourses, in which consumption within capitalist expansion could bring work to many across the globe, even if what it brought were classed, gendered, and racialized inequalities. What Rand calls a pop feminist notion of choice was used by Mattel by the late 1990s to sell multiple Barbies to each consumer-child. Mattel's CEO in 1997, Jill Barad, who started her career in fashion and cosmetic sales, deployed this pop feminism to sell Barbies. Under her leadership, the very successful slogan "We girls can do anything" was launched, with the new career-girl Barbie capable of moving up the corporate ladder or having any career she wanted, from doctor to astronaut. As Rand has argued, the fantasies that Mattel claims are universal were also hegemonic. According to Rand, the language of "infinite possibility" that Mattel deployed was used to "camouflage what was actually being promoted: a very limited set of products, ideas, and actions."[56] Rand suggests that even if subversive uses of Barbie were rampant, these did not change the ideological effects that Mattel promoted: compulsory heterosexuality, ageism, sexism, white superiority, capitalism, and the unequal distribution of resources.

This emphasis on American liberal feminism's discourse of "choice" as essential to women's struggles was understood by Mattel as a universal value that could be transmitted across the transnational connectivities and bring new consumers to buy the product in different parts of the world. In its annual reports, Mattel emphasized universality within claims of concern for the global welfare of children that were presented through organized events functioning as advertisements and also as public relations strategies. In 1990 Barbie hosted an international summit where forty children from twenty-eight countries discussed issues relevant to themselves. The annual report of that year described the event in the language of children's welfare and empowerment and concluded that the children "identified world peace as a principal concern." The summit's conclusions were similar to pronouncements by contestants at beauty pageants, where the most commonplace clichés are spoken to infuse the event with civic value. Although Erica Rand suggests that these clichés are "popular but largely uncontroversial forms of political consciousness" that Mattel used to reach more consumers, it is clear that the connection between consumption and politics, between support for Mattel and support for the concerns for welfare that Mattel expressed, was an important sign of the neoliberal context of its transnational consumption.[57] Consumer subjects were thus produced not merely through class positions but also through discourses of good citizenship and liberal values of equality and progress combined with a neoliberal feminism, all of which were seen as international and universal.

NATIONALISM, INTERNATIONALISM, AND BARBIE

*

In feminist activist and scholarly circles, Barbie has had a thorny history. *Mondo Barbie*, edited by Lucinda Ebersole and Richard Peabody, contains essays and poems that clearly delineate this relationship in the United States.[58] From feminist critiques of the body, to Barbie angst, to "deviant" uses, to Sandra Cisneros's "Barbie-Q" narrative of those who could buy only damaged or generic Barbies, this collection reveals Barbie's iconic status in the United States. A majority of critiques from American feminist circles have been directed at the shape of the female body as presented by Barbie and Mattel's relentless recuperation of gendered types in terms of a binary opposition between femininity and masculinity.

Recent work on Barbie has focused on gender as well as sexuality and race. I have mentioned earlier the work of Erica Rand, who argued that Barbie as white, young, blonde, straight, and normative has been ideologically powerful though it could not prevent all kinds of subversive "queerings" of Barbie play. For Rand, Barbie production and reception suggest that subversion works better than resistance to describe consumption practices in relation to this product in the United States. Although Rand suggests that the whiteness of Barbie occasionally incorporates the "exotic" or "foreign" as a comparison or foil, her work does not primarily focus on the globalization of Barbie or Mattel, although, unlike other commentators, she describes Mattel's rise as a multinational corporation with global aspirations. Yet globalization is an important matter, as colonial and postcolonial formations all utilized the white, blonde, straight, "American" female in various ways in creating new consumer subjects transnationally through global advertising and media.[59] Moreover, the use of women as labor in the third world by multinational corporations produced workers who could also be consumers, since consumer culture works through specularity, fantasy, and imagination.[60] For these workers, ideas of race within localized consumption encounter the racial divisions produced by corporate marketing and production processes. For instance, Louisa Schein has examined the use of white femininity in advertisements in post-Mao China as a "catalogue of consumption style" to be used by those she calls "consumers in training."[61]

Ann Ducille's work employs an intersectional analysis combining race and gender by critiquing Mattel's use of "diversity" and multiculturalism as superficial.[62] She argues that Mattel uses multiculturalism to commodify race and gender difference. Relying on the work of the anthropologists Jackie Urla and Alan Swedlund on the anthropometry of Barbie, which showed that the African American Barbie had almost the same body as the "regular" Barbie, except that its back was angled differently, Ducille pointed out that for Mattel, difference was merely a matter of costume (sometimes skin color is changed but not always).[63] Though wishing to retain the notion of a genuinely transformative multiculturalism, Ducille suggests that the practices of Mattel and other instances of corporate multiculturalism were "an easy and immensely profitable way off the hook of Eurocentrism that gives us the face of cultural diversity without the particulars of racial difference."[64] This kind of target marketing has increasingly used ethnic and sexual identities in the United States to sell products and seek new markets through diversified products, just as consumption practices were used by groups to differentiate themselves from others. As Ducille suggests, corporations such as Mattel have successfully been able to merchandise racial and gender difference, although it cannot be said that the merchandising has exactly the uses that were planned by corporations. Ducille's essay, for instance, emphasizes the place of experts who consulted with Mattel about "culture," such as the African American experts on children's play who believed in the value of a black Barbie as a role model. These experts became valuable transnationally as well as in the United States, where immigrants and racial minorities become target markets for consumer goods. Through the 1990s Mattel (and other corporations) used Indian companies and knowledge of transnationally connected Indians (including NRIS) to market their products. Transnational corporations relied on the work of NRIS as multicultural experts to mediate what came to be called "diversity" within corporate culture and to produce difference.

While Mattel hoped to benefit in the American market from participating in discourses of diversity, the "international," as an older historical construct, has been a staple within Mattel's Barbie product line as a plurality of homogenized, stereotypic "national" representations. This "international" produced a caricature of national and international stereotypes, with an Elke from Sweden, Mimi from France, Zizi from Kenya, Chelsea from England, and Stacey from the United States. Yet this internationalism was framed by an imperial discourse produced in relation to cultural contexts in the United States and racialized in American terms, in which, as Ducille pointed out, English Barbie is a lady but Jamaican Barbie is a maid.[65] Furthermore, to fit into the American context, all the international names were easily pronounceable by American consumers. This collection was also supposedly educational, since the annual report mentioned that "little girls can have tons of fun learning to become fashion models"; it is clear that this education can only produce consumers for the beauty and fashion industry.[66] Moreover, the "international" collection linked Barbie to the fashion industry and international beauty pageants in which racial, ethnic, and national differences are emphasized as well as managed.[67] This international array of Barbies could be sold outside the United States, much as in the fashion industry clothes made in many parts of Asia enable European and American fashion brands to become household names across the world. Brands such as Barbie thus produced not only workers but also consumers in Asian countries.

MATTEL IN INDIA: PRODUCING NEW CONSUMER SUBJECTS

*

By the 1980s, in any toy store in India's urban centers catering to the children of the middle and upper classes, one could find not only the whole array of Masters of the Universe dolls (which made implicit the idea of power, war, and imperial conquest, not only of the world but of space) but also a large range of Barbie dolls. These included the blonde Barbie, the brunette, and the bride dressed in white, but also one refinement for the Indian market: the Barbie in a sari.

While Barbie came to India in 1986–87, it was only known to the affluent section of the urban population, to those who traveled to the United States for various reasons, or to Indian immigrants living in the West. In 1991, after what Mattel called the "standard" Barbie had not sold very well, Barbie reappeared with "Indian" clothing, complete with sari, bangles, bindi, and black hair. While the Indian affiliate, Leo Mattel, based in Nagpur, continued to manufacture the dolls, the marketing shifted in the 1990s to an Indian company, Blowplast, presumably because it was believed to be in better touch with the Indian market and could therefore find more locally specific ways to sell the product. Early advertising strategies included print and TV ads and other promotions such as a Barbie Friends Club (now defunct) and a Barbie magazine, which promoted a greener world and health issues. The club sent out cards and "I Love Barbie" badges and had a database of about fourteen or fifteen thousand names—a relatively small number in India. Eventually there emerged five categories of Barbie: a "penetration" Barbie, low-end and most accessible, which had shoulder-length hair and western clothes but uncannily recuperated a gendered imperial discourse of nineteenth-century colonial expansion; long-haired "activity" Barbies, both black-haired and blonde, in a sari (figure 1); "theme" Barbies, such as Best Friend Barbie and Birthday Barbie; "Glamour" Barbies, such as Happy Holidays Barbie; and "Collector" Barbies, often in limited editions such as the Expressions of India series, in which Barbie wore native costumes from Rajasthan, Punjab, and other states, showing diversity in an Indian context (figure 2). Though Barbie's friend Ken did appear in "Indian" clothes, sales of Ken were small compared with those of Barbie.

Mattel targeted the middle and upper classes in India as well as the overseas and diaspora markets as it created Barbie in a sari and the new series of Barbie in various "ethnic" costumes. While the "penetration" Barbie sold in 1997 for about 99 rupees ($2), the traveling Barbie in Indian dress sold for about 250 rupees ($5) and the "Expressions of India" Barbie for about 600 rupees ($12). The availability of different Barbies varied with location. The most expensive Barbies, the Collector and Glamour dolls, were available only in the big cities. These Barbies, with depictions of ethnic and regional diversity, were aimed at NRIS and tourists from the West with dollars or pounds or currency more powerful than the rupee, and were sold in five-star hotels, airports, and other tourist areas. Given that with economic liberalization, as Arvind Rajagopal argues, consumption patterns changed and became more fluid,[68] Mattel's segmented products created new subjects of consumption from many segments of the population in the country and overseas. At present, these Barbies are available online at many websites that sell goods from India. They are priced somewhat higher and can be sent from India to anywhere in the world, though at many websites the prices given are in U.S. dollars, suggesting that they are intended for NRIS and collectors living in the United States.

Yet gaining a market for Barbie was difficult for Mattel. In the late 1980s there were about two hundred toy stores in all of India, their size ranging from 200 to about 1,200 square feet. Except for the major multinational brands Mattel and Funskool, no other manufacturer advertised, so it was left to these two companies to create the market they desired.[69] The unorganized

2. Barbie in Indian ethnic costume.

manufacturing sector, which once made most toys, was not able to compete with Mattel and Hasbro, since they possessed the molds for toys, unlike the local manufacturers that lacked transnational links. Whereas Indian versions of many toys popular in the West were available in relatively inexpensive versions made from sometimes obsolete molds from East Asia, by the 1990s there was a lack of molds available for sale. Most of the molds went to China, where a huge number of toys began to be manufactured for the global market. Also, the slim profits created obstacles for local manufacturers who were not able to buy very expensive molds.

The Indian government's decision to classify toys in the small-scale industry sector (which entitles manufacturers to special lower interest rates for loans and other advantages) became a problem for local manufacturers who did not want to lose this status but also could not expand into the export market. These manufacturers believed that the Indian toy industry could be as large an export industry as China's, but that the government's toy policy did not give them the support nor the incentives to export.[70] Local quality also did not enable the companies to export, the government having very little interest in toys or their safety; certainly, Mattel and Hasbro products were safer for children since they did not have small metal parts that could break off. Also, labor laws which forbade the manufacturer to lay off workers at the whim of the export market were seen by small business owners as discouraging for an export market.

The Indian small business community considered the toy business a risky investment, considering that even Lego in India has not done as well as could be supposed, even though it was marketed as an educational toy. This record is mixed primarily because children are not the subjects of consumption that they are in other parts of the world. The advertising and marketing practices of Mattel and Hasbro through the 1990s were aimed at turning children into consumers, and gendered ones, within the context of a more transnational media and culture. But this process had many obstacles. The marketing community itself did not see children as consumers; for instance, the "global" survey of consumer attitudes mentioned at the beginning of this chapter did not, in India, include anyone under the age of eighteen. Economic issues were also key, since the consumption of toys and products designed especially for children was not possible for any except the wealthy. Leo Mattel attempted to advertise toys as an "impulse" buy in urban markets, to make shopping into a pastime for middle-class Indians motivated by shop windows and displays to satisfy spontaneously created needs, and it took the lead in developing the toy market in India. Stores with elaborate displays that functioned as spectacles for passersby also appeared in the shift to a new consumer culture.

Highly specific middle-class cultural practices, such as the preparation of middle-class children for an intensely competitive academic arena which governs the future for many, dictated consumption within one class of consumers. Board games remained bestsellers, since they were seen as educational for both boys and girls and they amused middle-class children within the confines of the house, a key element for the gendering of girls. Stuffed toys were also successful, primarily because they were inexpensive and made by the unorganized sector. One industry expert's opinion was that toys were primarily sold as birthday gifts to the middle classes, and he believed that toys were bought for their size rather than their quality for the purpose of gift giving.[71] This small manufacturer quit the industry after some losses, which he blamed on the burgeoning industry in China, where all the molds were now being sold, on the very uncertain market in India, and on the recent recession. To this manufacturer, even the success of a Mattel or a Hasbro was not guaranteed in the Indian toy market. Since even at the end of the 1990s stuffed toys and board games sold more than Barbie, especially for birthday presents, his opinion was that Barbie's success was not assured.

Turning many classes of children into active consumers of global brands required changing familial aspirations and goals, interactions between parents and children, the segmentation of children's identities into age groups through consumption, and gender relations within the family. Market segmentation by age and gender as it slowly emerged in liberalized India meant that targets of media advertising on TV not only were women and men but also, increasingly, children. The process to incorporate these children into a national as well as a transnational consumer culture was under way in the 1990s, but the lack of an age-segmented children's culture, as it had developed in the West and Japan, prevented the formation of the child as consumer, and children remained unindividuated as members of families.

Given the mixed success of Mattel and Hasbro, the emergence of the child-consumer faces multiple obstacles, but with changes already occurring in cultural practices in response to the new economic conditions and to NRIS, some consumer segments are taking shape. An intensely transnational media, made possible by the presence of multinational media conglomerates and their local affiliates, has also been key. The Masters of the Universe toys produced by Mattel were quite a success in the Indian market, because they were based on a TV show that was frequently broadcast and quite popular. These toys sold well, partly because they were intended for boys, who I would assume, given the still pervasive gender discrimination, would get more discretionary income for toys than would girls.[72] However, these toys lost popularity when the TV series ended. It remains to be seen whether the Disney toys introduced by Mattel will be more successful, although the absence of a marketing blitz of the sort that accompanies every new Disney film was not the norm for India. Even so, with more TV channels like the Cartoon Network available and with Hollywood movies readily and easily available on video and DVD, toys based on TV shows and movies have increased in popularity.

There are signs that a "youth" consumer market is emerging, defined by age, ethnicity, gender, and class and analogous but not entirely similar to those in the West and Japan. This market is the result not only of the media advertising of Hasbro and Mattel but also of music culture such as that of bhangra music. Historically, there has been no specific market for youth and children in movies, magazines, fashion, or even books (apart from textbooks and other consumer items related to schoolwork), so that there have been no media representations of youth culture outside the productions of transnational media.

In light of these differences, the marketing of Barbie in recent years has used modeling and fashion culture to reach ever younger age groups among the middle and upper classes. Mattel participates in the production of consuming subjects who would buy its products by tapping into the gendered and classed forms that multinational culture in India has created. Thus not only is Mattel's Indian affiliate working to use the gender and class formations that took root in the 1980s and 1990s, but all of its advertising is geared toward this new Indian global consumer. This new consumer culture includes a "pop feminist" ideology which sees itself as transnational rather than diasporic in that it includes those living in India as well as its diasporas (figure 3). Advertising appears in women's and movie magazines like *Stardust*, *Savvy*, and *Filmfare*, since women are still seen as the primary consumers on behalf of children. These magazines are much more diverse and are renewing themselves through liberalization. Their direction is toward a specific form of patriarchal quasi-feminism that keeps a dominant patriarchy in place just as much as it does in the United States, where Mattel sells a huge number of astronaut and doctor Barbies. This neoliberal consumer feminism is taking its place alongside a much longer-established socialist and liberal feminism.

With a boom in what is called the "vanity industry" in urban, middle-class India, it is clear that urban consumption participates in and constructs new gender relations and ever-younger and gendered consumers. The appearance of advertising in many realms of the media means that appearance as symbolic capital has much more currency than it did, especially if women are to participate as workers in multinational corporations and

3. Advertisement for import-export company, "Prelude Reaches Out to the Family across the Community. Across Countries. Across Continents," *Elite*, February–March 1994, 4.

their affiliates. For women, this Indian consumer feminism, denoting a participation in a globalized economy for women not only as consumers but also as professionals (models, advertising executives, marketing experts, and small business owners, especially in garment manufacturing) is more and more the career goal of Indian urban women of the middle and upper classes, just as the role of working-class and poor urban women as factory workers and garment industry workers also increases.

For the urban upper classes, fitness centers are burgeoning in the metro areas; one estimate is that there are seven hundred in the metro area of Mumbai and five hundred in that of Delhi.[73] Magazines such as *Verve* aim not only for the metro consumer in Mumbai or Delhi but also for what is believed to be the "upmarket Indian woman globally, even the non-resident Indian," according to the managing editor of *Verve*, Neeru Nanda, who also describes this consumer as the "contemporary urban Indian woman with Indian roots and western exposure."[74] Lavish spending on advertising cosmetics and a growing Indian designer wear industry contribute to the demand for fashion and beauty pageants. In this context it was not surprising that the twenty-three-year-old singer Mehnaz Hoosein should have changed the name of her début album from *Main Houn Mehnaz* (*I Am Mehnaz*) to *Miss India* and that it went on to become an instant hit.[75] Ford Models, a global model search agency, established an Indian affiliate which hosts an annual "supermodel" search. The first search garnered about 200,000 applications from every part of the country.[76]

Leo Mattel's advertising campaign took advantage of the spiraling transnational modeling and fashion industry to increase interest in Barbie. In this new campaign, Mattel went to the urban schools in Mumbai to sponsor a fashion design competition. A fashion model dressed in Barbie clothes was sent to the schools to give away Barbie dolls and to initiate a fashion design competition among the schoolgirls. All entries were exhibited at two huge exhibition halls and the entrants and their parents were invited. A movie star, Hema Malini, was brought in to inaugurate the marketing event, which was conducted in urban schools in Calcutta, New Delhi, and Bangalore. Interschool competitions were encouraged, and the winners' designs were put together in fashion shows. Two famous models were brought in to judge the shows, and the winners from the Mumbai show were used in a limited-edition Barbie with the schoolgirl designer's name and school on the box. Mattel's slogan, "Fun and Learn," was used to encourage young schoolgirls to become fashion designers and to incorporate girls into a transnational garment industry. It is clear that Mattel's advertising utilizes the existing children's culture in which preparation for a career remains the dominant motivator for consumption, but what is specific to this new phase of economic liberalization in India is the intense interest among the middle classes in fashion and the garment industry as career options for women.

Localized gendering practices and economic liberalization have led to the promotion of fashion design and fashion modeling, as well as other less visible careers in the garment industry, as new opportunities for middle- and upper-class girls and women. New body images (thinner and taller) and new fashions (hybrids of European and Indian clothing acceptable in diaspora and urban India) proliferate. Transnationalizing incorporates di-

aspora fashion to present successful role models and opportunities, promoting "ethnic" looks and darker, Asian models in the West, who now
participate in the transnational garment industry much more actively. Gendered consumers, constructed by an Indian pop-cosmopolitan feminism
formed as much by Bollywood's as by Hollywood's circulating productions,
are participating as producers, workers, and consumers in the transnational garment, fashion, and beauty industry, to which Mattel is allying its
products. Ethnic and Asian "looks" have a market not only as exotica but
also because of the large diasporic Asian markets in many locations.

TRANSNATIONAL CONSUMERS AND DIASPORIC SUBJECTS

✷

In contrast to the 1980s, the emerging youth and transnational markets
and growing NRI culture in the 1990s suggested that Barbie sales might
improve. Two contexts are important: the transnational market for Indian
goods, and the changing marketing practices of Barbie, which tapped into
new subjects. Because diasporic and national formations were intertwined
in the cultural practices of Indian liberalization, the Barbie in a sari became
meaningful in new ways. It enabled, for instance, South Asian immigrants
in the United States to give their children what they wanted, the "standard"
Barbie, but with a difference that recalled their "traditional" culture—an
important aspect of the formation of diasporic ethnic identity in a highly
racialized America. In addition, national notions of female beauty became
transnational. The interplay of the "traditional" and "national" female body,
interpellated through Bombay cinema and its close and long-standing ties
to transnational connectivities of capital, media, and goods, circulates powerfully in the diasporas of India. In a national culture where unity and
diversity were seen as typical of India, the creation of ethnic "types" functioned also in a "diverse" and "multicultural" America. Within this Indian
diasporic culture in the United States, for instance, Hindi film dance became an emerging art form. Beauty pageants for Miss India USA and Miss
India America, as well as regional pageants like Miss India California, Miss
India New York, and Miss India Georgia, included performances of Indian
classical and folk dance and music, as well as Hindi film dance and music,
along with fashion shows displaying the latest trends from India.

While Barbie in a sari was a popular purchase for NRIS visiting India, the interplay between the diaspora in the United States, the multinationals, and transnational objects of desire is manifesting itself in even more complex ways. The "traditional" female icons of the Bombay cinema, their images based on Bollywood versions of Ajanta and Ellora figures, remain powerful but come into conflict with two diaspora cultures, those of the United Kingdom and the United States.[77] These two diasporas have influenced cultural productions such as music and fashion, creating a transnational music circuit more effectively than other South Asian diaspora cultures from East Asia or Africa, which emerged at very different periods of history and through different economic conditions. For many decades, the dominance of Bombay cinema, for one, has been in a complex relation with national and transnational culture since its audience has not solely been within India. In the earlier decades of the industry, the Middle East and Africa were important markets for Bombay cinema, and at present the video and DVD market overseas among the South Asian diasporas competes with the video and DVD market in India. Bombay cinema is also the main attraction on many TV channels shown in India, as well as on the Star TV network, based in Hong Kong and transmitted by satellite to the United States.

Since the 1960s, a time of powerful nationalist discourse when India was concerned with the "brain drain" of its intellectuals to the United States, Bombay cinema has concerned itself with "tradition" and westernization. However, this concern became both more intense and different by century's end. Several commercially successful film productions depict the main figures returning from the United States or even living there; one actor turned director even mounted a highly publicized search for an NRI in the United States and the United Kingdom to find a star for a movie about a girl searching for her roots. The diasporic characters are often shown coming into conflict with a culture seen as "traditional," so that the tradition-modernity debate becomes transposed into an Indian-western binary. However, as Purnima Mankekar has argued, some recent Bombay film productions have also shown that the diaspora can be purer than the "home,"[78] and both the awareness of a more transnational Indian audience and the influence of transnational capital that can be seen as responsible for the change. Yet for many, the nation as "homeland" continues to be a site that can be constructed as the "origin" or source of cultural nationalist formations, and notions of multiculturalism and ethnicity in sites such as England and the United States recreate these formations. In India these nationalist discourses also became communalist in tenor, creating communal "Hindu" identities rather than national "Indian" ones. These identifications have become widespread in the United States as well among diasporic Indians, as right-wing organizations seek funding and resources among those desperate to articulate an "authentic" Hindu and Indian identity as multicultural Americans.

The Indian fashion industry, using salwar kameez as a new South Asian transnational costume, spans the globe, selling to NRIS in the United States and the United Kingdom and to others in the South Asian diaspora. The emergence of ready-to-wear salwar kameez as the dress for those of Indian origin living elsewhere as well as for the many women entering the professionalized workforce in multinational corporations in India has changed the Indian garment industry.[79] This industry is located not only in India or Pakistan but also in London, and its fashion catalogues, printed on glossy paper, showcase expensive garments. The interest in "tradition" and "ethnicity" has heightened among cosmopolitans in India as well as its diaspora. What Naseem Khan has called "the fashion explosion" of the 1980s included movements to resuscitate older dyes in the manufacture of "ethnic" garments, as well as modifications of so-called traditional styles. But as Khan points out, the industry in London could not compete with lower-priced goods and the established retail outlets of its counterpart in India, where the desire for locally produced commodities combines with the lure of lower prices.[80]

While the clothing designed in the United Kingdom did not create any new statement of a "fusion" culture analogous to that of music culture, the negotiations that immigrant communities make between their communities of work and family lead to particular styles that enter into circulation transnationally; the change in the salwar kameez suit from a salwar to a more trouser-like cut is one example of this trend. Although the nature of fabrics and style might fuse working-class Indian immigrant culture with working-class Indian culture, much hybridity theory ignores these forms of syncretism for the more recognized hybridity of "East" and "West" as is evident in music culture. Diasporic negotiations are apparent in the many beauty contests proliferating among South Asian communities in the United States. The Miss India pageants in the United States present the

"American" female body ideal in a very different style inspired as much by Bollywood and urban Indian culture as by the Euro-American fashion industry. A diasporic aesthetic is linking up with disciplining female bodies through newer ideas of beauty not only because Indian women and men are visible in the European fashion industry but also because of new investment in India and because India is a large market for the American and European garment industry. The link between this diasporic female aesthetic and transnational corporations is also apparent in STAR TV of Hong Kong, which broadcasts beauty contests such as Miss India Canada.

India Today, a newsmagazine based in India, created a North American edition in the 1990s to actively promote these investments and keep up the interest of NRIS. Every issue contained many advertisements for real estate and mutual fund investments and new corporate issues from India, rankings of the investment climates in Indian states, and a list of possible corporate positions in India for NRIS. Many South Asian professionals discovered that multinationals allowed them to return "home" by offering positions within Indian branches and affiliates (which also, more recently, facilitated outsourcing). Since these professionals were paid in dollars, their economic status was far above that of Indians paid in rupees. Multinationals found it advantageous to use the expertise of immigrants who had worked in the West but had grown up in India and spoke its languages. Their affiliations, loyalties, and conflicts within the local and global economy became contingent and flexible; they purchased real estate in both the United States and India, especially in new housing developments in India similar to those in the United States. The prices of these developments keep out most middle-class Indians but not many of those living in India who have benefited from the liberalization of the economy.

These upper-class transnational NRIS, or "international Indians," as one glossy publication calls them, were targeted by the Indian state not only to invest but also to buy Indian goods. One publication by a group called Media Transasia out of New Delhi was called *Elite: For the International Indian*. The first two issues featured "successful Indians" on the cover: Zubin Mehta, the famous symphony conductor, with his wife Nancy (figure 4), and Arjun Waney, a garment entrepreneur, with his wife Judy (figure 5). Thus did the magazine define success as marrying a white "American" woman and collecting expensive Indian goods. This glossy magazine not

4. "Zubin Mehta Conducting the World," *Elite*, February–
March 1994, cover. Photo: Rishika Advani.

only sold India as a place for investment but also sold the lifestyle of the
"transnational NRI" in America, with advertisements for carpets, expensive
clothes, jewelry, furniture, and of course luxury tourism. Slim Indian models were featured wearing high-fashion Indian clothes that suggested an
India of "classical" music, fashion, and tradition; the clothes included saris
and salwar kameez as well as European pants and shirts for men and
women made out of silks with Indian motifs. The successful NRIS on the
cover, however, were featured with their white "American" wives, symbols
of their success outside India, suggesting that white femininity was important even with cosmopolitan rearticulations of gender relations within
transnational connectivities. Advertising of "global" brands, Hollywood
cinema, and a host of other cultural productions all utilized the white
female as the icon of consumer style,[81] as the élite traveler and entrepre-
neurial feminist.[82]

This "international Indian" was based not only outside India but also

5. "Arjun Waney, Raja of the Rag Trade," *Elite*, April–
May 1994, cover. Photo: Rishika Advani.

inside it, since transnational corporations hired immigrant professionals of Indian origin to work in India. Whereas earlier the corporations would send only white European or American executives, now they used "local" knowledges to send executives "home" or even to hire "local" talent. AT&T, Motorola, Digital International, and Pepsico were some companies with Indian expatriates at their head during this period. Companies ran advertisements in Indian newspapers in the United States to recruit engineers and financial executives. One advertisement in *India Today* read: "Everything that ambitious and achievement oriented Indians are looking for in the world's international business centers is now on the tap—back home."[83]

Unlike the successful NRI on the cover of *Elite* magazine, who was seemingly well settled in the United States, the other successful NRI was one who could return "home" with a position in a multinational corporation while drawing a high salary. (By contrast, the lure for multinationals of setting up manufacturing and other units in India was that at the lower levels, Indians were paid considerably less than their counterparts in the United States.) The higher-level professional jobs were said to offer the possibility of having a "traditional" family. An article in *India Today* stated that some of those interviewed by the magazine had taken jobs in India because of a concern for the consequences if their children grew up in the United States, "especially daughters." For these immigrants to the United States, as revealed in the article, the United States was constructed as a place where the "achievement-oriented" could fulfill their professional potential more successfully than in India. The American ethnic discourse of the model minority is operative here, and the professional immigrant's participation in the "brain drain," the article concludes hopefully, will be reversed once sufficient expertise is taken back to India.

For the transnational NRI, the "international Indian," the concern for Indian "tradition" and culture, and by extension for controlling the sexuality of the daughters and sons growing up in the United States, is crucial. In particular, women's sexuality was disciplined in diasporic locations through nostalgic representations of an Indian tradition of women's virginity and purity that were bolstered by the Bombay cinema's dominant discourses, and were negotiated in terms of a pure India where the daughter's sexuality is believed to be safeguarded and an impure West where it is constantly in jeopardy. Males were disciplined in families with the goal of making them professionals, policed rigorously through a "modern" heteromasculinity in which, for the middle classes, professions such as the sciences, technology, and medicine counted for success. With widespread homophobia among South Asian communities in the United States prompted by more visible gay and lesbian communities of color, the policing of male sexuality was also taking new forms. However, being an "American" professional was not seen as conflicting with being an NRI, or with any religious or class identity.

Magazines such as the North American edition of *India Today* were directed at the immigrant professionals who fit both the model-minority notion of ethnicity in the United States and the nationalist theory of the "brain drain." Those who were neglected both as audiences and as subjects were the two-thirds of the immigrants of Indian origin who were neither professionals nor from the upper classes. Indeed there are Indian immigrants who live below the poverty line in the United States, but these were not people at whom the Indian government directed its advertisements for investment in India. The exploitative conditions under which many working-class and poor immigrants work as undocumented or migrant labor are also neglected, though many families in India rise above the poverty level because of remittances from these same workers. The widespread exploitation of domestic servants brought from India to work in the homes of "international Indians" becomes the concern not of the Indian or U.S. state but of nonprofit organizations like Sakhi in New York and Narika in California. Nonprofits in many cities, established predominantly for women and by Indian women and other South Asian and Asian women, are the only ones addressing the underclasses of the globalized Asian labor force in the United States. Yet for these migrant workers, the pleasures and desires of consumption position them also as subjects of transnational connectivities.[84]

The presence of the national in the multicultural, of the "American lifestyle" in the "ethnic" and in the "global," reveals that nationalisms are crucial in this global economy. Many of multiculturalism's symbolic forms as they exist in the United States today, and in other regions as well, come from consumption practices. An examination of these practices reveals that America as a symbol of consumption style is both powerful and heterogeneous. As Stuart Hall puts it, the new cultural forms in the global mass culture are recognizable in their ability to "recognize and absorb . . . differences within the larger overarching framework of what is essentially an American conception of the world" in which capital has had "to negotiate, . . . to incorporate and partly to reflect the differences it was trying to overcome."[85] The conjunction of modernity and consumption has indeed come to be hegemonic. To be Indian or Pakistani or Bangladeshi in the United States means shopping at particular stores, be they Pakistani or Indian or Bangladeshi stores, wearing and buying salwar kameez and saris, and living in relation to an ethnic style, where style, as Stuart Ewen suggests, has emerged as the "predominant expression of meaning."[86]

In her book *Shopping for Identity: The Marketing of Ethnicity*, Marilyn Halter argues that while ethnic groups often resist a dominant consumer culture, they nevertheless participate in consumption to enhance and reinforce their ethnic identities, and thus use the market for their own ends.[87] The idea that consumption is about establishing identity has been argued by a number of scholars including Zygmunt Bauman,[88] Anthony Giddens,[89] and Mike Featherstone,[90] among many others. Although Barbie in a sari is marketed to an emerging consumer segment in India, it also becomes meaningful as a means for immigrant Indians to assert their identities in different times and places or even concurrently as Indians, NRIS, immigrants in the United States, and Americans. Thus Barbie makes possible all of these identities and in doing so becomes a more successful product. In tracing Barbie's travels in India, I have examined how a multinational corporation such as Mattel tries to be at "home" in India and thus participates in the emergence of a new gendered market segment and also in economic liberalization, inserting Indian women and girls into the transnational garment industry. Discourses of gendered beauty, employment, entrepreneurship, and consumer feminism traveling in multiple directions across transnational connectivities all enable the changing context of this new transnational culture to which Barbie provides an opening.

Yet these identities and subjects produced by the transnational connectivity of which Barbie is a sign are neither voluntary nor a matter of choice. Alan Warde, for instance, critiques Bauman's conceptualization of the consumer as a "free-floating agent" rather than engaging with the "constraints people face in their consumption practices as embodied persons rather than as ghostly abstractions of economics."[91] If, as many scholars have revealed, consumer choice is highly constructed,[92] and also emerges in relation to how identities themselves are produced through a nexus of nation, state, gender, race, class, and a number of other factors, then ethnic identities produced through consumption cannot be seen as being chosen or willed. The nexus of culture, ethnicity, nationalism, gender, and class (as well as a number of other social formations), as I have suggested in this chapter, has become entangled with political economy and the transnational movements of goods, bodies, and ideas to produce subjects and identities. Hegemonic discourses within transnational connectivities enable these movements and produce flexible subjects. For instance, for Indian immigrants in the United States a hyphenated identity may only be part of the story of subjects in transnationality. They are also the subjects of the Indian state and are produced in conjunction with the demands of the IMF as it articulates with the desires of diasporic nationalisms. Becoming

"American" by consuming Barbie, these hyphenated and immigrant subjects figure prominently in metropolitan discourses of the global consumer
in India and within many formations of Indian nationalist anxieties in
different sites. Barbie in a sari is thus simply one opening into our understanding of how consumer subjects and consumer nationalisms are produced in a transnational world.

chapter *three*

✶

Human rights discourse emerged in the last twenty-five years as part of a regime of truth that became what one scholar calls "the preeminent univer-salistic ideal within contemporary moral discourse."[1] It was almost the only way to address issues of social justice, oppression, and inequality within states and across them. The discourse had its beginnings in the UN Charter of 1945 and by the end of the century took on a renewed impetus with the UN World Conference on Human Rights, held in Vienna in June 1993. Human rights struggles came to be more urgent, as Rajni Kothari argued, when internationalism as a promise of equality, peace, and justice among states receded in a world of transnational corporations, fragmenting yet repressive nation-states, and emerging cosmopolitan groups.[2] Once used only by groups such as Amnesty International and Human Rights Watch, human rights discourse moved beyond campaigns for civil liberties and political rights to embody in everyday language what seemed just and mor-ally right. Powerful states used it to measure whether other states were democratic; training in human rights was given to police officers in India as well as to feminist workers in grassroots organizations. As a regime of truth and as an ethic that was believed to lie at the heart of a normative state and of a transnational civil society, and as a rationality with the goal of welfare and democracy motivating state and nonstate actors, human rights became transnationalized through powerful technologies of knowledge production in a number of regions around the world.

In a world in which welfare was dissociated from the state and became the work of those groups and individuals who saw themselves as "global citizens" with responsibilities beyond the state, the field of the social expanded into transnational domains. Managing the crisis of continuing inequalities, extrastate entities such as nongovernmental organizations came to be the transnational instruments of technologies of governmentality, creating and applying knowledges and techniques that promoted the welfare and security, rather than just the rights, of populations. Both NGOs and states used the concept of human rights not as a juridical instrument to ensure the rights of subjects but rather as an ethical regime that put into play a whole range of instrumentalizations of governance. Human rights became not a means of ensuring the rights of individuals or collective subjects but rather a claim of good governance by states as well as NGOs, showing that the juridical power could become governmentalized and move outside the plane of sovereignty. Thus the question was not simply whether human rights are universal, a key debate in this field, but rather which kinds of tactics and apparatuses they enabled as an index of the welfare of populations. Revealing once again the ways in which geopolitics and biopolitics exist through reliance upon one another, the governmentality of human rights is a key topic to understand the end of the twentieth century. In addition to the tactics of human rights governmentality, this chapter will also explore the subjects produced by human rights discourses, who saw themselves as autonomous individuals participating in the spread of liberal democracy around the world.

The deployment of human rights became pivotal in a number of struggles concerning refugee rights, environmental rights, global citizenship, food security, health care, and many other causes. In fact it was remarkable how many causes and organizations used the language of human rights as part of their platform for action. Human rights achieved a considerable amount of power as a discourse necessary to authenticate the extent of suffering and deprivation imposed upon individuals or groups by the state. As a result, human rights discourses were used in a number of sites around the world. From minority groups in India struggling for civil liberties to women's groups worldwide focusing on domestic violence and rape, it was clear that concerns for visibility and voice were addressed through this discourse of human rights that had once been used only for "political" violence as defined by groups like Amnesty International.

The recourse to rights from the sovereign state and the recourse to rights from the "international community" were connected, since they remained within the nation-state system. Yet they must be rethought, not only because so many millions of people did not belong to any state but also because these rights became a means to create new dominant groups who had a "voice" and thus promoted the liberal conceptualization of the "international arena" on the model of a state, with a division between the state and civil society. Furthermore, human rights regimes became powerful also because they envisioned political action in terms of the struggle for rights, and thus produced discourses that became normative in creating modern subjects. Articulating a cosmopolitan "global" ethic, human rights crossed many borders. Although, as Gayatri Spivak has pointed out, human rights left out the rural subaltern and recuperated a colonial relationship with the colonizing West, thus reviving the notion of the "white man's burden," it was difficult to dismiss human rights as simply an élite or neocolonial formation, since they made for a powerful discourse that circulated effectively across many transnational connectivities.[3] It became normative to discuss injustices of various kinds through the language of human rights, both in the West and in the non-West. Even scholars and intellectuals who designated human rights as a Eurocentric or neocolonial discourse argued that human rights instruments of some kind were a necessity.[4] Thus it was not just the "white man's burden" but the burdens of many kinds of knowledge producers that were linked in this debate on the relevance of human rights for ensuring the welfare and security of populations.

In all these contexts, what has to be examined is how and why this form of knowledge became governmentalized and, in connection with this question of power, what knowledges and modes of power it produced. Both its representational practices—that is, the ways in which the objects of violations were depicted—and its subjectifying practices need to be examined. Who was speaking for whom? What were the knowledges that enabled them to speak for others? What forms of violence did these representations perform? What techniques of governmentality could be identified in these usages? If it was not individuals or states but nongovernmental and non-profit groups that were making claims for others, then how were "local" and "grassroots" claims established? In the United States at the end of the century, where the "local" was being fought over by both left and right, these questions became urgent for defining the liberal positions being established on both sides of the political equation. Moreover, it became urgent to examine how human rights regimes emerged as a normalizing technology of a "global civil society"[5] or a "transnational civil society."[6]

In the previous chapters of this book I have examined how neoliberal cosmopolitanism is produced through transnational connectivities within cultures of consumption. In neoliberalism, the promises of rights and citizenship were believed to be achievable through the workings of market capitalism within what was commonly referred to as globalization. Within the context of this liberalism, human rights claims did not simply depend on the workings of the market[7] and the processes within what has been called globalization. "Globalization" was a fuzzy and somewhat misleading term, because it universalized what could be better understood as the movements of discourses and practices within specific transnational con-nectivities and the histories of these movements. These connectivities may include the practices of élites in different parts of the world, of neocolonial knowledge formations, as well as the practices of those who are nonélites. What was made possible within many wildly divergent transnational con-nectivities was not just economic disparity but also the subjects who were produced in different connectivities, making biopolitical formations visible and working to redress their effects—those subjects and practices seen as oppositional to the detrimental effects of continued imperial practices. In this chapter I turn to these movements, in particular the movements of women's rights as human rights, which I view as another discourse that moves through transnational connectivities, producing multiple subjects and governmental technologies at various sites and creating what is often seen as a "global" movement of women's rights as human rights that joined women from the global North and South in solidarity. For it was not only a North American or European "global feminism" that seemed to have adopted human rights as a dominant language to address gendered forms of violence, but also women's and feminist groups from many other parts of the world.[8]

In this chapter I examine human rights as a regime of truth disseminated
through transnational connectivities which came to power as a mode of
transnational governmentality producing technologies of welfare alongside
modes of disciplinary and sovereign power. Knowledge production about
human rights and their violations was undertaken by myriad institutions
within states and outside them—from governments to NGOs to activists to
academic researchers. Many of the researchers producing knowledges
about women's human rights in these institutional sites were feminists or
were part of feminist organizations. Others, who may not have identified
themselves as feminists, were using feminist goals and objectives in their
organizations to improve women's lives or challenge the patriarchal status
quo. In examining human rights as producing technologies of transnational
governmentality, I am interested in trajectories and tactics of feminist activism and knowledge production that came into existence in relation to the
ethical discourse of human rights. Human rights have become a key mode
through which governmental technologies have come into existence
through the discourses of liberal democracy as a source of freedom.[9] Feminist activism in human rights is an example of this governmentality, producing knowledges by subjects who saw themselves as ethical and free, and thus
as feminist subjects able to work against and within the state for the welfare
of women around the world. In examining feminist human rights activism
in this way, I collapse the distinction between rationalities of governance and
forms of contestation, seeing them as both inimical and interdependent in
ways that follow Foucauldian theorizations of liberalism and civil society. It
is precisely because this sort of distinction is untenable that we can understand how liberal feminist subjects could so easily move across public and
private spheres and across transnational connectivities, how they could be
both nationalist and internationalist, working against some nation-states
while sustaining others.

ETHICAL REGIMES: THE EMERGENCE OF
WOMEN'S RIGHTS AS HUMAN RIGHTS

*

Human rights discourses in their current form began when the UN General Assembly adopted the Universal Declaration of Human Rights in
1948. What has come to be called the International Bill of Rights includes

two international covenants dating from 1966, the first of which covers civil and political rights and the second economic, social, and cultural rights.[10] The first covenant, the Covenant on Civil and Political Rights, encompasses what some have called the "first generation" of human rights and sought to protect individuals from states. The second covenant, the Covenant of Economic, Social and Cultural Rights, is seen as second-generation because it focuses instead on economic rights, which have faced more intractable obstacles in their implementation than political rights.[11] In 1981, the Assembly of Heads of States and Government of the Organization for African Unity adopted the African Charter on Human and Peoples' Rights, with the goal of establishing regional cultural difference (from the Universal Declaration) while respecting historical tradition and the values of African civilization.[12] For some feminists, what became more important for women were the different covenants which specifically refer to women's human rights and which include the Convention on the Elimination of All Forms of Discrimination Against Women (CEDAW), adopted in 1979.

"Women's rights as human rights," an offshoot of what can be called the "human rights regimes"—by which I refer to the networks of knowledge and power that inserted these discourses into geopolitics—was a claim used by entities as different as the U.S. State Department and insurgency movements around the world. In addition to American women's groups and the UN, or the Amnesty International and Human Rights Watch groups that were at the forefront of this movement, women's and development groups in different parts of the world also took up human rights discourse, as did a number of NGOs, some working in human rights organizations and some in groups devoted to women's issues. In addition, the formation of many international and transnational women's NGOs within a global network, which exist in and against the nation-states, promoted new discourses of universality and sisterhood within many transnational connectivities.[13] Among feminist circuits, where the the personal and the political were not demarcated, it became increasingly common to argue that women's rights were human rights. As Charlotte Bunch, a feminist activist based in the United States, asserted, this meant "moving women from the margins to the center by questioning the most fundamental concepts of our social order so that they take better account of women's lives." This assertion claims that "women's issues are not separate but are neglected aspects of . . . global agendas."[14] The rationale underlying the claim was that human rights instruments when applied to women's issues could break down the distinction made by patriarchal states between public and private domains and thus address the violence and subordination of women within the private sphere. The claim in turn relied on arguments that states were unable to address the question of women's welfare because they were patriarchal and that women's groups were better able to address problems such as violence against women. Thus the rationale for the movements was what was seen as the failure of states to ensure the welfare of female populations, the inefficiency of the state, and its ideology of patriarchy.

The momentum building up to the Vienna declaration, as Elizabeth Friedman narrates, came from UN women's conferences such as the NGO meeting in Nairobi in 1985, as well as from concerns felt by women's groups across the world. According to Friedman, these groups felt that their state governments and the state systems were patriarchal and anti-women, and that nothing but international organizations and international rights instruments like CEDAW could help.[15] Friedman quotes Hina Jilani, founder of a group in Lahore, who argued that struggling against fundamentalist state and religious laws in Pakistan meant seeking a secular basis for struggle: "We felt that [international human rights law] were the standards that you wanted to make the basis [of women's rights], by saying that we don't want religion as the basis, we want equality and social justice in accordance with internationally accepted standards."[16]

In the South Asian context of which Jilani is speaking, where religious laws were supplanting so-called secular state laws (of course this is a problem not only in South Asia but also in other parts of the world including the United States), international law, seemingly above these contexts, became an attractive tool to obtain "equality and social justice." Implicit in the assumption was that international law was more equitable and just, even if there seemed no clear means of knowing whether it indeed was. There was considerable debate among activists and scholars about the efficacy of international law in its international manifestations, or in the national realm with which it was closely intertwined; however, despite the debate, many feminists still supported human rights instruments for feminist causes. Saroj Iyer, although arguing that human rights had been a limited concept in India since they had not addressed the problem of violence in the private sphere, believed that the "human rights community must move beyond its male-defined norms in order to respond to the severe and systematic violation of women's rights" in India.[17] Her view was that it was a patriarchal and corrupt judicial system that prevented women from achieving the rights guaranteed to them in the Indian constitution, and she called for expanding human rights frameworks to include women.[18] While for some feminists, feminist traffic with the state was always fraught, for others it was a necessity that must be undertaken, if only to expose the ways in which the private sphere was constructed by the state. Stanlie James argued that human rights covenants that focused on women's human rights, like CEDAW, were "constricted by weak enforcement provisions" and were not ratified by many states, but she also believed that they posed a challenge to gender oppression.[19]

Some feminists concluded that at best, human rights might be marginal to the interests of those they meant to serve; at worst, human rights laws could become tools to punish subalterns. Thus Adetoun O. Ilumoka argued in her critique of the use of human rights instruments in Africa: "In seeking to define acceptable change and the process for effecting it, the concept of human rights can be a powerful tool for legitimation of existing institutions and the concentration of power in the hands of powerful groups." Ilumoka stated that in Africa, the discourse of rights was more popular in struggles for political and civil liberties by élites, whereas the struggle for social justice was the discourse of more mass-based movements.[20] For Ilumoka, the liberal nature of human rights had depoliticized the struggle for justice.

Another question is whether human rights laws could even be enforced when powerful patriarchies within most states did not even allow existing laws to be effectively used to protect women. Was it only, therefore, a hostile political environment that prevented otherwise exemplary laws from becoming widespread in practice, so that these claims needed to be made only in states such as India? The question defies an easy answer because the implementation and construction of these laws are profoundly intertwined, so that the context is only what can be seen as the condition of possibility of the law. What Mary John called the "constitutive" nature of context changes how meanings are created through laws.[21] Furthermore, the hostile nature of legal systems in nation-states in Asia, Africa, and Latin America has not been the only obstacle to proper implementation of human rights instruments for women: so have the geopolitical agendas of the "international regimes" creating the laws. These factors were ignored when some argued, as Radhika Coomaraswamy did in her analysis of the situation in India, that human rights instruments could only become used where notions of human rights were widely accepted and where they could become "a part of the legal structure of a given society."[22] Unfortunately these formulations, once again, use the concept of "third world" non-European "backwardness" to explain why the "third world" lacks human rights.

To ask in which context these international laws could be utilized begs the whole question of the nature of nationalisms, the gender politics of nationalisms, and of course the geopolitical context of human rights discourse at the end of the century. While it might be accurate to state that the commitment of the justice and "law and order" machinery of many nation-states to women's rights and to women's freedom from oppression is not a given, this situation also would include the so-called West. Yet this "West" was often coded as being friendly to human rights. Thus the argument made by Kirti Singh with regard to India, that the most significant obstacle to securing rights for women is a "hostile state that is not actually interested in giving them any rights," does not clarify what makes patriarchal states different.[23] Consequently when Singh pointed out that although the Indian constitution guaranteed rights of equality to women, the inadequacy of criminal law and the misogyny of the legal system prevented the laws from being administered, one could point to many similar contradictions in other parts of the world. Yet in countries like the United States, with patriarchal and often anti-feminist legal cultures, feminist groups did not resort to claims of human rights violations since it was assumed that they did not lack human rights; it was taken for granted, however erroneously, that the American legal system and others like it were adequate to the task of ensuring the rights of women without resorting to international instruments or the UN.

To a certain extent, what was important about human rights discourse was the assumption that it would address not just the subordination and disenfranchisement of women across the world but also the kinds of knowledges it produced and the forms of rule and rationality that it presumed, and thus its functioning as a mode of governmentality under neoliberalism. Thus the power of human rights discourse was to represent women as a population, which is one way that Foucault defined governmentality, and also as sovereign autonomous subjects. "Women" outside the West, in human rights discourses, were represented as objects of charity and care by the West but could become subjects who could participate in the global economy and become global citizens; this was the "third-world" victim who had become a global subject. The apparatuses of welfare of a normative nation-state supported both projects of subjectification, especially with regard to women, and they did so through collaboration and conflict with earlier development regimes. Furthermore, in relation to its function as a mode of governmentality, the rapid spread and ubiquity of human rights discourse within struggles for women's rights must be noted. Thus for many of those working in campaigns for women's rights as human rights, it was important to claim that for "women" to be recognized as "human" they must become autonomous individuals who could recognize their oppressions and struggle to become citizens of a global civil society.

For many feminists, the promise of global citizenship through human rights remained a vital project. For example, Marjorie Agosin, in her book *Women, Gender, and Human Rights: A Global Perspective*, argued that "human rights, and particularly women's rights, must also be defined as being seen and treated as equal in the political and ideological as well as domestic and private arenas."[24] Increasingly, global citizenship was based on the assumption of a global feminism with common agendas for all women; within this feminism human rights became an effective way to address what Agosin called "a strong commonality that goes beyond national, economic, and social boundaries" and recognizes "the rights of women both in the public as well as the private sphere."[25] However, rather than see this global feminism as a ground for the claims of human rights to be made, one can instead see it as an effect of many of these claims. This global feminism is, however, not global; rather it is transnational, moving through particular connectivities through which communities of feminists are produced.

HUMAN RIGHTS AND DEVELOPMENT: POPULATIONS OF WOMEN

✳

If human rights produced the liberal subject of a transnational civil society, then the collaboration with development regimes, which represented women in the "developing world" as populations to be modernized, also

revealed its continuity with earlier projects of governmentality. Whereas the development regimes were all-powerful internationally all through the 1960s and 1970s, they became subject to critique from feminist and other quarters in the last two decades. These critiques argued that development, by using the West as a model of progress, implied a linear, environmentally destructive model of change based on Enlightenment notions that did not, as Gita Sen and Karen Grown revealed in 1987, advance the needs of women.[26] Thus, as Janet Momsen noted, after two UN "Decades of Development" led to declines in the living standards of women in most third world counties, development no longer has unquestioned legitimacy.[27] More recently, Arturo Escobar, Akhil Gupta, and other scholars have argued that the globalization of capital and the neoliberal policies of many states and international agencies in conjunction even with newer development regimes did not augur well for improving the lot of the impoverished in rural or urban sites in regions such as India[28] and Latin America.[29] In new development regimes, meeting the needs of women was deemed to be key to removing inequalities around the world. Thus by the last two decades of the twentieth century, the World Bank, the UN, and very many agencies devoted to development around the world turned their attention to women, claiming that development could only work well if women were given help; micro-lending, literacy, and contraception and other health services were all seen as means to this goal. A large number of agencies began keeping statistical information on women, and few development reports were produced without attention to women. All this meant that women (not gender, but women) became the dominant subjects of development regimes. At the same time as attempts were made to use the notion of women's rights as human rights to address a number of sources of women's subordination, development regimes gained new legitimacy to continue their task by focusing on women as their target population.

While the relation between human rights and development can be understood in terms of what Foucault calls the "schematism" that enables the exercise of power through its correlation,[30] scholars have also argued that human rights and development have been inimical to each other. However, the regime of human rights evolved in the shadow of development to address its limitations and to ensure the continued authority of knowledge production by the "developed world" over the "developing world" within transnational connectivities. In 1981 the International Commission of Jurists met at The Hague to argue that human rights and development needed to work together, because then human rights could work on problems as they arose rather than addressing just the symptoms, as human rights instruments did. In this way, development's neglect of the "human factor," which was a major critique of development regimes, could be overcome.[31]

Despite many critiques, development regimes remained powerful, gaining legitimacy through collaboration with human rights regimes. Both gained strength through the 1960s and the first UN Decade of Development, although the end of the 1970s saw growing tensions between these regimes of knowledge and the need to manage the conflict. The UN Commission on Human Rights in 1969 adopted a resolution that the universal use of human rights "depends to a large degree on the rapid economic and social development of the developing countries."[32] That same year, the UN General Assembly's Declaration on Social Progress and Development stated that "social progress and development shall be founded on respect for the dignity and value of the human person and shall ensure the promotion of human rights and social justice.[33] The reference to social justice here linked human rights to development, since it was believed that without some form of development human rights could not be universalized. Another connection was the recognition of a "Right to Development," which was articulated in a UNESCO meeting on "human rights and the establishment of a new international economic order" in 1978,[34] and was followed up by the Dakar Colloquium on Human Rights and Development organized that same year by the International Commission of Jurists and the Association Sénégalaise d'Études et de Recherches Juridiques.[35] The colloquium concluded that because human rights were an essential component, development requirements could not be used to violate human rights. Yet development was not seen as second to human rights, since, as the colloquium also stated, it was important to have a "free, active and genuine participation of everyone in preparing and implementing a development policy for the general good," and the goal of development to satisfy fundamental human needs should also be assured without impediment.[36] However, despite the tensions that existed at the time between the proponents of the two concepts, development and human rights are con-

nected through common knowledge formations based on linear notions of
progress that use North-South inequalities to claim that the North has
human rights (with a few aberrations) and the South needs to achieve them.

More recently, rather than discard development, human rights NGOs
have assumed the task of development while critiquing older versions of it.
As David Chandler suggests, the NGOs have established a "rights-based
'new humanitarian consensus'" which claims that its tasks are quite different from the more "people focused" approach to development prevalent
in the 1980s, which was based on "capacity-building," empowerment, and
the creation of civil society.[37] It is noteworthy that this new approach includes attention to women, which was deemed crucial within developing
countries. Chandler noted that "ethical" involvement of these human rights
NGOs relied on the creation of the third world victim as an object of rescue
by first world NGOs, and thus delegitimized nonwestern states and legitimized western activism. The move from "needs-based" to "rights-based"
humanitarianism, Chandler argues, led the way for the "military humanitarianism" of the western states in which development could come about
only through military action.

Despite these new approaches to development, some feminists did contest the belief that a development policy based on human rights would
support women and be substantively different from earlier efforts. Charlesworth, Chinkin, and Wright argued that the right to development remained
a problem for women, since it "draws no distinction between the economic
position of men and women."[38] Furthermore, this right to development
within neoliberalism was seen as bound also to economic and geopolitical
rationales. Within the "military humanitarianism" espoused by George W.
Bush's administration, women's human rights were used to justify military
intervention, as in Afghanistan. However, once this intervention was justified, women's issues and their participation in the rebuilding of Afghanistan and in liberal citizenship were sidelined. Women's groups claim that
the administration of Hamid Karzai has given no more than lip service to
women's demands and that in many rural areas, Taliban-era conditions
prevail for women.[39] Despite these uses of the discourse of development,
and despite the opposition to this discourse from a number of groups and
interests, the link between its technologies and the project of women's
rights as human rights made possible the regulative project of managing

populations through regimes of welfare that produced women as key subjects for governance.

THE RATIONALITIES OF HUMAN RIGHTS GOVERNMENTALITY: UNIVERSALITY VERSUS DIFFERENCE

*

Within the transnational connectivities of human rights discourses, the first rationality of the ethical regime of human rights is the division between the universal and the particular, so that the debate on human rights has often centered around its universal application and challenges to this view. Yet the debate on the universal applicability of human rights did not diminish the power of this discourse to become disseminated; rather it encouraged its entrenchment, since it produced cosmopolitans and their detractors at many sites. Thus one of the main geopolitical issues between states, for example the United States and China, was (and remains) the question of whether human rights is a universal concept or a western concept. A great deal of scholarly literature and political writing has been devoted to this topic.[40] The PRC government argued that human rights was a product of western culture, and that there were Chinese concepts that were different but similar. In the area of women's rights as human rights, the debate was over whether there was a common patriarchy, whether all women had a common source of oppression. Even if cultural difference was asserted, it was asserted that human rights could be commensurable across many social, geographical, and economic divisions. Or it was suggested that because of strategic political reasons, differences, whether cultural, religious, or national, had to take a back seat to universal precepts articulated as humanitarian rationalities. Thus in one version of this debate it was argued that human rights were necessary even as an imperfect tool, that is, even if they were alien to the cultures in which they were being used. This is the argument put forward by Pheng Cheah, for whom human rights was "double-edged but absolutely necessary."[41] Even though Cheah suggested that the global capitalist framework of human rights and the inequalities between North and South needed to be acknowledged, he remained committed to the belief that these instruments were crucial. Similarly, Ed Friedman argued that human rights were a utopian notion that needed to be

retained as such,[42] while to Susan Koshy human rights could only be retained as a Derridean "specter" that became an "ideal universality" in which
universality emerged and was displaced.[43]

Scholars such as Rajni Kothari argued that human rights were Eurocentric in many of their assumptions and goals, even though they might be
one of the few tools available to struggle for the rights of the disenfranchised.[44] As Kothari put it, the concept of human rights was grounded in
the assumption of an "individualistic ethic and takes as a philosophical
given that social formations are homogeneous and hence amenable to
universal formulations of individual and community, liberty and democracy."[45] According to Rhoda Howard, since human rights remained a product of liberal democratic states, they were a means to assert the rights of the
individual as a private, individual, or autonomous being.[46] Rights discourse
thus could not be adopted for the liberation of many of those outside
notions of a polity compatible with this view or of those who would argue
against this kind of universalizing. Consequently, Smitu Kothari and Harsh
Sethi argued that it was important to ask whether women in many parts of
the world could be seen as autonomous individuals (outside of the structure of the family) or whether their oppression in the family could be
addressed by asserting their autonomy from it.[47]

In response to the individualistic assumptions of most dominant forms
of human rights, the notion of "group rights" became a means to preserve
"tradition," for example in the struggles of the Native Indian groups in
North America. Based on cultural membership, group rights were asserted
by indigenous groups for a number of claims,[48] although some scholars
pointed out that these claims were often based on an essentialized notion of
culture.[49] However, as Rhoda Howard has suggested, these struggles could
create incompatibilities and conflicts over issues like group membership,
as well as redefinitions and representations of traditions that defined the
group.[50] Especially for those in subordinate relations to a hegemonic
group, this assertion of group rights could become problematic if it was
challenged by members who saw themselves as marginal to the group, thus
revealing how modernity's push to individualism could not be written off
within group rights claims in modern nation-states. However, some claims
of group rights were based on seeing the group as a collection of individuals
rather than as a collectivity that struggled against assumptions of individual

autonomy.[51] Yet while some scholars argued that group rights were op-posed to individual identity projects, producing an identity that was not that of an autonomous, political being, others concluded that in the current political and geopolitical climate, where multicultural nations were the norm rather than an exception, group rights needed to be taken very se-riously.[52]

It is not clear even whether the struggle for women's human rights was to be seen as a group right, since women could be seen as one group with a common tradition, and the term "woman" could carry within itself the notion of an autonomous individual.[53] Within modernity, women were constructed as a group of individuals who collectively articulated their op-pression in certain instances, so that their rights were often understood as collective rights rather than group rights. The emergence of collective rights galvanized the movement for women's rights as human rights to become a new paradigm for organizing women globally. The Beijing wom-en's conference in 1995 highlighted this framework as a unifying one, suggesting a new impetus in networking across national and international divides.

Yet the idea of collective rights assumed that females live their lives as "women" solely rather than as parts of other communities, or that women see themselves as autonomous individuals. It was certainly difficult to as-sume that the subjectivity of those persons termed "women" was con-structed solely by gender. The multiple subject-positions of persons termed "women" argued for differences that included gender as one aspect of their subordination. Thus, while we might understand the human rights of women as the struggle of a collectivity, the collective consisted of autono-mous individuals believed to be in a common struggle. Since it was not tradition or biology but gender that brought these persons together, it was necessary to understand gender as a highly contingent and diverse forma-tion that could not be understood outside its articulation with race, nation, religion, class, or sexuality.

In the case of women's rights as human rights, the forms of power that produced universality or commensurability were visible across transna-tional connectivities. It was clear that in presuming women to be subject to what is called "domestic violence" across national, cultural, social, and economic divides, the female subject was essentialized. Agosin, for example, suggested that the project of women's rights as human rights was

necessary because women were linked by their "invisibility" and "resili-
ence" as well as a "universal pattern of abuse"[54] resulting from the separation of public and private spheres. Similarly, in articulating the rights of
migrants and refugees in terms of human rights, commonalities were
created through narratives of gender oppression in prostitution or domestic service. The women's rights as human rights project universalized and
stabilized the category of "women" at the same time as it addressed their
situations in terms of a discourse of rights and civil society. In forming an
"international" struggle, in which all women from all nations could speak
to or understand each other or work together for a "common" goal, gender
was stabilized through practices articulated as human rights violations essentially linked to gender, for example widespread domestic violence or the
vulnerability to rape for women by militarized or nationalist power. Large
bodies of knowledge were produced to show these commonalities, in everything from poems and literary texts to photographs, statistics, and testi-
monies.

Some feminists were critical about such assumptions of universalism.
Writing about women's human rights in Africa, Adetoun Ilumoka stated,
"Once again, an attempt is being made to universalize this [women's rights
as human rights] agenda," and "to talk of universal women's rights pre-
sumes a self-conscious, coherent group of persons that cuts across class and
cultural lines and has an identity of interests."[55] Nivedita Menon argued that
human rights were being universalized by the "rich and powerful countries
of the North" and that rights "evolve in specific contexts and any universalization is bound to reflect the interests of dominant groups rather than
marginal ones."[56] For Susan Koshy, the opposition between universalism
and cultural relativism was itself "the ideological production of hegemonic
forces at various historical moments."[57] Yet the campaign for women's
rights as human rights formed an "international" struggle with women
from many nations, colonial and postcolonial, participating, although hier-
archically, in transnational connectivities that created a "common" goal. The
struggle to keep various kinds of difference alive in the women's human
rights arena was a difficult one, as Hilary Charlesworth suggested, made
even more difficult by the asymmetries of power of states, nations, and
groups.[58] It is these asymmetries that need to be highlighted as we examine

the technologies of governmentality through which human rights have worked as a regulative apparatus to produce feminist and "free" subjects.

MANAGING HUMAN RIGHTS: NGOS AND CIVIL SOCIETY

✴

The dissemination of women's rights as human rights occurred mainly through the work of a number of groups that constituted a sphere of action seemingly outside the nation-state but not outside nationalism. These groups, commonly designated NGOS, did not always work in consultation with the UN, as they were initially intended to do. A powerful mode of action was created by the claim that NGOS were an authentic and organic form of resistance because they were more connected to the women who were the objects of their welfare work. The NGOS were said to be more flexible because they were not connected to state bureaucracies, more efficient because they were "closer" to women, and less corrupt, and it was believed that they provided more efficient and cost-effective services for the states by employing a greater number of women who were often not paid very well. NGOS became the vehicles for providing welfare both for states who wished to privatize or reduce their welfare work and for international agencies and other groups interested in women's issues who believed that "developing" states were corrupt and patriarchal and thus would not help women. Furthermore, many NGOS came to see themselves as the saviors of women and as being above or beyond neocolonial differences of power.

As a result, NGOS and nonprofit organizations (as they are usually known in the United States) played an increasingly important role in the world and were believed to constitute instruments of care and action that stepped in to help those marginalized by states, multinational corporations, and the global economy. Women's NGOS expanded dramatically over the last decade of the twentieth century and into the present. Keck and Sikkink argued that transnational advocacy networks "helped instigate and sustain the change between 1968 and 1993" in the expansion of human rights within feminist activism, and that approximately "half of all international nongovernmental social change organizations work on . . . three issues" of women's rights, human rights, and the environment.[59] Sally Engle Merry suggested that the activities of the NGOS and the UN constituted "an international civil society actively engaged in expanding and monitoring human rights."[60] Mary Geske and Susan Bourque called this arena a "global civil society," although they argued that there was a gap between NGOs and grassroots organizations.[61] As Amrita Basu has suggested, women's transnational NGOs were extremely diverse as their numbers grew, and the results of their work were mixed, being less successful in arguing for economic rights and more successful in campaigns against sexual violence, for example.[62]

Especially in regions where the state was seen as weak or anti-feminist, and these were often believed to be the postcolonial states or the "developing countries," NGOs stepped in to do welfare and feminist work. In many parts of the world NGOs were seen as more efficient, less corrupt, and more flexible in response to needs. Munira A. Fakhro makes this point in noting the presence of NGOs working on women's issues in the Gulf states.[63] Even in countries like the United States, NGOs enabled the privatization of social work that neoliberal policies emphasized, while in other parts of the world these were often the only possible source of welfare. James Petras has critiqued this abandonment of the state as a neoliberal and imperial move by western states and the World Bank, although he too is quick to group neoliberal and imperial together in a conspiracy.[64]

Yet this move has also come in response to the increase worldwide during this period in the number of refugees and other displaced and stateless persons, most of them women and children. The number of refugees alone reached twenty million by the end of the century, and the work of women's and other groups to prevent the continued exploitation of refugees and immigrants grew as well. Groups known as transnational social movement organizations (TSMOs), such as Médicins Sans Frontières, which were coalitions or formal federations of national or regional nongovernmental organizations, increased as well. Yet it is problematic to suppose that these organizations were outside the knowledge and power frameworks of modern western expansion,[65] since they remained within the logic of governmental rather than state power, thus creating a continuum across the state and civil society.

The number of NGOs that were lobbying organizations, self-styled as apolitical, or were fronts for states, corporations, or even right-wing groups (including "hate" groups in the United States) also proliferated. Some of the groups that also called themselves "community" or "grassroots" organizations also had nonfeminist or anti-feminist politics. Yet quite often, even among so-called progressive women's groups, the connection to a "community" was taken for granted, so that critical reflection could only be framed as "academic" rather than as engagement with the context and content of the work. Many of the NGOs continued to rely on development policies, since development activities received funding from many sources and since development and modernization remained part of the project of welfare to be given to women in postcolonial states. Often it was not clear which community was being served by NGOs on the "international" circuit, and it was also not clear what was meant by the term "community." As Maitreyi Krishnaraj points out, the "proliferation of N.G.O.'s and the liberal funding they receive from donor agencies cast doubts on their role as the true spokespersons of people's interests. . . . Increasingly N.G.O.'s have become an alternative career route for educated persons with communication skills."[66] It can be concluded, however, that claims about efficiency and effectiveness were linked to claims of proximity to the "grassroots" or to some organic notion of "community." Many feminist NGOs (though not all) continued to claim that they evolved from the "grassroots," thus calling upon a romantic notion of community that had little to do with the day-to-day pressures of work and the constant search for resources experienced by most NGOs.[67] For those groups that wished to remain tied to their communities, it was difficult to refrain from having strong transnational connectivities, though there were also subaltern groups that did seem to be left out and to have low levels of connectivity or none at all.

We can, however, trace the movement of a group from its local beginnings to its incorporation within a global community of women. Many groups began as grassroots organizations working on local issues and became more cosmopolitan as they expanded their networks transnationally. In an account narrated at an NGO forum on immigrant and refugee women at the Vienna Human Rights Tribunal, two organizers from a Guatemalan refugee organization revealed how they expanded their project of repatriating refugees to understanding that their plight as women and refugees was common to many women across the world. They stated that meeting representatives of NGOs and the UN High Commissioner for Refugees (UNHCR) and "funding agencies and solidarity people" enabled them to become "literate" "decision makers" in their communities, while before they had

just focused on returning to Guatemala: "The UNHCR has given us protection, it has helped us find assistance in order to be able to train ourselves, to
be aware of our rights and to defend ourselves."[68] Thus new cosmopolitan
subjects were produced within transnational connectivities in which the
search for information, support, and funding sources (mostly in the West)
created new encounters and connections between on the one hand powerful organizations like the UN and on the other feminist organizations from
the West and small organizations in the non-West. The result was a project
of empowerment through the insertion into global regimes of women's
rights as human rights.

In the United States the continued binary construction of "activism" and
"theory" was another useful argument for the efficiency and effectiveness
of NGOS. Within many feminist institutions, members of NGOS were considered "activists" based on their putative closeness to the "grassroots."
This was because greater levels of funding and the professionalizing of the
NGOS within transnational connectivities created new networks and new
discourses of women as universal subjects of violence and as new global
feminist subjects. The process of professionalizing NGO work, therefore,
was an example of the governmentalizing of women's welfare, with a human rights ethic as its foundation. Professionalizing produced greater benefits, from more connections among those working in similar agencies in
different communities to new kinds of identification of transnational soli-
darities. Yet there were pressures to professionalize and to institutionalize
"activist" work in numerous areas, ranging from the search for resources
and grants to the establishment of networking capabilities. These pressures
created conditions for work that produced new forms of regulation and
increased the power differential between funders and those in the field, and
between those in the field and their helpers, who were of varied genders
and classes and races. Even in the United States nonprofit organizations
were only able to get funding if they created "five-year plans," had official
positions for interacting with other organizations, produced publicity mate-
rials, hired and fired the right kind of staff, had diversity goals, kept records
on every "client," and created goals for efficiency and productivity—all necessary if an NGO wished to participate in strong transnational connectivities. To become designated a "nonprofit" organization in the United
States required, among other things, designating a director rather than

working collectively. These requirements made the work of NGOS everywhere become "visible" to funders and donors as well as to other agencies; the struggle to be "visible" at the international level required establishing credibility, measuring and evaluating effectiveness, and using specialized language to explain both these achievements and the levels of subordination that were to be overcome. Women's rights as human rights came to be key to such a language, through which subordination and need could be conveyed across transnational connectivities.

It is important to examine the practices of nongovernmental organizations, not with the aim of adjudicating which are authentic but with the recognition that they were all part of the new governmentalized regimes of welfare work. Some NGOS had to negotiate the neocolonial contexts of first world or third world inequalities and the condescending attitudes of agencies in the first world, and all had to address the power differences between groups from the South and the North. NGOS everywhere lived with internal hierarchies: the main one was often that between those who were helped and those who did the helping, while others distinguished between different levels of workers, which often corresponded to class differences and to differences in nationality, religion, caste, gender, and race.

In the context of the United States, the state and the discourses of American nationalism produced female subjects who saw themselves as "free" in comparison to their "sisters" in the developing world, and these attitudes often pervaded the encounters between women's groups, as at the NGO meetings of the UN women's conferences. Since NGOS and the grassroots organizations in the UN women's conferences were separated from the working of the governmental bodies, it was possible to forget how nation-states, nationalisms, and their related institutions participated in creating subjects who participated in NGOS. Yet women from all over the world came to see themselves as a "community" through these encounters. Newer groups, including those working on lesbian, gay, bisexual, and transgender issues, also saw themselves as part of an international community. Paul EeNam Park Hagland, for instance, finds evidence that the transnationalization of human rights by NGOS could evade state control through the "active construction of community on a global scale," although he also argued that human rights instruments were not as effective for lesbian, gay, bisexual, and transgender issues because they were tied to state formations and were often unenforceable.[69] However, even the use of human rights in the women's rights struggle faced this problem, since few states enforced instruments such as CEDAW.

Although various kinds of nationalisms could not be eliminated within "global communities," it would be problematic to simply see these subjects of feminist NGOs as pawns of the state, since they both protested the state's policies and pointed out its inadequacies; however, they could also not be assumed to have escaped interpellation by the state and nation.[70] The influence of nationalisms and nation-states in creating certain kinds of NGOs and groups was an important one, visible most particularly in the United States and Western Europe within "global feminism": what Caren Kaplan and I have called the hegemony of first world women's groups to affect women's lives and women's groups worldwide by creating a "common agenda" that produced women as their subjects[71] and as a target population.

However, the cosmopolitan nature of human rights internationalism (which is distinct from other kinds of internationalism used by nonmetropolitan subjects) was visible in the claim that human rights instruments were necessary because "nonwestern" subjects needed them. The cosmopolitanism of claiming universal application because it was used by noncosmopolitan subjects who could be known and understood was apparent in much of the knowledges produced of deployments of women's rights as human rights. Internationalism represented the use of these instruments by "nonwestern subjects" as a mark of their undisputed applicability rather than as a discourse of power created by cosmopolitan knowledges. Bruce Robbins argued: "Rather than seeking a universal philosophical foundation for human rights, I take as my point of departure the existence of a provisional transnational consensus about human rights, legitimized in my view by the increasing participation of NGOS, *especially non-western ones* [my emphasis], and the existence of continuing dialogue about the limits and unequal applications of human rights instruments."[72]

Although Robbins acknowledged that there were limits and inequities in the application of human rights, and suggested also that universals are to be rejected, he claimed there was a consensus as well as a "dialogue" about the use of these instruments, rather than a relation of power. It would be difficult to conclude much about the political leanings of NGOS simply from the fact of their being "nonwestern." However, according to Robbins, these

NGOS "sufficiently demonstrated" their "autonomous political importance" at events such as the Vienna conference on human rights, so that the states have had to compromise with them.[73] NGOS are understood, despite their incredible variety, as being beyond the state and made up of actors who belong to no state and crucially to no nations, and thus can be the ideal cosmopolitans.

Absent in these articulations is an understanding of the institutionalized frameworks in which the articulation of human rights by "nonwestern" NGOS became possible. The networks of funding and resources that taught the language of human rights as a framework to voice demands have to be understood in greater detail. For example, the final document issued by the Working Group on Women's Rights of the NGO Forum at the Vienna World Conference in 1993 listed among its recommendations that "the World Conference should declare that human rights education is a human right and reaffirm that the UN and nation states have an obligation to disseminate human rights information, to support local NGOS working to create human rights awareness, and to help communities protect themselves against violations."[74] The Sisterhood is Global Institute in 1996 was working on a human rights manual designed to teach women in "non-western cultural contexts about general concepts of human rights and how to attain and protect those rights in their societies."[75] Called *Claiming Our Rights*, the manual was the work of a group of women, some of them Muslim, who incorporated their interpretations of religious texts into a manual intended for women in the Muslim and Arab communities. The institute, based in Montreal, has human rights education as one of its key tasks and has also published *In Our Own Words: A Guide for Human Rights Education Facilitators*.[76]

In the United States, the work of the Ford Foundation to promote feminist activism in both mainstream and poor, working-class, and minority women's projects through the 1970s and 1980s is well known, as is its project to promote feminist scholarship in universities through the establishment of research projects.[77] The foundation was also involved in international funding of women's projects and more recently in the funding of projects to promote women's rights as human rights. For example, the publication *Al-Raida*, published by the Institute for Women's Studies in the Arab World with Ford Foundation support, has spoken out strongly in favor of human rights as a tool to articulate women's agendas. An issue devoted to the topic, "Women's Rights Are Human Rights: Perspectives from the

Arab World," was published in 1996 and disseminated widely because of funding from the U.S. Agency for International Development.[78] The Ford Foundation also has a Peace and Social Justice Program, which takes a social justice approach to promote human rights. It has funded efforts to promote Afghan women's rights under the auspices of Equality Now Inc., conferences on "crimes of honor" in Egypt, and the Coalition for Women's Economic Development and Global Equality to "integrate women's human rights into all areas of United States international development policy."

Each year, the Center for the Study of Human Rights at Columbia University, with funding from the Ford Foundation, hosts a four-month intensive training program for human rights activists from a number of countries, who are taught to use human rights law and to raise funds. As the center states in its literature, "participants in the Human Rights Advocates Training Program study basic concepts of human rights, as well as hone skills such as fund raising, human rights reporting, and media advocacy. Activists also have ample opportunity to connect their own local- or national-level work with larger human rights struggles through meetings with international human rights institutions based in New York City and Washington, D.C."[79] The Human Rights Advocates Training Program brings in activists from a number of countries to train them to use human rights laws, and also, crucially, teaches them to seek funds on the basis of such discourses. Activists have to be fluent in English and thus may come from mostly the upper classes in Asia or Africa or Latin America rather than from the "grassroots." Programs like this one are proliferating in the United States and Europe to train activists from developing countries in the use of human rights instruments, especially among women's NGOs. Their growth illustrates the connections that can be made between the discourses of grassroots activism and first world discourses of human rights, connections that are a necessary part of the development of liberal democracy and civil society, while also illustrating the asymmetries of power between those who teach and those who are to learn.

THE STATE, NATIONALISM, AND INTERNATIONALISM

✳

The complex politics of United States feminism were visible in the work of many feminist organizations participating in transnational activism in human rights, even while the U.S. state reduced its support of the UN. At the same time, the role of the UN has changed in recent years, with increasing reliance on the the United States as the remaining superpower.[80] Yet in the United States itself, dominant attitudes to the UN remained mixed, as nationalism became fragmented by issues of minority rights and immigration, and as race, gender, and sexual politics pervaded all aspects of social and economic life. The state and the nation are not unified, as many take for granted.[81] Ed Friedman has pointed out that it was only after the American withdrawal from Vietnam and the subsequent crisis of the Vietnamese boat people, and the genocide committed by the Khmer Rouge, that a global human rights agenda was taken on by the United States as part of its international agenda.[82] Nevertheless, internationalism received little support among many groups from both the left and the right, which were enmeshed in problems that were seen as domestic and separated from international ones. White supremacist groups believed that the UN was an arm of a dangerous "new world order" infiltrating the white nation figured as America, revealing the split within racially dominant groups between a cosmopolitan class which directly benefited from international capitalism and noncosmopolitan classes that owed their privileges and powers to the existence of a white state.[83] Both Democrats and Republicans in Congress hesitated to support the UN under President Clinton, although Clinton himself was more of an advocate. Under George W. Bush, the contradiction between a white nationalism and a capitalist cosmopolitan class has been resolved by a move toward an explicitly imperial agenda that disdains both the UN and multilateral diplomacy. While conservatives in Congress, in their neoliberal onslaught on so-called wasteful bureaucracies that they asserted should be replaced by a private sector which is supposedly efficient, targeted the UN as a bureaucratic institution that wastes and misuses money, the Democrats, even under Clinton, found it difficult to give the UN what was owed to its maintenance.

This ambivalence toward the UN came at a time when human rights in the international arena were becoming an important tool for disenfranchised people to assert their claims against many nation-states. While organizations such as Amnesty International have waged decades-long battles for political rights, turning to the state and to the UN for redress, some assertions of rights discourse relied on concepts of socioeconomic rights by questioning the belief that nation-states could look after all their citizens, and supporting the rights of all those who were refugees or were displaced or stateless. This reanimation of the concepts of economic, cultural, and social rights in the 1990s caused consternation among conservatives especially alarmed by Clinton's assertion early in his presidency that the distinction between "fundamental" rights and socioeconomic ones should be dropped. Although the Clinton administration did not follow up substantively on this promise, the *Wall Street Journal* in 1993 prophesied that the result of this move could be that the United States would become "a virtual piggy bank for underdeveloped nations" that could "render the U.N. incapable of sorting out the most basic human-rights problem."[84] While the *Journal* argued that socioeconomic rights were less "basic" than political ones, and that the American practice of opposing any claims for economic rights needed to be continued, it singled out for particular condemnation the Clinton administration's support for collective rights such as women's rights and for creating a UN High Commissioner on Human Rights. Lumping "economic rights" and "rights to cultural difference" as conjoined (revealing that for neoliberalism these are inseparable) and foreseeing a veritable "Pandora's box," the *Journal* warned that collective rights discourse was powerful and dangerous, especially on issues like women's rights and violence against women.[85] This kind of right-wing discourse in the United States, which became policy in the administration of George W. Bush and also circulated among nonélite whites, was profoundly anti-internationalist and anti-UN. To struggle against this conservative take on the UN, many progressive feminists supported CEDAW and the "women's rights as human rights" approach and hailed human rights internationalism as the progressive answer to global inequalities.

Thus U.S. state practices reduced the power of the UN while increasing the supremacy of the United States as well as the power of feminists to organize and perform welfare work around the world. Some transnational connectivities became stronger even while the UN became weaker. But the history of the UN and its participation in advocating development and debt reduction programs through the World Bank and the International Monetary Fund, as Gita Sen and Karen Grown have indicated, was hardly encouraging.[86] The UN has been in existence for more than half a century, during which time, according to Rajni Kothari, initial gains in the lives of women in the 1960s and 1970s were reversed by increasing poverty, environmental destruction, and the exploitative practices of many transnational corporations.[87] Neo-imperial first world powers often utilized the UN for their interests, even though sections of the UN operated to rescue refugees or protest the actions of certain states. In general, recent UN work did not recommend it as the savior of the poor and the women of the world. Kothari argues that the period since the cold war "has given rise to a large and widespread upsurge of nationalist, ethnic, and religious turbulence . . . , which in turn is being used for establishing a new model of hegemony in which the U.N. itself is being made an instrument."[88]

In addition, the UN organizations devoted to women's and children's welfare, among them UNIFEM, INSTRAW, and UNICEF, had fewer resources and power than the Security Council, the General Assembly, and the IMF, suggesting that gender and women's issues were relegated to second place even in the UN. While CEDAW and other treaties provided accountability methods such as requirements that states report any infractions, women's rights organizations asserted that states did not live up to the convention. It has been noted that human rights provisions are weakest when there are few enforcement mechanisms attached to them.[89] According to Andrew Byrnes, "international pressure" was the best means to convince states to comply with treaties.[90] Yet the pressure was often dependent on the geopolitics of states and could only work effectively when states wished to protect or maximize their own interests. Thus, scholars of human rights came to believe that often it was only the powerful groups within the state system that could bring a problem to international attention.[91]

Because the UN itself was not a monolithic entity, the imaginary of the "international" represented by the UN was not unified. While the UN remained closely tied to the system of nation-states and the power of the Security Council for its highly politicized policies that generally benefited the first world rather than the third, UN agencies forged diverse paths and goals. Some UN agencies, including those dealing with women, children, and refugees, seemed to be critically aware of power differentials and the problem of economic policies that benefited the North at the expense of the South, while other more powerful agencies only reluctantly acknowledged these discrepancies. Only very recently has the World Bank recognized that structural adjustment programs being implemented the world over are neither justifiable nor successful. However, the IMF continues to implement these policies.

The international, even in its plethora of meanings, could not be seen as supranational since it was reliant on the system of nation-states for its existence and conceptualization.[92] While resistance to North-South inequalities was strongest in nation-states that composed the "third world," the struggle for rights relied on the system of nation-states that collectively made up the international as a geopolitical arena. In the era of multinational capital, it was problematic to assume that these nation-states could or would resist being integrated into an IMF-linked economy. Furthermore, to presume a unified opposition to the exploitation of the world's poor would also be problematic, since transnational capital created new subalterns and new cosmopolitans across national boundaries and North-South divides.

The internationalism that the UN produces could not be understood as the imaginary "family of nations" or as a global "community of nations." The international, as Jonathan Ree argues, does not transcend nationality but is a "global social organization that tries to generate a plurality of nations."[93] Liisa Malkki has pointed out that the global imaginary of the international is shared transnationally but "may have profoundly different significance and uses in specific local sociopolitical contexts."[94] Among white militia groups in the United States, UN internationalism signified a dangerous and threatening racial commingling of the people of the world, whereas for certain women's human rights organizations it implied a universal category of similarly gendered persons.

"International" alliances forged under the auspices of the UN enabled the deployment of imperial discourses by powerful states. The United States used human rights as a tool of geopolitics to assert is supremacy and its imperial projects. Louis Henkin reveals that the incorporation of human rights into American foreign policy began in the 1970s, when Congress enacted statutes in which spreading human rights was a "principal goal" of foreign policy.[95] Some scholars claimed human rights as a quintessentially American "value" rather than as a historically situated strategy in foreign policy. Samuel Huntington saw human rights as included in what he calls "American values" and argued that the United States needed to impose them across the world since "the survival of democratic institutions and values at home will depend on their adoption abroad." According to Hunt-

ington, these "values" were "universally valid and universally applicable"
and it was part of the "American" tradition to believe they are so.[96]

Yet the United States has not applied these "values" universally, nor has
it used them in ways unconnected to its geopolitical agendas. For instance,
of the many ways in which gendered inequalities are produced within
societies, it was in particular the sterilization of Chinese women, female
infanticide, and abortion of female fetuses in Asian countries that were
condemned and reviled by Hillary Clinton at the Beijing international
women's conference. Chinese women's rights abuses could be condemned
because they fit into long-established Western discourses about Chinese
women's backwardness and oppression, because they revealed the inadequacies of communist rule, and because they provided an opportunity to
castigate the Chinese government on its human rights record. American
media coverage during the UN conference indicated clearly that these colonial tropes and geopolitics were very much in operation. Thus it is also part
of the U.S. government's political strategy to position "America" as the site
for the authoritative condemnation of the practices in question. For example, the collaboration between trade and rights was viewed as effective
policy, even though it was presented as a conflictual one.[97] This strategy
consolidated "America" as the "land of freedom" whose representatives
could adjudicate the human rights violations of other nation-states and
consequently affect trade negotiations. Even though in recent years reports
such as *The Human Rights Watch Global Report on Women's Human Rights*
(1995) have condemned the abuse of women's rights in prisons in the
United States, the criticism has neither created much change in the treat-
ment of women in custody nor altered the policy of the United States of
using human rights to claim moral superiority. "America" has remained
hegemonically constructed as a land of freedom and rights through its
ability to adjudicate whether other countries and communities had them or
needed them, and through the work of many organizations and activists
committed to working for the human rights of women who were seen as
less free than Americans.

In India and many other countries, human rights became a necessity for
the state's efforts to establish its legitimacy at the national and international
levels and for groups and NGOs to position themselves as part of a civil
society separate from and in opposition to the state. Both national and

transnational NGOs in India, especially those working with women and those working on issues of civil liberties, utilized human rights instruments. A number of state organizations used human rights not as a tool for working against the state but to strengthen the power of the state and to manage its military more effectively. One author argued that the state must incorporate human rights into its policing mechanisms, and suggested that human rights instruments like CEDAW could work best when implemented by the Indian government.[98] Another suggested ways to make the police more "human rights friendly,"[99] to make India a state in which human rights were normative. Here human rights were understood not as rights acknowledged by the state but rather as an effective means to articulating geopolitically that the state was concerned and caring about the welfare of people rather than abusive and violent. This author argues that since the entity most often accused of violating human rights was the police, and since NGOs and individuals brought complaints against the police to the National Human Rights Commission, it was necessary to reform the police by educating them about both the Indian constitution and the international covenants. To further accomplish this task, a considerable amount of work on human rights training has since been done by the Indian Police Service. Thus Dr. S. Subramanian, a member of the Indian Police Service, writes in his two-volume training manual for the police that it is the remnants of "colonial traditions and practices" that have led to police violations of human rights and that training is necessary to eliminate these traditions and enable the police to adapt to "democratic traditions."[100]

These attempts to make the state friendly to human rights have been a powerful response to the work done by NGOs and human rights organizations to protest the power of the state. The Human Rights Commission was established in India in 1993 to guard against the violation of civil rights by police and paramilitary groups run by the state. Groups such as the Peoples Union for Democratic Rights and the Peoples Union of Civil Rights came about in response to the loss of civil rights under Prime Minister Indira Gandhi and have remained active to protest custodial deaths and rapes, and to investigate crimes committed by political parties and politicians against minority communities. A number of new groups were devoted to human rights, and the National Commission for Human Rights was established by the government, although it remained an advisory body able to only exert "moral pressure."[101] In some states such as Punjab, human rights instruments became tools for punishing enemies rather than ensuring the rights of individuals or groups,[102] although they were also used by Sikh groups in the United States to bring to the attention of the U.S. Congress the counterinsurgency practices of paramilitary forces in Punjab. Conservative politicians in the U.S. Congress such as Dan Burton, with political records unfriendly to progressive movements, immigrants, and minority communities, took up the charge to push the Indian government on its violations of human rights and thus helped to consolidate American foreign policy as one based on pushing democratization and human rights. Thus human rights instruments were used selectively by states for their own political agendas; in the application of these instruments, we can see the operations of disciplinary and governmental mechanisms as well as the production of liberal subjects across geopolitical agendas of states and NGOs.

GLOBAL FEMINISM AND HUMAN RIGHTS

✳

It is unfortunate but unavoidable that the "moral superiority" of American geopolitical discourse should have become part of the new global feminism in the United States (and worldwide, although for diverse agendas), constructing "American" feminists as saviors and rescuers of "oppressed women" elsewhere within a "global" economy run by a few powerful states. It is in these discourses that the linking of geopolitics and biopolitics is visible, since the production of free subjects who can save those suffering from human rights abuses sustains the widespread use of this mechanism of welfare. Among other problems, this new discourse of a global sisterhood misrecognized the ways in which many women were treated in the first world itself. For example, even though domestic violence was acknowledged as a very large problem in the United States, it was framed as a "health" rather than a human rights issue. Strategies to address domestic violence included the training of hospital and health workers, police, and judges but did not rise to the level of a human rights claim in the national or international legal system. It appears that human rights for women could become meaningful only through geopolitics—that is, in relation to women in the "third world."

However, even groups that were aware of histories of imperialism and that promoted a notion of "global sisterhood" between colonizing and colonized female subjects were unable to avoid governments' rationalizations of their practices by using discourses of diversity and pluralism. The Center for Women's Global Leadership, based at Rutgers University, which played a leading role in pushing this agenda in the United States, utilized very generalized language for organizing in the area of violence against women.[103] Its report on the campaign for women's human rights in 1992–93 stated that women's rights as human rights

> provides a framework of reference within which each women's group can place its own existing agenda. It also allows groups to link existing agendas of various women's groups together, to rally people around a common cause, and to project themselves as a unified and unifying force, thereby expanding the vision of each group.
>
> This framework helps connect feminist organizing to activism on other issues such as oppressed groups.... It appeals to universal principles and elevates women's rights to a level considered more legitimate by government officials and government policy makers.[104]

Even though this group incorporated anti-colonial, anti-racist concerns, its discourse of human rights internationalism claimed universalism by ignoring historical contingency and context, addressing difference solely within a notion of nonconflictual pluralism or even beyond relativism to a narrative of oppressions that could easily fit into a common framework rather than disrupting it. Whereas earlier forms of "global feminism" from the late 1970s and early 1980s, as in Robin Morgan's work, suggested that all women were "sisters," the impact of race-based and class-based critiques resulted in the formulation of a multiculturalist diversity, albeit without any conflicts or contradictions.[105] Crucially, therefore, this "common" framework which incorporated difference constructed "American" feminist subjects in the United States in particular ways and enabled them to become agents in the practice of "rescuing" victims of human rights violations.

Discourses of rescue erased histories of various economic, state, political, and cultural formations and human rights, as an ethical regime replaced historically contextualized analyses of women's lives. While groups such as the Rutgers Center for Women's Global Leadership struggled to expand the notion of violence against women to include social, cultural, and economic issues, it was also clear that differences between women were so great that socioeconomic rights could not rise to the top of the agenda. Given the power of liberal and cultural feminisms in the United States, and media that recognized only these feminisms, issues of domestic violence and rape became prominent within transnational feminist connectivities, leading to an erasure of other campaigns.[106] I do not suggest that these issues are unimportant, but that they became the main rationalities of addressing the welfare needs of women.[107] Researchers working in other parts of the world argued that domestic violence should be seen as a human rights issue.[108] Issues that emphasize difference or inequality between women in the North and South, or even difference within a nation-state such as the United States, could not receive sustained attention from dominant groups of women everywhere determined to create "common" goals.[109]

It was clear from events such as the UN women's conference in Beijing that in terms of a generalized discourse of women's issues, it was only in certain specific areas of activism, for example domestic violence and rape, that there appeared to be agreement among women from across the world. Domestic violence became an issue that produced women as a stable category and therefore as a population visible "internationally." Given the dominant focus of cultural feminism in the United States on rape and domestic violence as issues of the female body rather than as socioeconomic issues, many feminists in the United States, both from minority groups and the mainstream ones, pressed this agenda. Keck and Sikkink show how the transnational campaign on "violence against women" became a "global discourse,"[110] and Basu argues that some of the successes of transnational women's organizations have come in this arena.[111]

In India the term "domestic violence" became commonly used in the 1990s, as was the term "post-traumatic stress disorder" to describe the trauma caused by this violence.[112] A whole new set of terminologies and means to gather information on female populations came into existence, along with changes in ways of thinking about "victims" and "survivors" as well as new kinds of experts and information. New forms of governmentality were inaugurated by the project of eradicating domestic violence. During this period a concerted effort was made by a number of agencies around the world to collect statistical information on this topic. Development agencies were in the forefront; the World Development Report in 1993 found that "globally," rape and domestic violence contributed to 5 percent of illnesses among women between sixteen and forty-four years of age.[113] As Nikolas Rose argues about the role of statistics in the advent of psychology as mode of governmentality and as a "corporeal regime" that took root in the twentieth century, "statistical norms and values become incorporated within the very texture of conceptions of psychological reality."[114]

Yet this claim of commonality has proved difficult to translate into policy and action against poverty and other threats to survival. It cannot answer the problem of providing support to differently constituted women for whom domestic violence was manifested and acknowledged only within particular subject-positions. Undocumented women in the United States often did not acknowledge or report domestic violence for fear of deportation, and to address their needs meant confronting issues of immigration status and economic needs as well as psychological ones. It is at the level of analysis, policy, and services that U.S.-based nonprofit organizations working on domestic violence were quite conflicted, suggesting that coalitions and collaborations were complex even within the United States, let alone globally. Thus a seemingly global unanimity regarding the prevalence of domestic violence could only be apparent when specificities are not discussed. However in the interests of global unanimity, the language of women's rights used by some U.S. women's groups was startlingly full of laudable goals and short on specificities of how these could be achieved, rather like the language of intergovernmental agreements. If differences were mentioned at all they were contained within a nonconflictual model of diversity and pluralism. The many debates and differences among women across the world who argue for different ways to combat domestic violence are ignored, even though, for instance, the role played by the police to prevent domestic violence or come to the aid of battered women could only depend on the specificities of particular states and the particular role played by the police and the courts in these states.

Yet a unified and "global" movement against domestic violence was constructed, one based on an essentialized conception of the female body as one that is subject to violence. Marjorie Agosín stated that "domestic violence in the United States bears profound similarities with abuse of women worldwide. It is always the body that is tortured, abused, and punished in wars fought between countries, sects, or partners."[115] In these representations, women were universal and global subjects, made so by a universalized conception of the body, in which what differentiated the female body was the violence wreaked on it. This violence constructed the body as stable and essential, despite articulations of "cultural" differences which could be overcome by education and through transnational connectivities.

At the same time, other feminists in the United States, articulating differences based on race and class, disputed this essential subject as the subject of domestic violence. Kimberle Crenshaw argued that there were profound differences in how women acknowledged domestic violence, or found remedies for a violent situation.[116] For instance, resources were allocated to battered women of color and immigrant women only after a vigorous campaign by women of color and immigrant activists. It is also clear that too few shelters in the United States attended to the needs of immigrant women from Asia, Africa, and Latin America. Shelters offered psychological counseling when the most important priority in a woman's life could be getting training for or finding a job, reaching economic independence, obtaining legal immigration status, or finding day care and housing. Many of the short-term programs offered by a shelter did not provide this training, although there were notable exceptions.[117] As a result of these problems, women from different communities, such as South Asian women, set up their own shelters. Nevertheless, policy problems are continually arising in these shelters because of differences of class, nationality, religion, or sexuality.

The mainstream success of the battered women's movement, as indicated by governmental attention under the Clinton administration, led to other problems. The Violence Against Women Act allocated most resources to state law enforcement agencies and fewer to women's groups and to women's economic empowerment and education programs.[118] Furthermore, domestic violence activism in the courts within the United States utilized various kinds of cultural stereotypes; for instance, the "battered women's syndrome," as Jayne Lee has argued, deployed rigidified notions of a physically abused woman that jeopardized legal remedies for all those who departed from this description.[119] Those penalized by this dominant white stereotype included women from other cultures and races who are gendered very differently.

Thus in the "global" struggle against "domestic violence," we see a link

between those who recognized this as one of the main "problems" standing in the way of a better world constituted without gendered inequalities and those who, through this sort of recognition, constituted themselves as ethical subjects and thus as "global citizens" of an interconnected world. Collecting statistics on the incidence of domestic violence in various regions of the world, seeking more effective strategies for its eradication, networking to produce stronger connectivities through which domestic violence is recognized as a "global" and a human rights problem—all of these become the tactics through which the questions of violence posed by feminist movements become governmentalized.

I have argued in this chapter that human rights worked as a technology of transnational governmentality. While Foucault's theorizations of governmentality remained within the question of modes of power in which there emerged a close relation between social security and political security, human rights functioned to ensure the continued maintenance of the national-international order despite the many crises that threatened it—from the reduced power of some states, to emergent nationalisms, to new forms of imperialism. Akhil Gupta argues that "nations need the international system to engender, regulate, and normalize the feelings that are dubbed 'national' so that "governmentality is unhitched from the nation-state to be instituted anew on a global scale."[120] Yet what is clear in the discourses of human rights that I have traced here is also the power of the West and in particular of the United States to institute these new forms of governmentality that reshape the relations between the West and non-West, and between populations and states. The growth of new cosmopolitanisms was made possible by the discourses of global citizenship and autonomous individuality that were extended to those believed to have been left out of liberal citizenship, that is, women. The instruments of liberal citizenship were human rights and the work of transnational NGOs was to make possible these human rights to produce liberal subjects as objects and subjects of rescue, when states were seen as either being less efficient in this mission or as having failed outright. Feminist NGOs were constituted as key to this goal, and they worked to manage the "global" population of women whose welfare became increasingly their concern.

chapter *four*

★

In the previous chapter, I argued that human rights discourses evolved at the end of the twentieth century as an ethic of neoliberal governance that produced subjects who saw themselves as "global citizens" and "global feminists." In this chapter, I extend that argument to discuss how the crisis of a growing population of refugees was managed through the discourse of human rights to maintain the nation-state system, and to sustain national identities. What was also sustained was colonial projects such as the discourse of the humanitarianism of the West and its support of political freedoms, thus bringing together geopolitics with biopolitics in the making of modern subjects at the end of the century. Human rights, a juridical mechanism, change into a governmental tool when used to decide which persons can be granted refugee asylum. While human rights advocates argued in the late twentieth century that the refugee asylum system did not safeguard the human rights of refugees and that the nation-state tried to evade its responsibility of providing safety and security,[1] they retained human rights as an effective tool for addressing the refugee crisis. In these arguments, we can see that human rights instruments were mechanisms for managing this population; on the one hand, they were used to select a few refugees out of populations of tens of millions as appropriate for admission

into the countries of the West, and on the other they justified expanding the
criteria under which refugees could be defined. Such strategies were visible
most clearly in the 1990s in the debates regarding asylum on the basis of
gender oppression. Yet what was clear was that the mechanisms for refugee
asylum in the West worked through the production of knowledge generated
not simply by the state but by a number of nonstate transnational organizations and institutions that created transnational connectivities. Within these
technologies of governmentality an ethic of humanitarian concern was
expressed by organizations, NGOS, feminists, refugee advocates, and INS
workers, which enabled individuals within these organizations to create a
moral and ethical relation to themselves. However, this moral relation to the
Self could not be separated from the relations produced through human
rights instruments and their humanitarian ethics, between different national, racial, and classed subjects. Thus the goal of this chapter is to examine
the technologies used by individuals, groups, and states, and to bring together geopolitics with biopolitics through a use as well as a critique of
Foucault's theories of subjectification.[2] In addition, it examines how female
refugee subjects in the West were produced through gendered human
rights discourses, and how many were unable to become female refugee
subjects, thus raising questions about the work of discourses of cosmopolitanism and mobility.

As feminists critiqued the representation of the refugee as a male subject and produced alternate representations of female refugee subjects,
western states, such as the United States, used these critiques to select out
appropriately deserving female refugees who were allowed to settle within
their borders. Others were prevented from fleeing violence in their own
countries or from entering other countries as refugees.[3] By instituting
modes of adjudicating that specified which refugees had truly suffered
human rights abuses, the United States was able to contain the numbers of
persons entering the United States from Asia, Africa, and Latin America
while maintaining its nationalist discourse of being a country that supported freedom and humanitarian efforts. For instance, the Senate report
on the landmark Refugee Act of 1980 stated that the Act "reflects one of the
oldest themes in America's history—welcoming homeless refugees to our
shores. It gives statutory meaning to our national commitment to human

rights and humanitarian concerns."[4] Yet this "national commitment" relied on racialized and gendered regimes of knowledge based on human
rights, although in its claim to addressing the concerns of feminist refugee
advocates the U.S. state emerged as somewhat open to feminist critiques
and also willing to work with NGOs. Some of these changes into a humanitarian geopolitic occurred through the 1990s under the Clinton regime,
while George W. Bush's policies after 9/11 created new forms of surveillance and disciplinary power over a racial population designated as Muslim
or Middle Eastern. Discourses of "terrorism" and "security" began to justify the existing systems of controlling migration and "humanitarian action," as it was called.[5] Yet what is revealing is how the changes under
Clinton managed the growing population of displaced persons at the end of
the century, an issue often seen as a problem of dealing with populations on
the move. Living conditions for many across the world became even more
difficult because of the asymmetrical and varied intensities of transnational
connectivities created by mobile capital, faster communication technologies, and the increased visibility, made possible by the media, of disparities
in living standards among peoples of the world. Thus older and newer
modes of racialization, gendering, and class formations were combined
with constantly changing technologies of power that sustained the process
of producing national identities.

A great deal of knowledge was produced in many countries and regions
to address this sort of displacement as a "problem."[6] A number of studies
provided narratives, visual evidence, and statistical information to document this crisis. Some calculated the number of refugees, undocumented
workers, persons crossing borders, migrant laborers, and immigrants, and
the results were used to justify a range of policies, from stricter immigration controls to more liberal controls; yet even some more progressive
studies saw the large-scale movement of persons across borders as a problem requiring solutions.[7] The UN High Commissioner for Refugees was
one of the main organizations dealing with this issue as a problem. *The
State of the World's Refugees* (1995), subtitled "In Search of Solutions," asserted that the "scale and complexity of the global refugee problem" had to
be addressed by making the commission a "humanitarian" rather than
simply a refugee agency.[8] The strategy was to work with NGOs, the UN
Security Council, the World Bank, NATO, and other organizations to pre-

vent displacement and ensure the right of refugees to return. Rather than
understand that the intensification of transnational movements of capital,
media, and goods, and the crisis of the Westphalian system, were connected to the mobility of some persons and the immobility of others, this
report suggested, in the words of one chapter heading, the necessity of
"managing" migration.[9]

In this framework, then, of understanding how human rights discourse
worked in refugee asylum and how dominant frameworks of a benevolent
nation and state constructed unequal transnational subjects, I will focus on
the context of Sikh women from Punjab who claimed refugee status in the
United States during the 1990s. By examining the construction of these
gendered subjects as "victims of violence" or "victims of human rights
violations,"[10] institutionalized through a globalized discourse of human
rights feminism that was taken up by the U.S. state, I suggest how national
and international regimes of knowledge production create transnational
subjects. My analysis argues for the need to problematize the presumed
opposition between civil society and state, diaspora and nation, sexual subjects and national subjects, and feminism and nationalism/international-
ism. It also argues that the very concept of the "international" as a neutral
or supranational space has maintained the link between the geopolitics of a
universal human rights negotiated unequally between powerful states in
North America and Europe and the biopolitics of a cosmopolitan, humanitarian self concerned with the welfare of untold populations of poor, disenfranchised women in Asia, Africa, and Latin America. The debates in the
United States regarding the universal versus the cultural relativist notion of
rights miss the point that the universal as it was spatialized into the international arena was itself a transnationally powerful mode of knowledge. I do
not argue that there could be some area of human rights and refugee law in
which geopolitics and cultural difference could be eliminated[11]—that argument essentializes culture and populations. Instead, I argue that the mobilization by a nation-state such as the United States of human rights within
refugee asylum has produced transnational subjects which are both cosmopolitan and national; the politics of humanitarian cosmopolitanism has
existed alongside modes of power that are disciplinary as well as governmental.

Given that the focus of this chapter is the refugee subject in the United

States, I argue that transnationally produced knowledges articulated with one another to create the refugee subject and to construct those involved in the rescue of refugee subjects as subjects of the U.S. nation-state and of the "West." These subjects were produced through discourses of human rights as the means to address what has been thought of as geopolitics—what Gearóid Ó Tuathail regards as the ways in which the global political scene is "geo-graphed by foreign policy regimes of truth."[12] The links between American nationalism and human rights internationalism constructed this subject as a means to manage the population that was seen to be female and thus outside the concerns of any state or nation. While many nation-states ignored the welfare of their inhabitants, often by designating them noncitizens or lesser citizens, even so-called strong welfare states did not provide welfare or security of any kind, especially to racial and gendered minorities or to those fleeing violence in other countries. The construction of the refugee subject was thus a means to create technologies of transnational governmentality through which these populations were presumed to be taken care of by a number of projects that connect with each other: an international system like the UN, the humanitarian efforts of states and individuals, the work of NGOs. As Jennifer Hyndman has argued, it was the "very conception, organization, and deployment of humanitarian measures within distinct geopolitical and cultural contexts" that was the issue.[13] The refugee in the United States was the subject both of the state and of internationalism and a cosmopolitanism constituted through humanist discourses of rights and liberal freedoms that moved sometimes powerfully and sometimes less so within transnational connectivities. Neocolonial racial, gendered, and classed discourses operated within the networks of these connectivities through which individuals, groups, NGOs, and states communicated with each other. Thus my approach examines refugees not in the terms of their belonging to diasporic communities but as constructed within networks of human rights discourses that moved between states, communities, organizations, and individuals. While new approaches to the study of refugees focus on social networks that include refugees as integral parts of new migrant diasporas,[14] I argue that though refugees did participate in wider diasporic networks, refugees were specific subjects that indexed the crisis of the nation-state system in particular ways.

To explain how discourses moved within connectivities to produce transnational subjects who were also subjects of states, I will examine how the focus of a transnationally connected American cultural feminism on sexual

abuse as the dominant expression of the oppression of women became the
paradigmatic experience constructing the female refugee. By examining
the discourse of sexual exploitation within the production of the female
refugee, I do not mean to disregard the pain and suffering of sexual abuse
and violence. Rather, my goal is to understand how these discourses of pain
and suffering produced new subjects of transnational governmentality as
well as of American nationalism that was also raced and gendered. My
purpose is to examine how the agency made possible by contexts of "activism" and "public policy" could be understood within the framework of
transnationalized forms of governmentality in which feminist resistance
became part of the changing microphysics of power in managing populations.

In bringing together feminist advocacy and refugee narratives, my goal is
to examine the transnational connectivities that enabled gendered subjects
to move across borders. However, while this chapter is focused on the
narratives that enabled certain refugee applicants to receive asylum, it is also
an important reminder that there are many who are unable to cross borders
"legally" or even to remain in the United States. This inability may suggest a
weak connectivity or cosmopolitanism, in that these were subjects who
failed to become the subjects of the U.S. state. They are a reminder that
discussions of cosmopolitans as border crossers, or as internationalists, or
as national and international subjects, or as part of transnational migrant
networks, are often based on those who are seen as strongly connected
transnationally rather than on those who fail to connect or cannot cross
boundaries. They are also a reminder that nationalisms, states, gender, class,
and race interact in myriad ways to produce many different subjects, not all
of whom are claimed by state or nation. The problem lies also in the specificity of groups and in degree and intensity of mobility and connectivities; these
differences prevent us as knowledge producers from making some very
global claims. At the very least, in the context of this chapter, attention to
those who fail to make a successful claim of asylum tells us a great deal about
the nature of migrant networks and of the specificities of gendered, racialized, and classed subjectivities in relation to nation and state.

My focus is on advocacy for refugee asylum based on gender, on the
debates surrounding asylum claims, and on how these debates become
connected to the narratives of Sikh women from Punjab seeking refugee

asylum in the United States. I use the term "Sikh" as a religious subject (gendered male for the most part); in the last few decades the Sikh has become identified in specific ways as a figure of terror in the discourses of Sikh nationalism and the Indian nation-state. Within Sikh nationalism, the "Sikh" was a transnational subject created out of diaspora and homeland politics as well as state nationalism and religious nationalism. Human rights discourses have also participated in producing knowledge of Sikhs, as has the academic area known as Sikh studies. The masculinity of this subject is the point at which all of these knowledges coincide, and it is the problematic of what is left out of this normative gendering that I will examine in this chapter.

In the context of transnational knowledge production and Indian nationalism, it is important to examine the use of human rights discourses in India. While groups in India through the 1990s used human rights to combat the "law and order" machinery of the state, which regularly killed and tortured mostly poor people in jail, they also began to argue for the denial of rights to powerful Hindu fundamentalists whose strategy for asserting their claims against the interests of minorities was to demand their democratic rights.[15] In addition, the Indian state began to state its adherence to human rights doctrine by claiming, for instance, that human rights instruments were part of its training of police officers.[16] In this context, the denial of rights of those identified as minorities in the nation was also justified by a Hindu-majority state through representational practices in the media in which Sikhs and Muslims could be designated as "militants" or "terrorists." At the same time, Sikh groups in the United States who were organizing against state violence began to utilize the discourse of human rights after the Indian state intensified its counterinsurgency efforts. They did so to bring their issues to the U.S. Congress so that Washington would pressure the Indian government on its human rights record. While human rights discourses were not effective enough to prevent police terror or combat state discourses of "security" or even to address the needs of many who were jailed for being militants and continue to be in jail to this day, they were helpful in putting pressure on the Indian government to defend its human rights record. In addition, human rights discourses were used by Sikhs to get refugee asylum in the United States if they could prove that they were targeted by the police and the Indian state.

Such utilizations of human rights were not confined to India. Rather, the

knowledge of these utilizations moved through the transnational connectivities through which first Sikh men and then women were able to claim
human rights abuses by the Indian state and thus seek refugee asylum in
the United States. Transnational migrant networks were vital for Sikh nationalisms through the twentieth century, and Sikhs were able to constitute
themselves as adherents of a "world religion" and thus as a group with a
distinctive religious identity.[17]

Even as the knowledge of the United States as a destination for asylum
seekers moves through transnational connectivities of various kinds and is
supported by the U.S. nation-state's discourse of human rights as an
"American value," it works alongside the U.S. state's goal to keep the number of refugees (especially nonwhite refugees) as low as possible. Because
of these policies, many applicants fail to obtain asylum; some are deported
or refused refugee status. It is the mechanisms through which these claims
are adjudicated that provide us with an insight into the modes of governmentality that have become operative in dealing with what have been called
"displaced populations." Of course these mechanisms are ongoing and
changing, often with new state policies and personnel, and the country of
origin of those seeking refugee status changes as well, so that this research
on Sikh women refugees seeking asylum in the 1990s in San Francisco
may not apply to all kinds of other claims. Moreover, while my research
examines discourses visible in documents submitted to the INS (now part of
the burgeoning homeland security bureaucracy), I do not examine in detail
the other kinds of subjectivities inhabited by those seeking refugee status.
These other subjectivities are, however, visible by reading against the grain
of the official and NGO documents. The goal of this chapter is not to provide
a representation of migrant or immigrant Sikh women in the 1990s who
came to the United States but to examine how the Sikh woman as refugee
was constituted as a transnational subject of the U.S. state, of feminist
NGOS, and of human rights institutions.

STATELESSNESS AND THE CRISIS OF
THE NATION-STATE SYSTEM

*

By the end of the twentieth century there were many millions of refugees
around the world, and this number continues to grow. The question of the

refugee, of persons who did not belong to any sovereign state and who were not citizens anywhere, became another sign of the crisis of the modern nation-state and modern nationalisms, as well as of their continued relevance. Especially for notions of rights which arise in relation to concepts like sovereignty, nation-state, and citizenship, the existence of the refugee, as well as the tremendous rise in the number of migrants and immigrants, brought new challenges. While struggles for rights within nation-states that arise through new social movements revealed the existence of unequal citizenship and of subalterns within the nation-state, the presence of the refugee, one who may or may not return to "home" (as nation-state, or region, or place of residence) or may not have any nation-state or home to return to, led to new reliance on the "international" rather than the national as an arena for rights struggles. The rise of transnational corporations, of global NGOs, and of new regional alliances between states further proposed new questions regarding the international as a public sphere, especially in the circulation of discourses of the rights of citizens and noncitizens.

New subjects were produced both within the nation and in the realm of the international, among them the refugee as a universal subject, and in the United States the "illegal," the "alien," and the "non-resident" as problematic subject. In India, the nation-state designated as "refugees" those persons who moved from Sri Lanka, Bangladesh, and Tibet in the face of nationalist movements, but also created, as mentioned in chapter 2, new subjects such as the NRI and later the PIO, or person of Indian origin (a noncitizen who for $1,000 could visit the "homeland" or go "back home" for ten years without a visa). Other nation-states similarly proposed new categories of belonging and nonbelonging, including that of dual citizen (one who could hold citizenship in more than one country). At the same time, new modes of nonbelonging were also created for populations who live outside their country of birth.[18] In addition, persons were being displaced for a number of reasons that were hardly new, including economic necessity and state or other violence. For instance, Hindu nationalisms and collaborating state institutions in India recuperated "communal"[19] identities to designate all Indian Muslims as "foreigners" or "terrorists" and Sikhs as "militants" or "terrorists," both groups being seen as threats to the nation-state. Some of those so labeled remained within the nation-state and some left, fearing for their safety. After 9/11 the United States deported, sometimes formally and other times through less formal disciplinary mechanisms, more and more "illegals," and required Muslim males from most Middle Eastern countries to register with the Department of Homeland Security as subjects of surveillance.

Can we consider all these subjects cosmopolitans? While some may be cosmopolitans in that they could negotiate border crossings, they did not have the class formations of other cosmopolitans or their powerful national affiliations and could be differentiated from the cosmopolitan élite subjects of Western modernity. While cosmopolitan élites were produced in many parts of the world, new transnational subjects such as refugees could not be understood simply as cosmopolitans, though certainly, as Louisa Schein has shown, nonélite cosmopolitanisms, as James Clifford has called them,[20] were produced out of the necessity to negotiate both nationalism and transnationalism.[21] Even so, refugees were not simply cosmopolitans because they could negotiate border crossings. For one, they might have a vexed relationship to élite versions of cosmopolitanism, which defined ideas of displacement or exile for over two centuries.[22] Without participating in classed, racialized, and gendered connectivities as "world citizens," or by being outside the frameworks of nation or state, they were only sporadically part of postcolonial cosmopolitan knowledges like those discussed in chapter 1. There were also many narratives of failure within refugee stories— those who could not cross, or those who did cross and then failed to survive in the new land. Some migrants were more powerfully connected to transnational networks than others and thus might have stronger connectivities than others. With weaker links, some could not get documentation to live in a country as legal immigrants; some could enter without documentation yet develop stronger networks to obtain proper documentation. But even those who had weaker connectivities could not be understood as insular, immobile, and localized but rather as transnational subjects who remained in unequal and hierarchical relations to more metropolitan and élite forms of cosmopolitanism.

The relation of refugees to cosmopolitan discourses of international human rights is heterogeneous, emerging from historical and cultural contexts of internationalism as well as from very discrepant understandings of what "international" might mean. Thus it is useful to distinguish between the many subjects with stronger connectivities to these globalized regimes, for example global feminists, NGOs, academics, writers, consultants, and the various refugee subjects of different classes, races, genders, and sexualities. Indeed, since transnational governmentality signals how the geopolitical-biopolitical link, as I have described it in previous chapters, was produced through discourses of western humanitarianism embedded within American imperialism, these varied subjects connected and communicated with each other.

The female refugee subject was the product of a variety of discourses produced transnationally, which were combined in the context of internationalisms, feminisms, and nation-state practices to become institutionalized knowledges. Which subjects were more easily hailed as refugees is a question that can be answered by examining the historical links constructed through collaborating and different patriarchies, nation-states, and politico-religious institutions. Thus particular subjects were more likely to become refugees than others in a given situation, and gender was certainly one of the factors governing who might be inserted into these positions.

CRITIQUING REFUGEE DISCOURSE

✳

Many dominant representations of human rights discourse in refugee asylum constructed Europe and North America as the primary destinations of refugees and thus as primary "havens" that "protect" those escaping human rights violations. While these countries gave asylum to only a small portion of the world's refugees, they were influential in creating the definition of the refugee. It is often forgotten, especially in the anti-immigrant and racist rhetoric within these countries, that North America and Europe have extremely strict refugee asylum laws which are well known around the world[23] and which are designed to keep people out rather than bring them in. Anthony H. Richmond calls the regulation of migrants and refugees by western countries a "form of global apartheid."[24] Many countries in Asia and Africa have taken many more refugees from neighboring countries and no doubt will continue to do so. In fact, Western European nations gave asylum to a tiny portion of the world's refugees.[25] The often cited division between the western "host" and the nonwestern "guest" erased the fact that most refugees were taken in by poor neighboring countries rather than Western Europe or North America. Many scholars argued that refugee protection systems of various kinds were not able to deal with large numbers of displaced persons;[26] especially for those entering the West, refugee asylum was granted most often to individuals rather than groups, although there were some exceptions to this policy.

The legal definition of the refugee forged in the cold war in treaties such as the Fourth Geneva Convention has come to define what it meant to be a refugee. The legal scholar Patricia Tuitt has argued that the "desire to define the refugee . . . is intimately bound up with the desire to exclude" those economic migrants who are nonwhite.[27] According to Tuitt, "legal definitions of refugee tend to focus on dominant societal images—connoting masculinity, adulthood and conventional sexual and social mores."[28] Tuitt reveals how legal definitions of the refugee produced by the Geneva Convention created a limited notion of the category, with the result that solutions to the growing number of refugees in the world were jeopardized. In particular, she critiques the utilization of the Geneva Convention by the Western European states as further limiting, and suggests that changing refugee laws and addressing the racism implicit in these laws might be a way to reduce the refugee "crisis."

While Tuitt addressed legal definitions, other scholars such as Liisa Malkki pushed many of these arguments in a different direction, engaging with the question of the nation-state and of internationalism that Tuitt did not address. Malkki argued that a "whole internationally standardized way of discussing people who have been displaced across national frontiers has emerged in the course of the last several decades," in which refugee has become a category of persons who are seen as a "problem" and as an outsider to the nation.[29] In her ethnography of Hutu refugees, Malkki found that refugees were actively reconceptualizing themselves as "a people" and as a "nation" in quite heterogeneous ways. The refugees in the town where Malkki did her research inhabited what she described as "multiple, shifting identities" rather than seeing themselves as refugees. Constructed as outsiders to the nation-state in which they lived, they also created "a lively cosmopolitanism" different from that of the refugees residing in the camp. Malkki shows convincingly that internationalism was conceptualized in many divergent ways and that the "problem" of the "refugee" was a consequence of the internationalism of the nation-state system.

While Malkki described refugees in Africa rather than those seeking asylum in the United States, there were nevertheless many parallels. The

similarities were especially visible in a text that Malkki discussed as a particularly problematic representation of refugees. Published by Zed Press
and entitled *Refugee Women*, this text posits what Malkki terms the "universal human" believed to lie beneath all depictions of the refugee.[30] Although
Tuitt and Malkki both see the refugee subject as normatively male, this text
also includes a normative description of the female refugee, especially the
nonwhite, nonwestern refugee seeking asylum in the West. This figure was
very similar to the Asian woman as Other that Sherene Razack described in
her work on refugee asylum in Canada. Razack argued that when Asian
women sought refugee asylum, they were compelled to represent themselves as victims and their cultures as pathological.[31] Razack concluded that
a combination of racism, sexism, and imperialism produced such constructs and that these overdetermined racialized representations emerged
in the legal arena, especially in refugee asylum cases or in domestic violence cases involving nonwhite, immigrant women.[32]

America as the freedom-giving, immigrant nation was also an important
discourse that emerged within refugee asylum narratives in the United
States, producing the Asian, Arab, Islamic, or third world female refugee as
a figure who moved from incarceration to liberation. Even narratives by
American feminists presented the United States as providing freedom,
especially sexual freedom to women, and reflected a belief that in the
United States women could be free of their homophobic and "traditional"
patriarchies and able to articulate identities, for example as lesbians, which
they could not articulate in their "home" countries.[33] The construction of
the American woman as free and her nonwhite, nonwestern "sister" as
unfree has been integral to the geopolitical-biopolitical link that was so
important for American empire. At the same time, this link constucted the
humanitarian self, bringing freedom through work in transnational NGOs.
In doing so, as one scholar has pointed out, transnational NGOs often
enforced western models of the modern heterosexual family structure
within refugee camps.[34] In addition, they also utilized other normative
narratives; for those seeking asylum on the basis of sexual identity, a version of the "coming out" narrative might be necessary. A good example of a
narrative of refugees moving from incarceration to freedom was the work
of the psychologist Olivia M. Espin, who worked with immigrant women
on issues of sexuality.[35] Espin's argument was that in these cases the "crossing of borders through migration may provide for both heterosexual and

lesbian women, the space and the 'permission' to cross boundaries and transform their sexuality and sex roles." The concept of "transforming" is a key aspect of refugee discourses that involve movement into the West. In moving from one nation-state to another, refugees may indeed have to change narratives of subjectivity and identity. However, it may not be a transformative experience of moving from repression to freedom; rather, it may be an experience in which one kind of state-national discourse of sexuality may have to be negotiated through another one. How changes of this sort may be experienced can be seen as neither uniform nor liberating.

Thus Espin's claim that "women who come from 'traditional' societies" find new alternatives open to them implies that it is western modernity that offers opportunities. Rather than suggest that modes of modernity and traditionalism exist in all countries, this "American" narrative of Western migration and movement articulates a discourse of mobility in which migration can be mapped chronologically and spatially as a movement from "traditional" to "modern," from "East" to "West." This discourse of immigration has been pervasive in the United States; it has become normalized and narrated by all kinds of subjects.

This sort of recuperation of America as a place of freedom for women has been used in some measure as the grounds for the American role as the world's policeman of human rights, a position that the United States has struggled to keep. In recent years, with the growth of the battered women's movement in the United States, attention has been given to problems of domestic violence and rape, but the socioeconomic concerns of poor and nonwhite women have been ignored in favor of a "common" problem of women. Even scholars who have critiqued the normative representations of the refugee continue to frame their understanding of violence against women in terms solely of "rape, physical abuse, murder,"[36] thus recuperating the hegemonic universal subject "woman" as a victim of oppression, a subject that was understood as a global standpoint for gendered identity.

GENDERING THE REFUGEE SUBJECT

✳

Human rights discourse was foundational in creating the refugee subject by supporting liberal subjects not simply through the state but also through the work of NGOs such as Amnesty International and Human Rights

Watch. While projects of economic rights or environmental rights or sexual rights have been more recent manifestations of human rights discourse, in the area of political rights there emerged a transnational consensus regarding the preservation of political rights through human rights instruments. Although a so-called Asian rights debate challenged the hegemonic construction of this project through liberal western philosophies (concededly in terms of other hegemonies), yet even in the Asian context the notion of political rights as human rights became foundational in creating the category of the refugee.

Most laws governing refugee asylum in European and North American countries followed the United Nations Convention Relating to the Status of Refugees (1951) by defining a refugee as one "who owing to a well-founded fear of being persecuted for reasons of race, religion, nationality, membership of a particular social group or political opinion" cannot get protection in the country of his or her nationality and is unable to return to it. The United States used this definition as foundational to its own laws. The "refugee" was defined in the Refugee Act of 1980 as any person outside his or her country "who is unable or unwilling to return to . . . that country because of persecution or a well-founded fear of persecution on account of race, religion, nationality, membership in a particular social group or political opinion."[37] The act provided guidelines under which asylum could be granted while leaving the burden of proof on the applicant and also adding some constraints to the ability of the INS and the attorney general to grant asylum.[38] Legal scholars argued that persecution was "the sustained or systemic violation of basic human rights demonstrative of a failure of state protection,"[39] and that an understanding of the term "persecution" "requires the general notion to be related to developments within the broad field of human rights."[40] The denial of political rights as human rights was taken into account in granting asylum in the United States, although the refugee claimant had to establish the connection between persecution by the state (or at least inadequate state protection) and the loss of rights.

The geopolitical interests of the United States lay not merely in refugee asylum but also in refugee protection in other countries, since one concern was to prevent migration to the United States and to other western states. Especially in Africa, the U.S. State Department expended a great deal of effort within the continent in collaboration with the United Nations High

Commissioner for Refugees in creating and protecting refugee camps. A statement made by the U.S. delegation to the UNHCR Standing Committee on International Protection in Geneva in 1998 clarified the focus on the relation between human rights and refugee protection: "Safeguarding human rights is necessary to prevent conditions that force people to flee and if they have to flee, the right to seek and enjoy asylum is fundamental."[41]

Given the huge number of refugees in Africa in the 1990s, the very small quota for African refugees to the United States was startling. Clearly a racialized American policy was intended to keep refugees within Africa, and the U.S. State Department went to great lengths in that direction. A comparison with the situation in Eastern Europe and the State Department policy for that region makes evident this "raciology" (as Paul Gilroy terms such uses of racial categories).[42] For the years 1996–98, the extraterritorial refugee quota for all of Africa was 6,500–7,000, compared with about 2,000–4,000 for Latin America, 10,000–20,000 for East Asia, and 40,000 to 50,000 for Europe.[43] It was ironic, in light of these policies, that in anti-immigration discourse in North America and Europe through the 1990s, refugees were represented as hordes of nonwhites infiltrating a white nation, although it was clear that a large number of extraterritorial refugees from Europe during that period could pass as white, particularly those from Eastern Europe.

The U.S. State Department policy on refugees not only participated in creating and upholding racialized immigration policies but also opposed international human rights regimes during the cold war and supported totalitarian regimes. In the 1980s, for instance, refugee asylum cases from El Salvador, then an ally of the United States, were seldom granted, so that all those who had suffered from human rights violations there were denied asylum whereas those "escaping" communism were easily given asylum.[44] In these cases the policies of the U.S. State Department and the INS were in opposition to those of global human rights NGOs, rather than more closely aligned as they were under President Clinton in the 1990s.

As human rights regimes became more prominent in the 1990s and were recast in new formations, they collaborated with new social movements. Or rather, one can say that new social movements seized upon human rights as a powerful discourse with which to articulate new identi-

ties created within social movements. An excellent example is the imbrication of the U.S. state practices and a racialized American nationalism with
cultural feminism's articulation of a universal and essential female subject
through women's rights as human rights discourse in the emergent concept of gender-based asylum.[45] In this form of asylum, feminists struggled
to address the problem that a large majority of refugees were women and
children while the refugee was, as Malkki and Tuitt have suggested, a normative male subject. Feminists argued that it was the nation-state's patriarchal practices that created the gender inequities and that the state must
therefore be made responsible for redressing them. These claims were long
overdue, feminists asserted, because women's circumstances had long
been ignored by a patriarchal U.S. state. To this end, in 1989 the Women's
Commission for Refugee Women and Children was created in New York
under the auspices of the International Rescue Committee. This organization's goal was to carry out the recommendations of the UNHCR's Guidelines on the Protection of Refugee Women, which were released in 1991.
Through the 1990s, campaigns and research by feminist legal activists and
women's NGOs about women's rights as human rights (especially after the
Vienna human rights meeting in 1995) pressured the INS to reconsider its
refugee asylum guidelines to include women's exploitation and oppression. Through the work of Nancy Kelly and several others, the Women
Refugees Project in Cambridge, Massachusetts, presented guidelines for
including gender considerations in asylum policy.[46] A number of law review essays argued for including gender as a category for refugee asylum.[47]
As a result, there were changes in asylum determinations as well as in the
processes used to manage asylum claims.

   These feminist struggles around human rights and refugee issues led to
many changes in the last decade of the century in U.S. state practices under
the Clinton administration. These changes included greater consideration
by asylum officers when they heard women's claims, the use of women
asylum officers to conduct interviews in gender-related cases, and recognition of gender-based asylum in guidelines for asylum officers. Asylum
could be claimed on the basis of belonging to "social groups" that were the
target of gender persecution where states had not protected them. One can
see that refugee laws presented certain possibilities foreclosed by immigration based on family unification policy, which is based on and enforces

heteronormativity—it could enable gays and lesbians to enter under certain strict guidelines.[48] Moreover, most family unification categories required many years of waiting, since the processing was not a priority and the number of claims granted had been reduced. Refugee asylum thus could be a means for women and gays and lesbians to enter the United States unconnected to a heterosexual family, as members of "social groups" that had suffered human rights abuses.

Arguments by feminists for consideration of gender-specific violence also became translated into law. Since sexual violence was identified in the Vienna Declaration and the Beijing Declaration as a violation of human rights, state practices around asylum issues were modified.[49] In Canada, gender-based violence was seen as grounds for asylum claims. The Canadian model was adopted by the INS, which issued guidelines for its asylum officers, instructing them in gender and cultural considerations when deciding asylum claims. These guidelines brought to the notice of asylum officers such documents as the UN declaration that emphasized the need to incorporate the rights of women as human rights, the Convention on the Elimination of All Forms of Discrimination Against Women (1979), and the Canadian Guidelines on Gender-based Persecution.

As a result of the organizing by feminist legal advocates and NGOs, most visible in the Vienna conference on human rights and the Beijing conference on women, violence against women, particularly sexual violence, had been identified as a human rights violation. In 1988 the first International Consultation on Refugee Women was organized by the NGO Working Group on Refugee Women and produced a report advocating the "protection needs" of women refugees. Recommendations included expanding the category of "social group" to include women, new standards for adjudicating claims involving women, services for "victims of violence and sexual abuse," and a move to the rhetoric of humanitarian needs based on "protection."[50] Legal activists had struggled for many years to expand the legal definition of the refugee to include women escaping violence that was not only "political" in the way it had been defined by patriarchal states but was visited upon women by "virtue of their gender." As the UNHCR argued, "While some of [these] women flee persecution which is not gender-specific, others flee a particular form of persecution which targets them as females."[51] North American feminist activists critiqued not only the separation between public and private that underlay the supposed gender neutrality of civil and political rights but also argued that the "liberal ideology underlying much of the discourse on civil and political rights views the law as a mean of regulating State intervention in private life and fails to acknowledge the role of the State itself in constructing the separation of the public from the private."[52] Jane Connors argued that the emphasis on civil and political rights in refugee asylum was biased, because it did not emphasize the "affirmative duty of the state to ensure rights" or acknowledge that women may suffer not simply from the loss of civil and political rights but "as a result of severe disadvantages . . . in the economic, social and cultural field."[53]

It is not only the division between public and private spheres that was attacked by feminists but also the ways in which women were not seen as a "social group" that could suffer persecution based on gender. Pamela Goldberg argued that violence against women was often not a private act since the state could be seen as accountable in perpetrating it.[54] According to Goldberg, membership in a particular social group was often the reason why women suffered "intimate violence." Anna Ervolina argued for an "expansive interpretation of the 'social group' category that recognizes the unmerciful and inhumane acts of violence inflicted on women wordwide."[55] Other legal activists added that the grounds of holding political opinions opposed by the state were inherently problematic, because women could be persecuted if their partners, families, and friends had political opinions being repressed by a state. In these cases, women being raped and tortured not for their own political beliefs but for the beliefs of family members should also be given asylum. Maureen Mulligan concluded, consequently, that rape should be accepted as a form of persecution and as a violation of human rights, and that the "well-founded fear of persecution" standard should include rape especially when the state did not punish the attacker or when the woman's life was threatened if she prosecuted her attacker.[56] Other scholars understood the issue in terms of the "failure of refugee and asylum law to recognize social and economic rights," and of the ways it "privileges male-dominated public activities over the activities of women which take place largely in the private sphere."[57]

Although courts in the United States did not endorse the use of gender alone as a "social group" suffering persecution, they incorporated some modified use of it in relation to some groups of women.[58] The Board of

Immigration Appeals granted asylum in cases of "female genital mutilation" and "violations" of cultural mores.[59] In the latter area, a Moroccan woman with liberal Muslim beliefs was granted asylum in 2000 after putting forward credible evidence that she had suffered persecution and had a well-founded fear of future persecution on religious grounds at the hands of her father, who held orthodox Muslim views concerning the proper role of women in Moroccan society.[60]

However, there was a split between cultural feminists who saw women as a group marked by ahistorical and universal oppression and feminists who examined gender as a historical category. The influence of feminist theorists of postcolonialism and colonial discourses was important in shifting the grounding of feminist advocacy from an essential subject to a more contingent and shifting one. For example, Jacqueline Greatbatch critiqued the cultural feminism of many advocates of women's refugee asylum. In her essay "The Gender Difference: Feminist Critiques of Refugee Discourse," Greatbatch argued that gender-related persecution and the relationship between women and the state were widely divergent and had to be historically contextualized. Thus it was not useful to argue for a separate formulation of refugee asylum based on the division between private and public spheres, since these could not be separated. While the legal definition of the refugee was problematic, it could not be corrected by a definition based on women's separate experience or on women's culture, but rather by developing a "comprehensive profile of gender-based refugee claims," recognizing women as a social group, and effecting a "liberal reading" of the definitions in the Geneva Convention.[61] Despite these differences among feminists, for liberal feminism human rights remained key to establishing asylum, and within most of these debates refugees were seen as the victims of globalization rather than as subjects of transnational or national networks of knowledge production.[62]

GENDER-BASED ASYLUM AND U.S. STATE PRACTICES

✳

After adopting its new guidelines, the United States granted asylum on the basis of gender in fewer cases than opponents of the guidelines had initially feared, since the claims were difficult to make.[63] There was also opposition to the claims, since it was believed that they relied on opposition to "tradi-tions" and thus could be made by millions of potential asylees[64]—reflecting a concern about letting in larger numbers of refugees. However, a state-ment made by the U.S. delegation to the Meeting of the Standing Commit-tee on International Protection in Geneva in 1998 made clear that feminist advocacy had had an effect: the delegation claimed that U.S. policy in the area of refugee asylum was partly intended to "keep women and children at the center of protection and assistance planning and programming" and to prevent "further exploitation of girls and re-recruitment of boys into armed gangs."[65] Here the gendering of young refugees is done by creating new representations in which young males are producers of violence (with a visible racialized link to domestic discourses of nonwhite urban underclass as gang members), and females are victims of violence.

In reviewing the impact of the guidelines from May 1995, when they were issued to asylum officers, to 1996, the time of the report, the INS found that about fifty claims of gender-based asylum had been filed, and these, according to Lori Scialabba, deputy general counsel at the INS, were "among the most difficult" cases. The influential cases cited by Scialabba include those involving claims that under Islamic moral codes feminism is a political opinion. Whether asylum was granted often depended on how the social group persecuted by the Islamic government was defined; in one case the group was defined as "Iranian women who refuse to conform with the government's gender-specific laws and social norms." Another related case occurred in Arlington, Virginia, where an immigration judge granted asylum to a woman who, according to Scialabba, "opposed restrictions on women in Jordan and whose husband had severely abused her both in Jordan and the United States."[66] The judge determined that the applicant had a well-founded fear of persecution on "account of her opinions about the role and status of women in society, which endowed her with both a political opinion and membership in a social group comprising women who are challenging Jordanian traditions." The INS did not appeal the deci-sion. As Audrey Macklin points out, even though the woman in a case like this one was not protected even in the United States, where the violence continued, the grant of asylum rested on the construction of Jordan as a nation and state where women were not protected.[67] The decision was consistent with legal scholars' arguments for expanding the category of "social group" to include women seeking asylum from a country that has "historically ignored violence against women."[68] It was also consistent with the construction of a world divided racially between western rescuers and their objects of rescue from the countries of the global South[69]—a construction grounded in what Gayatri Spivak has called a "sanctioned ignorance," in this case of the history of violence against women in the United States itself.

"Female genital mutilation," as it was popularly termed, was another area where gender-based asylum cases were won. A great deal of work was done by feminists to argue for asylum for those who had been identified as having suffered from this violence.[70] Scialabba's mention of genital mutilation cases indicates how much attention was given to this issue, far beyond the number of cases the INS dealt with. Fauzia Kasinga made national headlines when she won her case before the Board of Immigration Appeals after being imprisoned by the INS for two years.[71] A second case cited by Scialabba involved a Nigerian woman who obtained a suspension of her deportation order after she asserted that her daughters would suffer extreme hardship if they had to undergo genital surgeries on their return to Nigeria. The discourse of "mutilation" and the popular feminist outrage in the United States and globally against this as an abhorrent practice influenced these cases; fascination with these cases among the public and the news media also led to frequent and neocolonial references to "FGM" as an example of "African savagery" that must not be allowed in the United States. While no doubt the practice was terrible, the discourses and the preoccupation of the media with it remain to be examined in a historical context.[72]

The other two cases touched on by Scialabba involved "spousal abuse" and "coercive family planning practices." The latter term is familiar because the U.S. state has long accused the Chinese government of engaging in it; as for spousal abuse and domestic violence, these have become part of an evolving and emerging body of asylum law. Whereas earlier spousal abuse claims had been denied on the grounds that they amounted to personal and not political persecution, the gender asylum claimants argued that they were protected under asylum law because their gender motivated spouses to harm them. In a related reformulation of law, women battered by citizen or immigrant husbands who had used the immigration process as a weapon of power could get domestic violence waivers through an amendment to the immigration law enacted in 1994. Thus in December 2000, the attorney general and the INS announced a new regulation recognizing that "victims of domestic violence may, under certain circumstances, qualify for asylum under the Immigration and Nationality Act."[73]

The cases that Scialabba cited could fall roughly into two categories: (1) those representing and creating nonwestern women as victims or as feminists in struggle against their traditions or nations or nation-states, and thus assuming either lack of agency or an agency that was alien to their own societies; and (2) those that emerged out of the recent global womanist and feminist struggles against domestic violence and rape and violence against women. It is worth pointing out that cases involving gay and lesbian asylum, in which asylum was granted to women who identified as lesbians and who came from an Islamic country, were not mentioned by Scialabba as "gender-based asylum." Whether the category of lesbians persecuted in Islamic states comprised a social category that falls under gender-based asylum or under political asylum is not clear; perhaps what is necessary to point out is that the guidelines for gender-based asylum had an impact on the cases of all women seeking asylum, whether or not these cases explicitly stated they were using the gender-based asylum claims.

The cases mentioned by Lori Scialabba at the Geneva meetings suggest that the use of the gender-based guidelines in the United States, as in Canada, recuperated the victimized woman as paradigmatic refugee. The representation of the non-West as a space of oppression, and the West as a site of freedom, figured prominently in this discourse of the U.S. state, where feminist ideas gained some ground, and where both the INS commissioner and high-level officials in the INS were, in the Clinton administration, women.[74] The result of these state practices was that many women's nonprofit organizations seeking to help immigrant and refugee women, and working to give them "access" to resources, ended up teaching the narrative of this state and thus assisted in producing gendered subjects of the nation-state. Razack has shown that in Canada (and the United States is similar) the nation-state's production of these gendered bodies, with the collaboration of some feminist and medicalized discourses, almost always rendered this female body as one marked by a pathological violence.[75] Audrey Macklin has argued that the binary structure of refugee discourse, in which a refugee-producing country could never be a refugee-accepting country and vice versa, meant the denial of violence against women in the refugee-accepting countries.[76] Although Macklin overlooked that most of the refugee-producing countries in Asia or Africa have also been refugee-receiving ones (India is an example since it has taken many refugees from Bangladesh), and as a result described refugee activities solely as movement from South to North, she made the important point that the consequence of the binary was to ignore the failure of the Northern states to protect women from "intimate" violence. Thus she found that "gender persecution will be most visible and identifiable when it is committed by a cultural Other." As Karen Engle argued in her discussion of various rights approaches to debates around what is called "female genital mutilation": "Just as Human rights advocates might keep women at the periphery, if not exclude them altogether, women's rights advocates keep the Exotic Other Female at the margins."[77] Engle showed that women's rights advocates categorized variously as this Exotic Other a female subject who supported actions that the advocates were working against and who was seen as inaccessible or as the victim of false consciousness. This intense interest and absorption with the geopolitics of gender became important for women's own construction as feminist subjects of the American state. The collaboration between feminist NGOs and the state has been critiqued as well. Thomas Spijkerboer has argued that asylum depends on concepts of ethnicity and gender to which applicants must conform, that feminist critiques of international law have not paid attention to their grounding in the West, and that awareness of this grounding would strengthen their critiques.[78]

The critique also has to take note of the ways in which refugee claimants were asked to testify against their own nation-states but to support and bolster the narrative of the U.S. state as a haven of freedom and democracy; given the often marginal relation of displaced women to any nation and to whatever state they are located in, this may not be a difficult narrative for women to deploy. The use of "expert testimony" from anthropologists, literary scholars, area studies specialists, and other academics also bolstered problematic notions of culture. The practices of the U.S. state thus deployed a modernist construction of cultural difference between East and West, North and South. For instance, the INS guidelines to asylum officers suggested that asylum considerations should include "the laws and cus-

toms of some countries [that] contain gender-discriminatory provisions,"
since "some societies require that women live under the protection of male
family members"; the clear implication was that the United States remained free of similar provisions.

In the cases of asylum because of sexual orientation, women from Islamic states had some success in claiming that they were persecuted in
their own nation-states and that their lives were in danger. For the most
part, it was only for women from Islamic countries that this narrative was
successful. While the United States continues to demonize Islam, the narrative of Islamic states as the enemies of feminists and women was supported by many feminists from those countries as well as from women's
NGOs, which saw themselves as international or transnational. Yet the notion that these countries are "traditional" and that "modern" states have
more freedom for women has been critiqued extensively by many, from
"U.S. women of color" to postcolonial feminists to immigrants speaking
from firsthand experience. As these critiques have suggested, no society
could be understood as uniformly "traditional" or "modern"; in fact, as
Minoo Moallem has pointed out, Islamic states incorporate some very modern forms of governmentality, and thus are also modern.[79]

TRANSNATIONAL CULTURAL POLITICS AND REFUGEE CLAIMS

✳

Under U.S. law there are two ways in which an asylum claim can be heard.
There are "affirmative" claims in which a person applies directly to the INS
for asylum: these claims are heard by an asylum officer and are believed to
be "non-adversarial."[80] There are also "defensive" claims which arise when
the INS has begun a deportation proceeding and the claimant has to seek
relief from deportation. These hearings are conducted before an immigration judge and, if appealed, go before the Board of Immigration Appeals, a
twelve-member panel whose decisions are binding on the INS.[81]

To indicate a "well-founded fear of persecution," the evidence to be
presented before the asylum officer might include U.S. State Department
country reports and information from domestic or international human
rights monitoring agencies, academic institutions, or other NGOs. Information from the asylum seeker must be credible and evidence from friends

and relatives is accepted.[82] The U.S. Court of Appeals recognized in 1984 that corroborative evidence was not required if the claimant's testimony was persuasive or credible.[83] Claims of human rights violations, especially through torture or political detention, were often part of narratives that resulted in the granting of refugee asylum.

In a practice that has continuities with early-twentieth-century Chinese immigration to the United States, when immigrants were detained on Angel Island and had to prove through examination by authorities that their papers were legitimate, getting through the INS remains a major hurdle: the hearing is like an examination that must be passed if a claimant is to avoid being deported. Asylum officers, even in supposedly "non-adversarial" situations, have to make determinations about the veracity of claims and whether they fit legal and cultural standards. The so-called non-adversarial process simply means that lawyers are not involved in arguments on both sides; it does not mean that the process involves equal parties. Since the INS rejects many thousands of claims and deports a large number of those who seek asylum, the asylum officer has a great deal of power. Often the asylum officer is the only person before whom a claimant is heard, although recent changes in refugee law mean that officers at an airport can hear a claim and make a judgment of deportation before it moves through the DHS. While standards of credibility have also changed, allowing credible claimants to present contradictory information because of fear or trauma, asylum officers have regularly demanded that claimants not depart from the legal and cultural conceptions that the officers have held or from the historical accounts presented by experts or by the State Department.

The credibility standards of current U.S. refugee asylum laws require that human rights violations, as defined in the Geneva Convention, become the measure of the necessity for rescue. Thus asylum officers' task is to figure out whether human rights violations have taken place. Questions of credibility are important, especially since the job of the asylum officers is to judge who has really been persecuted. In their determinations, cultural and political questions become key measures to assess credibility regarding human rights abuses. By recuperating global feminism's universal female subject through the guidelines for gender-based asylum, U.S. state practices located rape as a determining factor of gender difference in these claims. Even in political asylum cases, where gender-based asylum is not the basis of a refugee claim, American cultural feminism and its emphasis on rape as a primary determinant of violence against women mean that other forms of violence do not have a comparable impact at asylum hearings. The threat of rape has become the most important determinant of persecution for women, and the raped woman the paradigmatic female refugee. A woman's credibility thus has often depended on her ability to convey the threat of rape or the experience or trauma of rape to the hearing officer. Although, as Eithne Lubhéid points out, only "certain instances of rape are deemed to merit asylum," it is striking that rape became the paradigmatic way to establish persecution if the claimant is a woman.[84] Credibility regarding rape became one of the criteria for defining the truly deserving refugee as the one who had suffered human rights abuses.

SIKH WOMEN AS REFUGEE SUBJECTS
✳

The example of Sikh women from Punjab who sought refugee asylum in the United States in the mid-1990s is instructive in showing how this female refugee American subject is produced transnationally. While in the early 1990s many men from Punjab were applying for asylum because they presented claims that the Indian state persecuted them, by the mid-1990s some women began applying for asylum as well. Here we are not talking about vast numbers, although it is difficult to obtain information on the number of people already in the United States who are given refugee asylum. One U.S. State Department document from the Bureau of Democracy, Human Rights and Labor mentioned that as of 30 September 1995 there were 8,789 applications from Indian citizens pending before the INS asylum officers, and that 3,209 applications were filed in Fiscal Year 1994; out of these the report estimates that 65 percent of applicants were Sikhs.[85] However, the report does not state how many of these applicants obtained refugee asylum. These numbers suggest that refugees from South Asia may not be very numerous, especially in comparison with other groups. From 1996 to 1998 the annual ceiling for refugee admission from a category called Near East/South Asia was approximately 4,000, with a majority coming from Iraq and Iran.[86]

According to the INS and community workers in legal nonprofits, the

Sikh women stated that they were being persecuted because of their families' vulnerability to the police for three main reasons: (1) A family was "amritdhari," or baptized Sikh (formal baptism is done not to all Sikhs but only at the person's request). (2) Family members were believed to be supporters of the movement for creating Khalistan, a separate Sikh nation. (3) Someone in the family was a member of the All India Sikh Student Federation (AISSF), an organization which became more political as the Indian government began to target as "terrorist" all Sikh young men who wore turbans and beards.

It has been widely documented that in the 1980s and through the 1990s security forces were deployed by the Indian government to put down a Sikh insurgent movement for autonomy, and all political and civil rights were taken away from those living in Punjab.[87] The Indian parliament in 1985 enacted the Terrorist and Disruptive Activities Act (TADA) to control what it called "terrorism" in Punjab, where the so-called security forces (charged with combating the "terrorist" threat to the state) could detain anyone. Especially under the notorious police chief K. P. S. Gill, himself a Sikh, the police let loose a reign of terror that deprived everyone living in the state of any civil rights. Checkpoints manned by police with machine guns sprang up at city intersections, rural roads, and highways, and anyone could be harassed at random, then asked for a bribe or thrown into jail. Police were given rewards if they killed the insurgents, and this of course led to police becoming bounty hunters. In a regime of terror by the police, no one was safe who lacked some access to power. Anyone could be designated a terrorist and shot, and it was particularly the randomness of the police violence that was most effective at disciplining the population. While in the postcolonial state the rule of law is often no guarantee of rights, and the poor in the third world (and particular nonwhite groups in the first world as well) live under repressive conditions every day, for many others even the networks that often protect those with access to state power were rendered ineffective.

While the randomly applied police power which terrorized the population worked effectively to repress the insurgent movement, refugee asylum law as defined by the United States (and the Geneva Convention) deemed it impermissible and demanded that states permit the same level of political activity as might be sanctioned by liberal democracy. In a number of applications for refugee asylum made by Sikh women at the time, we can see the narratives produced to obtain asylum. In the applications, even if gender-based asylum was not being claimed, a clear gendered narrative is visible that relies on the legal activists' arguments mentioned above. For instance, applicants for refugee asylum often narrated that they had been thrown into prison, and raped or threatened with rape while in custody, not for their own political activities but for the activities of fathers, brothers, or husbands. Most of the Sikh women seeking refugee asylum presented themselves as political workers in the AISSF, although these narratives were risky since the U.S. State Department identified some groups within this organization as "terrorist" groups. The Indian state used terms such as "terrorist" and "militant" to refer to enemies of the state, as did the Indian media. The widespread reach of the Punjab police in collaboration with the Indian government made it impossible for these refugee applicants to flee to anywhere in Punjab or in India, given the highly publicized cases in which the Punjab police hunted and killed suspects in regions as far away as West Bengal state. Refugee applicants stated that only after a bribe had been paid to the police were they released and then, with the help of an "agent," put on a plane to the United States, sometimes leaving behind children or elderly parents.

The suddenness and number of these claims led INS and immigration lawyers to believe that some of the women were not "credible." U.S. government reports corroborated this concern. Thus the U.S. State Department report on country conditions in India stated, "Close study of hundreds of applications filed by Sikhs indicate that many applications are identical or follow a well-established pattern. There would appear to be a high level of misrepresentation in many applications and many applications appear to be fabrications."[88] Both for the INS and for legal aid workers, the task then became to figure out who was telling the truth, so that only those who they believed were really suffering human rights violations could be helped.

It is also because of geopolitics—because of relations between India and the United States and because of the production of the "terrorist" as the leading post–cold war threat to national security both in the United States and India—that the refugee narrative became convoluted in some instances. Since the U.S. State Department in its reports designated the brutal counterinsurgency campaign by Indian security forces as an "anti-terrorist" campaign,[89] it concluded that the articulations of Sikh nationalism were waged through "terrorism" in the Punjab rather than through political struggle, and that this violence was a long-standing problem within Punjab: "Ethnic strife and separatist violence in the state of Punjab has been one of India's intractable problems. . . . But fear of domination by India's Hindu majority and economic concerns have fueled discontent and strife. A separatist movement using terrorist tactics but supported by only a minority of Sikhs exploited this tension for its own purposes." The use of terrorism here articulated this movement to the geopolitical role of the United States in the struggle against "terrorism" globally.

The issue of "credibility" along with the need for applicants to prove that they were not terrorists created new narratives for refugee asylum. The need to establish a link between political action and state persecution ignored how random police terror became the chief means to subjugate the population. Sikh applicants for refugee asylum had to prove that they were persecuted by the Indian state for expressing political opinions but that they were not part of so-called terrorist groups.[90] Thus if they were in the AISSF, they had to be careful when saying what kinds of work they had performed and which groups of the AISSF they were working with, and they had to express political opinions in a way that the immigration officials would see as legitimate. The narratives of both men and women applying for asylum claimed only that they were persecuted by the state for working on voter registration, putting up posters, making speeches, participating in peaceful protests, and so on. Anything else was suspect, but it was also not enough to state that the police could persecute people just to blackmail them into giving money or goods or other favors. Furthermore, since the U.S. state extradited some so-called terrorists at the request of the Indian state, the slippage between the shifting and uncertain categories of "political worker," "nationalist," and "terrorist" produced a great deal of anxiety for applicants. The problem was that a claimant must not have participated in any activity against the state he or she was fleeing from, although the refugee was by definition escaping from what were conceded to be repressive practices by the state. So claimants had to be nonviolent and the state they were fleeing violent, but if that violent state demanded extradition, with documentation (and the credibility of this documentation was not often questioned), the claimant had to be extradited.

In this way, although refugee claims also problematized state practices, nation-state sovereignty was protected.

Given that the designation of what constituted a "terrorist" group was a political and geopolitical act, since in post–cold war geopolitics, "terrorism" has emerged as the "Other" of the international network of nations that participate in the UN, the designation of a "refugee" distinguished from a "terrorist" reflected a contingent and shifting political agenda that could not be seen as neutral or even humanitarian. Human rights violations by a repressive state were not acknowledged if an act against the state could be designated a "terrorist" act; again, the supranational claims of human rights discourses could not succeed against the maintenance of nation-state sovereignty.

For the Sikh women claimants, the particular logic of refugee asylum claims was a new discourse that they had to learn to become gendered subjects of the U.S. state. In its country reports the U.S. State Department during this period represented Sikhs as normatively male and political agency as also male. Without a comparable historical representation of women's political agency, Sikh women were unable to claim refugee asylum on the basis of political activity. However, because of the uncertainty and newness of claims of gender-based asylum, almost none of the Sikh women claimed this category for asylum, remaining with political asylum laws. Yet to a certain extent the narratives they used were gender-specific, since they were based on rape or the threat of rape by state police. The legal scholar Nancy Kelly has argued that there could be gender considerations even without a claim of gender-based asylum: "Even when the applicant's gender is not central to her persecution or her fear of persecution, however, there may be gender-related aspects to her case."[91] Rape therefore became a central narrative in these cases, and was used to articulate sexual difference within the supposedly gender-neutral category of political asylum. Consequently, other ways in which women were gendered were erased by the simple binary of global, reified, and ahistorical male and female subjects. In this binary, the women had to negotiate between presenting themselves as political victims and presenting themselves as political actors.

Some INS asylum officers, especially those in San Francisco, wished to be helpful and unprejudiced. In order to do so, they used "community experts" to gain the knowledge that they feared the State Department reports had left out. They expressed concern that they needed to know more about the lives of Sikh women so that they could find out which cases were deserving or whether a claimant had truly been persecuted. While the standard for "credibility" allowed that claimants may not be wholly "truthful" at certain times, given the circumstances of repression that they might have endured, asylum officers were still required to make judgments about credibility, and the immigration judges could also deny relief from deportation if they did not find a claimant to be credible. In San Francisco, where many Sikh women applied for asylum, most asylum officers and legal practitioners believed that a majority of the claims were false and thus created their own narratives about what was credible and what was not. Since alongside the humanitarian impulse of some asylum officers and the legal community was the INS's mandate to only give asylum to those who had really suffered human rights violations and to keep the number of refugees quite low, asylum officers had to turn down a majority of claims. However, the problems for the claimants went beyond the difficulty of establishing credibility at the hearings. Even obtaining legal services became difficult, since women had to prove credibility even to get past the paralegal at the front desk in the office of a lawyer or legal aid organization.[92] For instance, if a women had sought legal help from other members of her gurudwara (the Sikh temple), she was not thought of as credible since it was believed that contacts were available there that would help formulate spurious claims. This suspicion regarding community sources did not extend to legal sources, because going directly to a lawyer was believed to be a better indicator of credibility. One could, of course, conclude that going directly to a lawyer was class-specific behavior since those with more resources would go to lawyers and others would seek help wherever they could find it. The Sikh "community" was thus represented as a site where fictional narratives were generated, rather than as a location where newly arrived migrants participated in transnational connectivities and learned how to "access" the state and the narratives and language they were required to speak in order to remain in the United States.

The basis of these widespread doubts within the INS and the legal community about the credibility of Sikh claimants was the charge that most of these narratives were too similar. While asylum officers seemed to be questioning why many of the claimants had the same narrative, believing that it was being generated within the community in the United States so that "illegals" could remain in the United States, the determination of asylum clearly necessitated telling the same story. Since this narrative was the hegemonic narrative of the Sikh woman refugee, to depart from it meant risking deportation. Claimants could not depart from the cultural or historical narratives given to asylum officers by the U.S. State Department; if they did, they risked losing their "credibility." The "information" that asylum officers relied upon to judge credibility was generated by "consultants" that the INS used as well as by country reports compiled by the State Department. As this information circulated, there were common assumptions about the "traditional" cultures of Sikhs as opposed to the "modern" West. In these narratives, Sikh patriarchy was represented as homogeneously violent and the women as its victims. These beliefs were obvious in the questions that asylum officers asked me when I agreed to be an "expert." While these questions seemed aimed at obtaining the best kind of information to "help" women, they assumed that patriarchy was not being negotiated by Sikh women but rather that Sikh women were helpless before Sikh patriarchy.

This "cultural" narrative that represented "the Sikh woman" was created by human rights NGOs, global feminists constructing "traditional" cultures, and the mostly male "community consultants" brought in by the INS. Within these narratives, a victim of human rights violations was constructed: this victim was either raped or threatened with rape and could then be rescued by the U.S. state if she represented her experiences in the proper language of human rights and women's rights. For Sikh women, agency had to be restrained to the proper modes of political protest, the proper "culture" of Sikh women. Within these asylum claims, this figure of the "Sikh woman" was narrated as a victim, for the most part politically active only in putting up posters, but also someone wholly identified in relation to family, obedient to the menfolk, and remaining within the household, veiled and shy. She was governed by "shame" and "honor," those anthropological constructs through which "traditional" cultures are identified, was subservient, yet had to explain how she came to take flight to another country. She had to explain that she had a well-founded fear of persecution by the state because of her political actions or because of the political actions of members of her family, but that she was quite uninvolved in more fierce forms of protest; she had either been raped or threatened with rape.

Whereas the male refugee had to show persecution because of political opinion, this gendered female refugee could simply be a victim, persecuted because of family connections rather than for her own beliefs or actions, and threatened with rape by the police. If she could not articulate this narrative within the asylum hearing and before the immigration judge, she could easily be deported. Any departure from a narrative of the victim and she might be termed a "militant"—a terrorist, a designation which was a constant danger for any Sikhs seeking asylum. The safest narrative thus minimized all kinds of agency, although the agency might have been found in the narratives of flight and migration—those aspects of the story that had little to do with human rights discourses and in which the INS officers had little interest, and which were unspeakable for many reasons.

Consequently, INS and State Department knowledges produced a raciology in which Sikh refugees were constructed as uniformly devout, all of one caste and class (that of rural small farmers), without differences of sexuality or religious affiliation. Although many forms of belief have been subsumed under Sikhism, the transnational discourse of Sikhs was as a homogeneous collectivity. The only difference produced was that between the baptized (rigorously devout) and the unbaptized (casually devout) Sikh, a binary in which the baptized Sikhs were presumed to be either refugees or terrorists. Religious affiliations also became very clearly defined as stable identities rather than a set of shifting practices.

All the questions posed by asylum officers during a discussion with a community "consultant" revealed similarly ahistorical views. As a "consultant," I was asked to respond to questions such as what the age of marriage was for Sikh women, whether a single woman could relocate in India, what percentage of adult women in Punjab were unmarried, and most centrally, which "sexual violations" were committed by the police or during custody.[93] All these questions assumed a homogeneous, ahistorical Sikh "culture," and an undifferentiated Sikh female subject. Another set of questions posed by another officer did assume that Sikh women could be political activists, but also assumed that within the realm of activism, "women's rights" struggles were opposed to and separated from struggles for "Sikh rights." Asylum officers seemed to have little knowledge of class, caste, and gender issues in Punjab and how these were altered with historical contexts, and had no knowledge about the many kinds of Sikh communities in the United States. Thus while this refugee process was part of a long history of transnational connectivities, Sikh women were seen as victims of static and unchanging cultures.

THE TRANSNATIONAL GENDERED SIKH SUBJECT

*

Although I have focused on representations produced within and by the U.S. state, these representations came from a variety of sources, which included NGOs, individual "consultants" and scholars, the State Department, and a variety of media sources. In describing the counterinsurgency movements carried out by the state in the early 1990s in Punjab, Human Rights Watch/Asia and Physicians for Human Rights documented the torture of women detained along with family members by the police for extortion. These NGOs continue to represent women as victims of their state and, sometimes, their culture, or as nonpolitical innocents. Yet these reports also revealed other forms of gendered agency and other representations of the "Sikh woman." An analysis of one such report on Punjab revealed subjects who were most interesting because they were not the "objects" of concern of these global NGOs or global "victims" or even "innocent" bystanders of state violence, as most women refugees are deemed to be.[94] Gendered agency seems to be much more diverse and complex than most of these discourses of the transnational Sikh female subject would suggest. In one most revealing incident, the human rights groups obtained evidence from a female police officer who was married to an undercover agent and who told the group quite a few details about her husband's activities, which included many human rights violations. In another incident, the wife of a policeman told human rights advocates about how the police were rewarded monetarily for killing "militants": "My husband twice received Rs 3000 for the people he killed."[95] Thus while the human rights narrative about Sikh women represented them as tortured and raped, other forms of gendered agency, complex and problematic, slipped into the narrative, disrupting the representation of a normative female Sikh subject.

Human rights NGOs in India produced a related but different subject from that produced by transnational human rights NGOs when they focused on Sikh women. Since Sikh males have been represented within British colonial and Indian nationalist discourse as hypermasculine and aggressive, Sikh women are discursively produced within postcolonial India as both oppressed and masculine. Consequently, the report by the Citizens for Democracy group based in New Delhi depicted these women as courageous in the face of police terror, but courageous as mothers and as wives rather than as Sikhs: "Lonely, overworked, harassed daily by the Army and the Police, dishonored, beaten up for not being able to produce the men who have been missing—they came to meet us out in the open regardless of the fear of the police."[96] These narratives do include reports of being raped, what we are told is translatable as being "dishonored" by the police. The section on the women concluded that "the list [of requests for help] is endless—so is misery and so is fortitude and magnificent pride." Here, instead of the passive "Asian woman" of the U.S. state narrative, we have a narrative of the women of Punjab as proud and stoic, a construction that came out of British notions of the people of Punjab as masculinist and tough.

These are of course women from the same part of India that underwent the partition in 1947, where, situated in border states, notions of women's bodies and their sexualities were most carefully and problematically disciplined by the emerging nation-states. The work of Ritu Menon, Kamla Bhasin and Urvashi Butalia as well as many others on the partition revealed how the sexuality and sexual agency of women from the region was recuperated by national and state narratives, as well as how women's narratives often contradicted these state narratives; they reveal that women's narratives often subverted the narratives of the state that constructed religious, national, and gender subjectivity as unchanging and static.[97] The Recovery Operation, in which women kidnapped were to be returned to their proper "families," was much more about consolidating patriarchies of kin and nation-state, as Veena Das argues, rather than about the well-being of the women.[98] The women themselves had sometimes developed relationships with their kidnappers or formed new families and were resistant to being returned. Questions of a monolithic religious identity were irrelevant to them; what concerned them was how to create some kind of possible future when often their relatives were the source of violence. The subjectivity of women was also defined, both in the narratives of partition and in the representation of the event in postcolonial Punjab, by sexuality, in terms of reproduction within which women were objects of violence.

The question of the sexuality of women in Punjab remains to be examined. Historical and cultural evidence in Punjab has noted that many practices around marriage and sexuality did not conform to the notion of the brahmanical Hindu woman, especially in areas like the remarriage of widows. Since widows could, under colonial rule, inherit property, women tried to keep their property and their sexual autonomy. Prem Chowdhry described this period as a time when "dual control . . . of their rights of inheritance and their sexuality was openly contested by the widows [in colonial Punjab,] resulting in prolonged legal battles and open confrontations."[99] Women who became widows worked actively to retain their sexual and economic autonomy against the wishes of their families to perform "levirate" marriage in which they could be remarried to one of their dead husband's brothers and so lose control of property. So many women tried to be autonomous, and women's acceptance of their unchastity became such a common way to refuse remarriage, that the colonial government had to take action against this practice.

While I don't wish to suggest that the nineteenth century provided more sexual autonomy for women in Punjab, this narrative about other kinds of sexual subjects suggests that there are more negotiations that we can focus on to problematize the production of state subjects. Furthermore, historical information is important in revealing how narratives of the state and nation have collaborated with human rights internationalism and global feminism to consolidate the production of the Sikh woman sexualized solely as a victim of violence.

If community and grassroots organizing was based on this subject of violence, then we need to pay attention to the various discourses of nation, community, and family within which conflicting and intersecting subject-positions are produced. Thus the forms of agency that I have mentioned above, which may suggest the failure of the women to fully become the subjects of the U.S. state, become important areas of feminist analysis, for they indicate that agency may not be contained by one nation-state.

Refugee advocates and feminist and immigrant-rights NGOs struggled to provide "access" to the U.S. state for such subjects. In providing these resources, both internationalist and nationalist discourses represent the Sikh woman as a victim of violence. Often, it is when "access" cannot be provided that we see a glimpse of subjects beyond the state and nation; the failures of an NGO working with women can also be illuminating. A major failure for NGOS in the United States occurred when a woman was unable to explain her experiences to the INS officials or to the immigration judge in the language in which rape could be understood to be traumatic in American contexts, or if her actions did not fit the representation of a proper female refugee as a victim of violence—if, for example, the woman had left her children behind to seek asylum in the United States, if she did not seem to American "experts" to have been traumatized by her experiences, if she refused psychological counseling, if she had begun to live with another man in the United States to whom she was not legally married, if she had tried to hedge her bets by having a child with the man she was living with in the United States, if the counselor was unable to understand her experience of trauma, or if the middle-class experiences of the community worker failed to connect with the many negotiations that a woman needed to perform in order to survive. It is in these failures that agency could be theorized, although we may still not find our subject of resistance.

chapter five

TRANSNATIONAL AMERICA:

RACE AND GENDER AFTER 9/11

★

After the events of 9/11, it was clear that the technologies for the production of American nationalism were many and diverse. It was constructed through various representations not only in the United States but also from other nations and other nationals; within transnationality, the discourses of American nationalism that circulate within networks and channels of cosmopolitanism and of consumer culture were visible as never before. In the dominant media representations after 9/11, we can see clearly the articulation of this nationalism as defined by hegemonic state power, the investments of many inside and outside the United States in the idea of "America" as a liberal state, and the productions and circulations of a transnational media and consumer culture. Although these constructions of America have a long history, their specificities and reliance on consumer culture, as well as their racial and gendered history, make them quite different from other nationalisms. As a superpower and policeman, a multicultural nation as well as a site of hierarchical racial and gendered formations, America the nation-state, along with American nationalism, produces identities within many connectivities in a transnational world, whether as the source of imperial power or as a symbol of freedom and liberty. It is a signifier of many diverse meanings, but some of these meanings are more hegemonic than others in particular sites and time periods. It is both the difficulty and the necessity of identifying these hegemonic meanings that is my topic here, as I examine American nationalism in the twenty-first century around the events of 9/11 as exceptional when compared to nationalisms in other sites, while also sharing some of the normative ways in which all nationalisms have come to be constructed within transnational connectivities.

In particular, I want to discuss how America as a nation became a site for the articulations of gender and race after 9/11. My attention to representational practices in the immediate aftermath of 9/11, in particular the powerful discourses of multiculturalism, do not mark this as an event which changed American nationalism or American imperialism. Rather my intention in this final chapter is to show how a large part of what happened then was a continuation and a fulfillment of neoliberal practices that had arisen in the last decades of the twentieth century and that I have described in the first four chapters. Thus 9/11 does not mark a break, but a fulfillment of some of the directions taken by neoliberal American nationalism, in particular the articulation of a consumer nationalism, the link between geopolitics and biopolitics, and the changing and uneven gendered, racial, and multicultural subjects produced within transnational connectivities.

While race and gender have to be changing to work as the regulative apparatuses of a powerful state, they are also connected to earlier technologies of race and gender and thus must be understood in relation to questions of governmentality. We can understand gendered and racialized subjects not as autonomous projects of resistance but as subjects that develop in relation to modern regulative and disciplinary institutions. Following the work of scholars such as Tim Mitchell and Ann Stoler, I want to bring together ideas of colonialism and hegemony with questions about governmentality to see not only how racialized and gendered subjects emerge in relation to contexts of state power but also how these subjects are created within realms of social life that seem unrelated to state power.[1] In particular, I want to connect American imperialism with the articulation in the United States of a group including "Middle Eastern men," Muslims, and those who "look Middle Eastern or Muslim" as a racial and gendered category created by disciplinary power, racialized nationalism, and the geopolitics of the U.S. state. In doing so, I argue that this racial formation resonates with American multicultural nationalism through consumer citizenship by means of a transnational consumer and media culture. Nationalism thus does not evolve out of one imaginary community but rather is produced through the changing specularity of consumer culture and contingent community affiliations created by new and historical hierarchies of race and gender, which extend beyond the boundaries of the nation-state.

The issue of the relationship between forms of governmentality and the state is a contentious one. Scholars such as Nikolas Rose argue that there is not a clear link between the two, since forms of power are never that linear.[2] Others, including Achille Mbembe, use Agamben's notion of "necropolitics" to argue that "necropower," that is, the "maximal economy now represented by the massacre," characterizes the new form of decentralized state power that produces what he calls "death worlds."[3] If Rose's notion of governmentality takes shape in sites where freedom marks the modern individual whose practices of making choices constitute modes of regulation, that individual can only be in dynamic relation to a site of unfreedom in which the loss of "choice" and the loss of "freedom" is always a threat and thus acts as another mode of regulation. Thus it cannot be said that the governmentality of freedom can be mapped onto first world sites or the decentralized "death worlds" of "necropolitics" onto third world or postcolonial sites. Rather they work together within a particular context, bringing together biopolitics and geopolitics through the imaginaries produced by consumer culture's media worlds, the coercive powers of states, and the possibilities produced by growing nationalisms.[4] In particular, media technologies of various kinds, from radio and television to the internet, and their sounds and images that pervade rural and urban areas in the first world and the third, have transformed the biopolitics and necropolitics of power. Furthermore, the powers of freedom, as Nicholas Rose calls them, that produce modes of governmentality are undertaken not simply with the sovereign right to kill but also through the right to save. Modes of humanitarianism, for example human rights regimes, produce unequal subjects as well. To exclude any consideration of these subjects might lead us to see them simply as oppositional to the state. Though they might be in opposition to Mbembe's concept of necropolitics, they may not be in opposition to all forms of power that produce inequalities between the global North and the South. Rather, it is the interrelation between the sovereign right to kill and the right to rescue that constitutes modes of modern power, whether by states or by other institutions of power.

Thus even within colonial regimes, missionary discourses and discourses of rescue, civilizing the natives, education, health, and reform proliferated not only to create different cadres and classes of colonizing and colonized subjects. Elsewhere I have argued that within British colonialism in the nineteenth century, the freedom of the English woman became constituted in relation to the unfreedom of the colonized woman.[5] The practice of unveiling the "veiled woman" or the woman in "purdah" became a technology of colonial power exercised both to "save" and to destroy at the same time. Furthermore, saving the veiled woman became a project of reform, undertaken by anti-colonial nationalists as well as by colonial authorities. Thus one can argue that forms of governmentality produce nationalisms and the practices of state power, and that connection was visible within contexts of imperialism and in the realm of culture.

Modernity has been both hegemonic and enabling, especially in the ways in which colonial powers imposed and enabled the development of modern subjects as intrinsic to the "white man's burden," as Rudyard Kipling called it, of "civilizing the natives." While some scholars of colonialism have argued that "colonial modernity," as Dipesh Chakrabarty terms it, is not synonymous with the modernity of the colonial powers,[6] Ann Stoler has shown that the biopolitics of self-disciplining of the Dutch in Indonesia cannot be dissociated from the sexual and racial politics of colonial rule and the formation of a European self.[7] Chakrabarty and Stoler both argue for a difference in the formation of modernity if imposed through colonial rule but also see modernities as constitutive of each other; as Stoler puts it, "the colonial order of things" was historically not coterminous with European genealogies although constitutively linked to them.[8]

Within many debates on Foucault's work regarding the genealogy of the modern self through the conceptualization of governmentality, there is a productive focus on the forms of selfhood and self-making that are central to modernity, as well as some concerns about Foucault's erasure of the difference between colonialism and imperialism. Such a difference matters not simply in producing genealogies of colonized subjects in the nonwestern world, but also, as Stoler argues, in producing genealogies of colonizing subjects. Thus it is not just that modern subjects were produced in relation to concepts of race and gender that were seen as evidence of superiority, but that many other arenas of self-production and regulation were involved in producing these subjects. In addition to examining what Stoler calls the "intimacies" of colonial rule (which pertain to gender and sexuality and which political theories often ignore as trivial), we also need to pay attention to everyday aspects of social life that seem unrelated to ruling powers of the state.[9] At the same time, these practices of self-regulation cannot be dissociated from institutions of state power in which the regulatory mechanisms become technologies of hegemony.

Multiculturalism has become one such technology in the United States as a state project, produced through the census, laws, and provisions governing immigration and "protecting" minorities to create racialized and gendered subjects who see themselves as "American" at some points and as different kinds of Americans at other times and places. However, it is not just the practices of the state that produce these subjects, but also strategies of self-identification and difference through practices of belonging to groups and communities, many of which are materialized within consumer culture's use of "choices" in the formation of both individual and collective identifications. Through concepts such as "cultural citizenship"[10] and "hyphenated" or "mestiza" identities,[11] new social movements based on racial, gendered, and ethnic identities have shown both their links to the American nation and their struggles with its affirmations of white supremacy, asserting a differently racialized and ethnic origin as well as challenging the liberal state. While these political movements challenged the normative white, male, heterosexual, Anglo-American citizen and the liberal ideas of equality that were claimed as central to the U.S. state, the hyphenated subject of resistance to the state has been itself proved to have a heterogeneous relation to the nation and state, sometimes affiliating itself to it but also claiming a position outside it. Transnational movements of ideas, goods, labor, and capital have altered these subjects, making them more flexible and dynamic in relation to multiple identities, nationalisms, communities. Rather than simply become hybrid subjects that incorporate one or two races or nationalisms, these subjects of new forms of transnational governmentality are flexible and changing, moving from one subjectivity to another, able to coexist with contradictory and diverse subject formations.

Multiculturalism in the United States has produced dynamic and contingent subjects of this sort, within which the hyphen ceases to be a sign of resistance to the American nation but rather becomes also the marker of a contingent ability of those with such an identity to switch from one side of the hyphen to the other but at other times to challenge the American nation with this contingency. This changing affiliation is made possible through popular media and consumer culture, which become sites through which nationalism is purveyed but also changed. In the weeks following 9/11 these subjects emerged in relation to the articulation of changing racial and gendered formations. These were produced both through state-produced and older, racialized forms of surveillance and the criminalization of new bodies, and of embodiments of masculinity and femininity, and also through forms of self-regulation and self-making that followed these events. Thus to understand gender and race as varieties of regulatory formations that took root in specific historical periods, I examine the modes of governance through which they appeared. Multiculturalism enables the production of the sovereign subject through a variety of means, one of them being the ways in which the managing of risk and danger are connected to classifications of race and gender. It is a racial and gendered notion of danger that I want to suggest produced racialization in the late twentieth century, and this notion of danger then became allied with knowledges, visibilities, and institutions as technologies of power.

If scholars have identified "risk" and the "risk society" as a powerful form of governmentality that has become associated with a wide range of mechanisms of power, the concepts of "danger" and "security" are allied. Through the twentieth century, risk emerged not only as a mode of judging actions and events but also as a biopolitical mechanism. While scholars like François Ewald argue that "risk" works as a synonym not for danger but for chance, randomness, and thus "accident," and that a technology like "insurance" arises to deal with this accident,[12] how then do we understand the incarceration and criminalization of certain kinds of bodies which are identified as inclined to commit violence or having tendencies of violence essential to them? If we examine one mode of addressing risk not through insurance but through incarceration, then the synonym for risk is not chance or randomness but danger and "terror," and the means for securing the population from this danger is the incarceration of other populations judged by various modes of expertise as dangerous. From the "criminal" at one level of risk for violence to the "terrorist" at a higher level representing a risk to the nation, we can see the progressively higher levels of risk associated with particular bodies within specific locations. While the "crim-inal" might still have recourse to some legal rights, the person designated a "terrorist" has lesser recourse, since he or she is believed to be more of a threat to the health of the nation.

Understanding "risk" in this way can enable us to see how the identifica-tions of "populations at risk" are allied to the idea that racial and gendered (and often sexual) minorities are a danger to themselves and others, and thus have to be subject to forms of state, community, and self-regulation. Whether through education, medicine, or participation in consumer cul-ture and consumer citizenship, these populations are at once racialized and gendered by these technologies but also given the possibility of self-regula-tion to "improve" themselves. While multiculturalism offers the possibility of "improvement" through consumer culture, one that has used specific technologies in countries such as the United States, the United Kingdom, and Canada (in contrast to the ways in which multiculturalism became a national project in postcolonial India), the transnational figure of the "ter-rorist" suggests that it is a figure of such high risk to the nation and state as to be beyond redemption, fit only to be incarcerated immediately or de-stroyed. The flip side of this danger is thus the "security," happiness, and freedom to be felt by those who incarcerate bodies designated as "risk-producing."

Security thus brings together both the possibility of happiness and the freedom made possible through protection from danger through the prac-tices of the individual. Race and gender become modes of knowledge that produce the figures of danger and risk through technologies of surveil-lance, visibility, and, importantly, self-regulation. Just as the Benthamite project of rule meant understanding that "we must mean by liberty, a branch of security," Foucault's project was to understand "liberty as a con-dition for security" so that from the eighteenth century onward, as Colin Gordon puts it, "security tends increasingly to become the dominant com-ponent of modern governmental rationality: we live today not so much . . . in a disciplinary society as in a society of security."[13] In such a society of security, a liberal society, the work of disciplining populations becomes shared by many, although it is not, as Gordon suggests, replaced by another rationality. Why and how this kind of project becomes shared is to be understood, in the context of the United States in these early years of the twenty-first century, through the dissemination of knowledge and informa-tion made possible by a wide array of institutions and authorities—those who see themselves as "Americans" (not necessarily those who endorse some or all state practices) in a variety of ways. Thus if "risk" is a regulatory mechanism that works by identifying racialized and gendered embodi-ments of danger, the identification is undertaken by a wide range of sub-jects and practices, including the state.

Moreover, the counter to these identifications of dangerous bodies as a "risk" to the population becomes evident through recourse to other regu-latory mechanisms that provide protection. Whether these are religious practices of identification or spirituality, the use of "choices" provided by consumer culture, the endorsement of the nation-state as the primary in-stitution of power, or the endorsement of the free individual as sovereign—these are all practices that continue to be available to individuals. Thus if African American males have been incarcerated in ever larger numbers in the United States through the twentieth century because they are seen as presenting a "high risk" for inflicting violence on the population, we have come to see race and gender as the system of classifications that is also a changing, historical mechanism, based on a continued production of knowledge in a variety of fields. In the process, race and gender produce powerful discourses that enable others to share this knowledge of the threat and act on it, and thus to become secure by managing this threat. The Muslim as terrorist and the person who "looks like a Muslim" as a racial figure of the "terrorist" are thus now part of this visual history within consumer culture of managing and disciplining those who are believed to pose the highest risk to the nation.

9/11 AND THE AMERICAN WAY OF LIFE: PRODUCING SECURITY, FEELING SECURE

*

George W. Bush and his cabinet members in the month of September 2001 defined the "American way of life" as a "love of freedom" and belief in safety as a condition of living. Donald Rumsfeld, secretary of defense, in a press conference on 24 September 2001 mentioned that the goal of the "war" against "terrorism" was to ensure the continuation of the American way of life, which meant to him that every American could be "free." He followed up this talk with a short piece on the Op-Ed page of the *New York Times*, in which he stated: "Our victory will come with Americans living their lives day by day, going to work, raising their children and building their dreams as they always have—a free and great people."[14] This freedom, as Rumsfeld further elaborated in a talk on National Public Radio in the week following September 11, meant that people getting on airplanes could reach their destinations and parents sending their children to school would be sure of their safety. Given that the Bush administration supports the widespread use of guns among the population, this rhetorical strategy reso-nated in numerous ways. It was a reminder of violence as a "usual" occur-rence in the United States as well as a technology of power that enabled the "law and order" apparatus of policing and surveillance and incarcerations of adults (mostly nonwhite) and children. But Rumsfeld's words also posed questions regarding what was meant by the term "freedom," given that there was little evidence that what he meant by this term was the separation of civil society from the state, a separation which is the basis of liberalism.

Bush's and Rumsfeld's statements constructed a national identity through discourses of political freedoms and liberties, even as the Bush administration planned to restrict civil liberties in the "war against terror-ism" and even though various U.S. governments historically have partici-pated in restricting the rights and liberties of others across the world. The U.S. nation-state and American nationalism have produced the term "Amer-ican" as a discursive regime in which oppositions like "terrorism vs. se-curity," "good vs. evil," and "civilized vs. barbaric" have captured popular and state discourse. Yet this discursive regime becomes powerful not merely through force or military might, nor simply through the discourse of human rights and welfare, but through cultural formations within which the close relation between consumer culture and citizenship has allowed all kinds of identifications with America, in the United States and also in many other nations and regions. If the phrase "American way of life" became one of the main discourses used by politicians to justify a wide range of actions, from threats of bombing to reductions of civil liberties in the goal of attacking "terrorism" to racial profiling, supported by many liberals and conserva-tives, against "those who look Arab or Muslim," it is because this discursive regime has circulated within a transnational network of consumption linked

to democratic citizenship. As political freedoms are not the agenda of the
Bush administration, freedom has come to include the freedom to consume, since this seems to be the arena in which the liberal idea of "choice"
has become operative in new and powerful ways. It is a consumer nationalism, untethered from but also supported by the boundaries of the nation-
state and linked to nationalisms that provide identities. These identities are,
however, not stable or essential but provisional and thus powerful because
they cannot be avoided, while at the same time less powerful since they are
also contingent and provisional. The centrality of race, class, gender, and
religion to these forms of citizenship suggests that we need to rethink
multiculturalism in relation to governmentality as a process of modern
subject formation, as well as the state practices that use these subjects and
contribute to their formation.

Consequently the "American way of life" is much more than just a
political identity to be defined solely in terms of political freedoms. It encompasses economic, social, and cultural as well as political dimensions.
For Raymond Williams, the phrase "way of life" implied a whole gamut of
experiences of work in the home and outside, leisure activities and participation in public life as well as ideas of morality, beliefs, and emotions.[15]
But even for Williams, the "way of life" becomes too benign a concept when
he uses it as a descriptor for working-class lives in England that are understood simply through class and not through their articulations within European imperialism or through racial identifications.[16] Even so, Williams's
concept can help us to analyze the "American way of life," as referring to a
number of linked aspects that constitute modern subjects. These aspects
create a crucial connection between the "belief in democracy and freedom"
cited by Bush and his administration and all that enables a particular version of this belief to circulate both nationally and transnationally. This
"American way of life" links foreign policy and economic power to the
moral and secular discourses of democracy, rights, and freedoms, and the
patterns of work, leisure, and consumption that insert the individual into
the nation.

In this context, as so many have noted, although the protection of civil
liberties has been only selectively available to certain groups and not to
others, "freedom" as a central aspect of American nationalism has a genealogy within popular culture in the United States. The production of Ameri-

can culture and American subjects was also the work of technology and communication within popular culture through the twentieth century. Historians such as John Bodnar and Warren Sussman argue that in many kinds of displays, popular entertainment, and leisure activities, there was a concerted attempt to produce a national culture.[17] Eric Smoodin reveals that through the second half of the twentieth century, patriotism became attached to spectatorship in all kinds of cultural activities.[18] In all these cultural productions, "freedom" as a specific kind of "choice" was created as a symbol of nationalism. It is this "freedom" that links consumer culture within popular media to struggles for democracy and that has circulated through the world through the efforts of the U.S. nation-state and through the cultural productions that articulated American nationalism.

The "American way of life" is always being constructed and in process. It relies on the link between consumer culture (especially transnational media of various kinds), individual and group experiences, state practices, the economic realm, and the global economy that gives these discourses the power to produce subjects. Put this way, another signifier for the American way of life is the American Dream, a phrase that connotes much more explicitly the close relationship between American national identity and consumer culture, as well as the ways in which American identity as a form of consumer nationalism makes possible this nationalism's protean tendencies, visible in recent years in its ability to disseminate the power of the American Dream to many who have never lived in or visited the United States.

It is because of this transnational investment in America that 9/11 created a variety of responses across the world. While the nationalism of so many, including the Bush administration, was critiqued by those who deplored the recuperation of binary discourses from European colonialism's civilizing project, there also emerged a new transnational solidarity with America in many parts of the world, a solidarity that contributed to the formation of an "American," exceptionalist nationalism that was the dominant discourse after 9/11. Representations of sympathy worldwide were featured prominently in the press. *Le Monde*, the French newspaper, on 13 September claimed that "We are all Americans."[19] The *San Francisco Chronicle* for 14 September used the headline "Global Grief" over photographs of mourning all over the world. It had a large image of a grieving woman in

London who was holding an American flag, and smaller images of cere-

monies of grief in India, Germany, the West Bank, and Russia. The Allianz
Group, a multinational corporation with companies based in Europe and
North America, took out a full-page advertisement in the *New York Times*
stating: "The citizens of the world must never forget this tragedy. Right now
we are all Americans."[20]

While these representations of global mourning appeared on the front
pages of newspapers in the United States and elsewhere, another common
discourse in some parts of the world was that people living in the United
States finally experienced the violence that so many across the world live
with daily. From yet others, for example the commentator in *Le Monde*,
there was a call (however short-lived) for a new international alliance of the
"civilized" against the "barbarism" and "madness" of the "fanatical," and
thus support for America as a democratic and civilized country. There
seemed a new affirmation of America as an "experiment in democracy"
that needed to be supported from many directions. The condolences, sympathy, and support from all parts of the world illustrate that nationalisms
are supported not only by cultural formations within national boundaries
but also by those living outside them, and, in this instance, by those who
believed themselves to be connected to America even if they abhorred the
imperial policies of its government. American nationalism was recon-
structed through the representations of sympathy and support from citizens of other nations.[21] While these were also acts of solidarity with a
particular idea of America, many other nation-states used the new alliance
against "terrorism" as an opportunity to repress insurgent movements and
thus to support nationalist projects of state power in many parts of the
world. In India, for instance, the Muslim as terrorist has become a discursive regime produced by right-wing Hindu groups and the Indian state.
There the figure of the "Islamic terrorist" is an already familiar representation within dominant media, so that 9/11 provided an opportunity for its
further demonization.

For these more specific reasons, but also because the images of 9/11 and
the Twin Towers were instantly flashed across the globe through television
and other media, there were many people across the world who felt a horror
that they would not have felt for others suffering from violence in other
sites and times. The global media were saturated with images from New

York and Washington, and many millions across the globe sat by TV sets waiting for news of the survivors and the suspects. For many in the United States with relatives and friends in other parts of the world, news of the unfolding events that morning came from our own transnational connectivities through long-distance phone calls from those watching the evening news on television. Many more waited with worry and concern to hear that their loved ones in New York were safe, since New York is a primary destination for migrants. Thus America was a sign for much more than a territorially bound nation-state, becoming a nodal point in a networked "world culture" that brought together people from different nations and races in its cities. The sights on TV brought together those cosmopolitans who felt in solidarity against the "barbarisms" of the world with those who watched for news of relatives or with those for whom watching America on TV screens might have become a regular part of daily life.

Within the TV spectacle of the unfolding events, race and gender were mobilized for different audiences across TV channels and programs and corporations. As the victims of the attack on the Twin Towers and the heroes who were produced in the aftermath, individuals were shown to be heterosexual, firemen were sanctified, and the histories of racism within firehouses across the nation were ignored. Photo mug shots of the attackers in the newspapers showed them to be all males, presumably Muslims, represented as fanatical, well trained, dangerous, and thus barbaric. In these representations, the figure of the terrorist was created, though there were many debates as to whether these were disaffected youth or middle-class, educated professionals. What resulted was a racial formation of all Muslim males, whether rich or poor, as terrorists, made barbaric by allegiance to religion and thus as different as possible from the civilized, cosmopolitan Westerner and the secular American nation. Thus within the racial hierarchies of the United States, another racial formation was created that produced a new Other (albeit from an old history); at the same time new "Americans" were constructed through their solidarity with those who died or suffered in the attacks and through their difference from the "terrorists." A cartoon in the San Francisco Chronicle on 9 November illustrates how hierarchies of racially defined "cultures" as they were in earlier eras of western colonization produced an American nation (figure 6).[22] That is, when the Middle Easterner or Muslim becomes a threat, racism against

6. Aaron McGruder, "Boondocks," *San Francisco Chronicle*, 9 November 2001, D19. ©2001 Aaron McGruder. Distributed by Universal Press Syndicate. Reprinted with permission. All rights reserved.

other nonwhites does not occupy "domestic" politics as much as it did before, and other groups can be mobilized to be American in order to produce the non-American, racially identifiable Middle Eastern Muslim male as a new category of visibility. Minoo Moallem has called this a "neo-racist idiom, which has its roots in cultural essentialism and a conventional Eurocentric notion of "people without history."[23]

TECHNOLOGIES OF RACIAL AND GENDERED IN/VISIBILITY

✳

The creation of the Middle Eastern Muslim as a terrorist recuperated in new ways an old category of the Oriental. Within the territorial boundaries of the United States, to look "Muslim" or "Middle Eastern" was not a sign of cosmopolitanism; instead the Muslim or Middle Easterner became American nationalism's new racial Other. Being brown or "looking Middle Eastern" becomes a new racial formation which includes South Asians, Arabs, Iranians, and many others. Not that this racialization is new; it is a recuperation of much older colonial legacies brought back to serve new purposes. The Oriental Other has been an aspect of Euroamerican culture for over two hundred years, but in the United States, the "Oriental" by the middle of the twentieth century was either the East Asian or the Southeast Asian, reflecting the imperial ventures of the United States in the Pacific during the cold war.[24] Europe's "Orientals" have not been the predominant target of racism, although the Islamic Other has certainly had a lively representational history within popular European culture through the last two centuries.[25] However, this orientalism was not a categorization based on language, or blood, or continental origins, but one based on facial characteristics of beards, dark eyes, and turbans, or on discourses of fanaticism and violence, as well as origins in West or South Asia or the Middle East. Within orientalist representations in popular culture, for instance in Walt Disney's *Aladdin*, a mix of tropes from orientalist narratives create a Middle Eastern figure in terms of racial difference that pertains to a hybrid of cultures ranging from Indonesia to India to North Africa to Turkey. This figure was gendered through representations of masculine violence, fanaticism, and barbarism. Histories of racialized representations within popular culture can explain also why the U.S. state began to secretly incarcerate a large number of male migrants and immigrants from countries as diverse as Pakistan, India, Saudi Arabia, Kuwait, Jordan, and Yemen. It can also explain why phrases such as "kill the ragheads" became favorites of many U.S. troops in Iraq, recalling these histories of orientalism as well these new technologies of media visibility.

How did this racial formation become visible within the media and popular culture? One example reveals how the representational practices worked by recuperating older racial technologies of criminalization and visibility. Racial profiling, long under attack in some parts of the United States, became acceptable to many who might earlier have objected to the practice. Along with that, detentions by the state were widespread, and undertaken without any shred of evidence. Sikh men, with turbans and beards, bore a special burden of "looking Muslim" given that Osama bin Laden, who was accused by the United States of masterminding the attacks, also had a turban and beard. A widely circulated media photograph of a Sikh man taken off an Amtrak train for carrying his ceremonial knife was especially problematic, since the photograph did not inform us of his ethnicity or religion (figure 7).[26] The accompanying article merely mentioned, in a striking example of orientalist journalistic practices after 9/11, that the arrested person had "no apparent connection to this week's terrorist attacks." The journalist did not mention that the man was a Sikh or that the knife he carried was a ceremonial one that was an integral part of an orthodox Sikh's attire. The photograph that was printed showed him looking down, not meeting the gaze of the photographer or viewer, in an image that we see quite often when criminals are taken away by the police. Con-

7. "Man on Train Not Linked to Assaults," *West County Times*, 13 September 2001, A16. Photo reprinted with permission of AP/World Wide Photos.

sumers of media—which is all of us—have seen this pose most often when the criminal is an African American, and we have come to learn the language of these images. We know, for instance, that not meeting the gaze of the camera, or looking away from the camera, or even hiding the face from the camera signifies guilt. This image, though its caption stated that the man turned out to be innocent, showed a furtive and guilty man.

Although the Sikh was later released, the widespread circulation of this photograph over news wires that showed him in the stance of a criminal and did not mention who he was might have led, according to many in the Sikh community, to the killing of a Sikh man the following week in Arizona. Similar incidents galvanized Sikhs as well as other non-Christians, including Hindus and Muslims, across the United States to organize against this new racism. While internet messages from Asian-American groups organized to combat hate crimes circulated to encourage people to report violence and created important sites for struggle, worshippers in Sikh temples were told to be careful, not to go out alone anywhere, to carry a cell phone if they could, and to report any incidents against them. Many did follow the cautions, although others felt that it would be impossible to perform their jobs if they had to follow them all.

Another way to struggle against racism was to display the sign of allegiance to the American nation: the flag (figure 8).[27] In such cases, those

8. "Joginder Singh, a Sikh from San Jose," *San Francisco Chronicle*, 18 September 2001, A13. Mark Constantini / San Francisco Chronicle. Reprinted with permission.

who "looked Muslim" had to signal their allegiance to "America" and to being "American" by the same logic of visibility that marked them as racially unAmerican, in order to avoid becoming victims of racist violence. Thus mosques, temples, taxis, dwellings, restaurants, and some ethnic grocery stores had American flags, which also covered so many bodies, white and nonwhite. America had claimed, finally, even the multicultural spaces that many believed would be able to resist nationalist belonging. Sikh temples posted signs that said "God Bless America," assuming that religiosity attached to nationalism might provide protection against this new racism, and that distinctions between Sikhs and Muslims could be clarified. Within a long history of Asians in the United States, where Chinese and Japanese have not been distinguishable and have come to see themselves as united in a struggle against orientalist ideologies, such a distinction has been difficult to sustain within popular media.

This new racism, the effect of the resurgence of American nationalism, also brought with it representations of a shift from a hyphenated to a

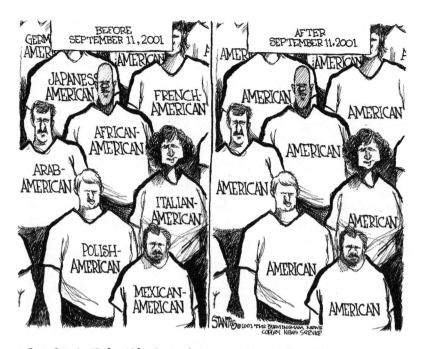

9. Scott Stantis, "Before/After September 11, 2001," *Contra Costa Times*, 22 September 2001, A21. Reprinted with permission of Copley News Service.

singular American identity. Such a shift was visible in the images in newspapers, which represented nonwhite immigrants with the U.S. flag on their bodies. There were reports that African Americans, other Asian-Americans, and many immigrants were also stating that in such moments they were "just Americans." It was reported that the man in Arizona who murdered a Sikh man had a Spanish surname and when he was arrested stated, "I'm a damn American all the way."[28] Thus within popular culture, multiculturalism's work was to show that "we are all Americans" after all; multiculturalism, in a moment of crisis, could call forth American nationalism (figure 9).[29] Although African American and Asian-American groups denounced this racism by linking it to their own histories, the images in the media told us quite a different story of multicultural America as producing united and patriotic Americans.

The fear of the terrorist Other exacerbated the circulation of discourses of security and the regimes of knowledge of the Other that created fear within the public. For these racialized groups who shared visual characteristics of this Other and who came to belong to this group of those who "look" Middle Eastern or Muslim, fear compelled many to display the signs of "Americanness" on their bodies to counter the color of their skins. Thus newspapers reported that so-called Sikh-Americans and Arab-Americans were stating that they too were "American." Such a claim of a shift in identity to American identity was made differently by those who were the targets of racism and the new racial visibility that they had not known before. "Flying while brown" became a problem for many who had thought that such pathologies only were directed at African Americans or at Latinos. Hundreds of incidents of racism by the public, by airlines, by politicians, and the widespread approval of racial and gender profiling suggested the limits of discourses of multicultural America. They also revealed the technologies of power that could be exercised against the Other within the United States though not outside it. The proliferation of the American flag on so many bodies, white and brown and black, testified to this shift. Multicultural America was used as a discourse to counter racism, yet all those multiculturalists were to visibly signify their allegiance to America, much as Japanese-Americans showed their allegiance by fighting in the Second World War and their deaths and their acts of bravery had to connote this allegiance. The flag was represented as signifying the truth of loyalty and national allegiance rather than multiple meanings which could also be used to conceal rather than to reveal. Yet for so many immigrants, the contingent nature of transnational citizenship enabled many to wear the flag both as a protective device and also, for some, as an affirmation of their future in the United States.

There were some attempts to suggest that the flag was a sign of grief rather than of patriotism, and that displaying the flag was one way people could express their sense of solidarity with those who suffered in the hijackings and in New York. However, given that the flag was also circulating as a discourse of militant, white, masculinist, and heterosexual Americanness, such recuperations were often relegated to minority opinions. The new ubiquity of the flag, which appeared on front pages almost every day for almost two weeks since the attack, was striking—since it also appeared on houses, in neighborhoods, and in stores. One of the first images after the events of the day that was widely publicized was that of rescue workers hoisting the flag over the ruins of the World Trade Center. The image clearly

10. Joe Rosenthal, "Raising the Flag at Iwo Jima." Photo reprinted with permission of AP/World Wide Photos.

evoked the photograph by Joe Rosenthal of the American flag being raised
over Iwo Jima toward the end of the Second World War, one of the most
famous photographs in the United States (figure 10). Recalling bravery in a
context of war, the photograph of the rescue workers and the flag was
widely published. Other images that appeared in the *San Francisco Chronicle* showed multicultural America. One set of photographs juxtaposed the
image of a young white man in a militant stance, waving the flag as cars
went by, with that of a young Filipino wearing a shirt with the stars and
stripes on it, holding a baby wearing a similar patterned cap.[30] The juxtaposition of the two images—the militant, shouting young white man and the
subdued Filipino—was striking, in that it suggested the ascendancy of militant, white nationalism and the inability of nonwhites to speak out since the
only discourse possible was that of American nationalism.

Despite such images of brown silence and fear, representations of nonwhites in the media showed either male terrorists (complete with mug
shots) or flag-draped Americans with families. A good example was the
front-page photograph in the *San Francisco Chronicle* for 19 September
2001. Here the flag was draped as a scarf over the head of a young woman,
Marla Kosta, hugging a man during the pregame ceremony of the first
baseball game held after September 11 (figure 11).[31] The woman was clearly
moved by the ceremony and conveys her sorrow in the image. Her legit-

11. "It Was Time to Play Ball Again at PacBell Park," *San Francisco Chronicle*, 19 September 2001, § A, p. 1. Carlos Avila Gonzalez. Reprinted with permission of the San Francisco Chronicle.

imacy as an American is confirmed by her heterosexuality but also by the flag covering her hair. That the photographer's name indicated that he is of Mexican or Latino heritage suggests that it seemed important for the newspaper and the photographer to state that people of all origins were also covering their bodies with the flag.

In the context of the potential for a wider anti-immigrant backlash, given the precarious state of the economy, such visibility seemed prudent. Thus the display of American nationalism signified by the flag occurred within the context of the discourses circulating in the mainstream media, by politicians, and by countless others who did not have to display their special allegiance since they looked visibly "American" simply because they were white. Whites, blacks, East Asians—such groups were at this moment deemed safe from "terrorist" tendencies by default, and thus "Americans" also by default, a surprising phenomenon for those who have been criminalized and incarcerated throughout American history. Yet at this time, in what George Bush, ignoring the many conflicts occurring around the world, called the "first war of the twenty-first century," the enemy was a different Other. For many

persons, the flag did not always signify what they might have wanted it to: the flag, like other objects, has always been open to resignification, though as a national flag it is resignified in more limited ways. Instead of connoting allegiance to America, it reveals both its racism and the vulnerability of nonwhites to it, as well as their desire to survive through negotiating this racism. Thus much as hegemonic representational practices tried to connect the flag to patriotism to America among all races, white nationalism effectively prevented the stabilization of such a meaning.

The discourse of grief from New York also suggested that it was mostly families, individual and corporate, heterosexual and white, who had been torn apart by the bombings. It was only later that some media attention was given to the many other workers, naturalized citizens, undocumented workers, and visitors, who were not white and had also perished. Buried in the newspaper reports of the hijackings was the story of one man who was gay and who had left behind "friends" in San Francisco (never termed family, community, lover, boyfriend, or any other term that would have indicated his sexual identity). The media did not show images of these friends; rather we only saw his grieving mother. Images of mobilized troops also showed the heterosexual family once again being torn apart by these events. The front pages for 20 September of two newspapers in the Bay Area, the *West County Times*[32] and the *San Francisco Chronicle*,[33] had identical images, both taken from the Associated Press, one of a black family and the other of a white family, holding babies and saying goodbye. Once again, the heterosexual American family, white and multicultural, was shown to be suffering and torn apart because of an attack by the "Middle Eastern" Other.

CONSUMER CITIZENSHIP AND THE NATION

✳

Even as the media were representing white and nonwhite bodies covered with the American flag, the flag also emerged within consumer culture. It was visible not only in TV commercials but in print media and the internet. Tourist destinations, sports associations, department stores, small retail outlets—all had the flag in their advertisements. The Bush administration said that it was patriotic to shop, to lift up the economy even though with thousands of layoffs, consumer confidence was quite low. Saks Fifth Avenue advertised in the *New York Times* with an image of the flag and a quote from Franklin Delano Roosevelt: "There are those, I know, who will reply that the liberation of humanity, the freedom of man and mind is nothing but a dream. They are right. It is the American Dream."[34] Here was explicit the link between the warlike stance of the United States, recalling the Second World War, the flag, and the American dream as the guarantee of the freedom to consume. It was striking that the ad contained no images of goods sold in the store (although a week later, the flag had disappeared from this regular advertising spot, to be replaced by fashion shots). Similarly the department store Lord & Taylor took out a full-page ad in the *Times* that featured the flag and the statement: "In unity we stand as Americans. Together, we shall overcome and ultimately triumph over the tragedy our nation has endured."[35] Orchard Supply Hardware had a full-page ad in the *West County Times*, stating "United We Stand," with the flag covering half the page and the name of the company in very small letters in the bottom right-hand corner. Other retailers used the flag to show that they were American as well. Cost Plus World Market, selling goods made cheaply across the world, had a flag with "Americans Unite" on 20 September in the *San Francisco Chronicle*, and ran this ad several times.[36]

The blow to the U.S. economy and the many thousands of layoffs suggested that most people did not have the confidence to go out and spend money. While flag sales and gun sales were up, sale of other goods went down (though we are told that sales of American-brand cars went up). The American dream, for all the rhetoric of the politicians, was in danger in the first few weeks after September 11, though it had already begun to falter even before with the deepening recession. Feeling American did not mean that everyone had confidence in the American dream. Consumer culture's role in producing "American" democracy and national identity was highlighted in the Bush administration's statements urging the public to "go shopping" and return to "life as usual" even in the face of an economic recession and large layoffs.

Bush's exhortations to go shopping to lift up the economy and have faith in the United States resonated in complex ways. First of all, the emergence of the flag as an advertising strategy enabled this symbol to be circulated much more widely as advertising in addition to "news." Given that the

connections between civil society and corporate and state institutions have
led to an American form of democracy in which consumer culture makes
possible all kinds of identities including national identities, it follows that
shopping would become a civic duty. After all, how else would the American way of life and the American dream be imagined as nationalism and
embracing diversity if not through consumer culture? Stores in downtown
San Francisco circulated shopping bags with the words: "America Open for
Shopping." To be American was thus to go shopping as usual.

*

If we are to rethink consumer citizenship and multiculturalism through
dynamic and changing racial and gendered formations, we cannot assume
that civil society and the state can be seen as separate from each other. Many
of our notions of struggle within democracy are understood through the
concept of a civil society separate from the state. But what are we to make of
a society that is pervaded by consumer culture's images, narratives, spectacles, technologies? How are liberal versions of individuality and group
identity made possible through the visual and written technologies through
which discourses of lifestyles, communities, selves circulate? And how is
the necrophilic state underwritten by the freedom-granting biopolitical capabilities of the liberal state and the imaginaries of emerging and continuing nationalisms? What work does culture do in these new formations of
racial and gendered power? Perhaps once again, we need to question the
separation between civil society and the state, or between the state and
multinational corporations, arguing for the way in which nationalisms produce identifications that reveal continuities between these two supposedly
disparate realms. Thus I have examined the interarticulations between the
democratic politics of a liberal civil society and new social movements and
consumer culture, not only to think through how the political is made
possible by the market but also how consumer culture has a hand in producing political subjects and identities. While classical liberal political theory has understood social rights as opposed to market relations,[37] by the late
twentieth century and the early twenty-first consumer culture had become
central to liberalism and neoliberalism, promoting endlessly the idea of
choice as central to a liberated subject and enabling the hegemony of both
capitalist democracy, American style, and the self-actualizing and identity-

producing possibilities of consumption, American style. Consequently, if there are some who, we are told, "hate America and all it stands for," then we also know there are many who cannot afford to hate America, and many in the United States and outside who come to mourn its perpetration of violence and feel a solidarity with it that they would not feel for most other countries around the world.

notes

✶

INTRODUCTION: NEOLIBERAL CITIZENSHIP: THE
GOVERNMENTALITY OF RIGHTS AND CONSUMER CULTURE

1   Cordula Tutt, "Can There Be a German Dream?" *San Jose Mercury News*, 20 August 2001.

2   I use the terms "America" and "American" to refer to the U.S. nation and its imagined community. I do realize that the term is problematic in relation to its erasure of other countries of North America and the continent of South America, but I use it as a term that best describes the kind of nationalism that I am discussing. When I refer to the state, I use the term "United States."

3   The relation between technological prowess and masculinity in East Asia and South Asia is important to examine—why, for instance, do most "tech workers" come from these countries? Just as the discourse of "Asian femininity" creates the woman worker as the ideal submissive worker on the global assembly line, this masculine formation has become similarly normalized. Though it is not the main concern of this chapter, it is certainly something that bears greater study.

4   My thanks to Sukhminder Grewal for information about this term.

5   Bob Fernandez, "A Profitable Business: Tech-Worker Imports," *Philadelphia Inquirer*, 25 February 2001, 1.

6   Castells, *The Rise of Network Society*; Castells, *The Power of Identity*.

7   Marchand, *Advertising and the American Dream*.

8   Halter, *Shopping for Identity*; Hennessy, *Pleasure and Profit*.

9   Kaplan and Pease, eds., *Cultures of United States Imperialism*; Berlant, *The Queen of America Goes to Washington City*.

10 Slater and Taylor, eds., *The American Century*.

11 Lisa Lowe, *Immigrant Acts*.

12 Marshall, "Citizenship and Social Class"; Rawls, *A Theory of Justice*, 221.

13 There is a vast literature on these topics for which I will only give some main texts. For feminist debates within second-wave European and U.S. feminism, see Carole Pateman, *The Sexual Contract* (Cambridge: Polity, 1988); Seyla Benhabib,

Democracy and Difference: Contesting the Boundaries of the Political (Princeton: Princeton University Press, 1996); Phillips, *Democracy and Difference*; Iris Marion Young, *Justice and the Politics of Difference* (Princeton: Princeton University Press, 1990); Chantal Mouffe, ed., *Dimensions of Radical Democracy: Pluralism, Citizenship, Community* (London: Verso, 1992). For debates on multiculturalism, ethnicity, and citizenship, see Kymlicka, *Multicultural Citizenship*; T. K. Oomen, *Citizenship, Nationality, Ethnicity* (London: Basil Blackwell, 1997); essays in Hall and DuGay, eds., *Questions of Cultural Identity*.

14 See the discussion of feminist responses to universalist theories in Phillips, *Democracy and Difference*, 54–74.

15 Barbalet, *Citizenship*.

16 Mouffe, "Democratic Politics and the Question of Identity," 33.

17 Isin and Wood, *Citizenship and Identity*.

18 Ibid., 154.

19 Ibid., 156, 160.

20 Kymlicka, *Multicultural Citizenship*, 124.

21 Laguerre, *Diasporic Citizenship*, 8–13.

22 Ong, "On the Edge of Empires."

23 Isin and Wood, *Citizenship and Identity*, 19.

24 Ibid., 13.

25 Ibid.

26 Berman, *All That Is Solid Melts into Air*.

27 Hall and DuGay, eds., *Questions of Cultural Identity*, 6.

28 This phrase has been theorized a great deal as a result of its use by Gayatri Spivak. See Gayatri Chakravorty Spivak, Lola Chatterjee, and Rajeshwari Sunder Rajan, "The Post-Colonial Critic," in Spivak's *The Post-Colonial Critic: Interviews, Strategies, Dialogues*, ed. Sarah Harasym (New York: Routledge, 1990), 109; for one example of its use see Emma Perez, "Irigaray's Female Symbolic in the Making of Chicana Lesbian Sitios y Lenguas," *Living Chicana Theory*, ed. Carla Trujillo (Berkeley: Third Woman, 1998), 87–101.

29 Ricardo Alonso-Zaldivar, "Refugees on Hold and at Risk," *Los Angeles Times* (Orange County Edition), 7 July 2003, § A, pp. 1, 10.

30 http://www.dhs.gov/dhspublic/display?theme=9 (visited 5 March 2004).

31 http://www.dhs.gov/dhspublic/display?theme=13 (visited 5 March 2004).

32 http://www.dhs.gov/dhspublic/display?theme=9&content=1075 (visited 5 March 2004).

33 Neil Smith, *American Empire*, xv.

34 Stuart Hall, "The Toad in the Garden."

35 Rose, "Government, Authority and Expertise in Advanced Liberalism."

36 Foucault, "The Birth of Biopolitics."

37 Grewal and Kaplan, "Introduction: Transnational Feminist Practices and Questions of Postmodernity."

38 Dillon, "The Security of Governance."

39 Mill, *The History of British India*.

40 For more on this, see Caren Kaplan's work in progress. Also delivered as a lecture at the University of Arizona, March 2004.

41 Michel Foucault, "Governmentality," *The Foucault Effect: Studies in Governmentality,* ed. Burchell, Gordon, and Miller, 87–104.

42 Larner, "Neo-Liberalism."

43 See Arjun Appadurai, "Deep Democracy: Urban Governmentality and the Horizon of Politics," *Environment & Urbanization* 13, no 2 (October 2001).

44 Stoler, *Race and the Education of Desire.*

45 Mbembe, "Necropolitics."

46 Neil Smith, *American Empire.*

47 Hardt and Negri, *Empire,* xv.

48 Ibid., Preface.

49 Gopal Balakrishnan, "Hardt and Negri's *Empire,*" *New Left Review,* September–October 2000.

50 For more on this critique of *Empire* see Maurer, "On Divine Markets and the Problem of Justice."

51 Hannerz, *Transnational Connections,* 6.

52 Castells, *The Rise of Network Society.*

53 See for instance the website on African connectivity: http://66.102.7.104/ search?q=cache:00FMnj4c9uYJ:www3.wn.apc.org/africa/+conne ctivity&hl=en&ie=UTF-8 (visited 16 March 2004).

54 http://www.satn.org/about/separateconnectivity.htm (visited 16 March 2004).

55 Mosco, "Webs of Myth and Power," 37–60.

56 Shields, "Hypertext Links."

57 Mbembe, "Necropolitics."

58 Rose, *Powers of Freedom.*

59 It is because of the incredible variety of these assemblages that we cannot presume the creation of a "multitude" single-mindedly "capable of autonomously constructing a counter-Empire," as Hardt and Negri state in their preface. This cosmopolitan multitude seems uncannily like an internationalism that is not a new idea; "global citizenship" is an idea that has been around for a long time and is the product of the very histories of imperialism that *Empire* argues have become redundant. Instead, this book argues that "global citizenship" has emerged in a neoliberal version in which the old inequalities of European and North American imperialism can be recuperated.

60 Gibson-Graham, *The End of Capitalism.* Critiques of mainstream liberal feminism in the 1990s included works based on race and sexuality and the works of postcolonialist and post-Marxist thinkers. Scholarly works that became influential were Mohanty, Russo, and Torres, eds., *Third World Women and the Politics of Feminism;* Spivak, *Outside in the Teaching Machine;* Judith P. Butler, *Gender Trouble: Feminism and the Subversion of Identity* (New York: Routledge, 1999); Grewal and Kaplan, "Introduction: Transnational Feminist Practices and Questions of Postmodernity"; Mouffe, "Democratic Politics and the Question of Identity"; Mouffe, "Democratic Citizenship and the Political Community"; and the work of Jacqui Alexander and Chandra Mohanty, as well as poststructuralist feminists such as Caren Kaplan.

61 Finnegan, *Selling Suffrage,* 12.

62 Ibid., 27.

63 Ensted, *Ladies of Labor, Girls of Adventure*, 6.

64 Ruiz, " 'Star Struck.' "

65 Waters, *Globalization*, 140.

66 Ewen, *Captains of Consciousness*, 42.

67 Appadurai, *Modernity at Large*, 81–83.

68 Marchand, *Advertising and the American Dream*, xxii.

69 Berlant, *The Queen of America Goes to Washington City*, 14.

70 Ritzer, *The McDonaldization of Society*, 1–13.

71 Waters, *Globalization*, 145.

72 Scanlon, *Inarticulate Longings*, 4–9.

73 Barns, "Technology and Citizenship."

74 Castells, *The Rise of Network Society*, 364; Lash and Urry, *Economies of Signs and Space*, 220–22.

75 This is a growing literature and I will cite only a few texts out of many: Appadurai, *Modernity at Large*; Miller, ed., *Material Cultures*; Ang, *Watching Dallas*; Tarlo, *Clothing Matters*; Cohen, Wilk, and Stoeltje, eds., *Beauty Queens on the Global Stage*; Sinclair, Jacka, and Cunningham, eds., *New Patterns in Global Television*; Hendrickson, ed., *Clothing and Difference*; Burke, *Lifebuoy Men, Lux Women*; Goodwin, Ackerman, and Kiron, *The Consumer Society*; Miller, ed., *Worlds Apart*.

76 Grewal and Kaplan, "Transnational Practices and Interdisciplinary Feminist Scholarship: Refiguring Women and Gender Studies."

CHAPTER 1: BECOMING AMERICAN:
THE NOVEL AND THE DIASPORA

1 "Migration of Natives and the Foreign Born: 1995–2000," Census 2000 Special Reports, August 2003.

2 Said, "Reflections on Exile."

3 Pollock, "Cosmopolitanisms," 578, 582.

4 Appadurai, *Modernity at Large*.

5 Mankekar, "Brides Who Travel," 755–61.

6 Caren Kaplan, *Questions of Travel*.

7 Caren Kaplan, "A World without Boundaries."

8 Ibid.

9 Lisa Lowe, *Immigrant Acts*.

10 Pollock, "Cosmopolitanisms."

11 Ibid.; Cheah and Robbins, eds., *Cosmopolitics*.

12 Caren Kaplan, *Questions of Travel*.

13 Brennan, *At Home in the World*, 36–44.

14 Mukherjee, "American Dreamer."

15 Amitav Ghosh, *In an Antique Land*.

16 Mukherjee, *Jasmine*.

17 Divakaruni, *The Mistress of Spices*.

18 Visweswaran, "Diaspora by Design."

19 Macaulay, "Minute on Education of India."

20 Chatterjee, *The Nation and Its Fragments*, 35–75.

21 Rushdie, *Midnight's Children*.

22 Chakrabarty, *Provincializing Europe*; Chatterjee, *The Nation and Its Fragments*, 117–236.

23 Dharwadkar, "Print Culture and Literary Markets in Colonial India."

24 Ibid.

25 Helwig, *An Immigrant Success Story*, 4–5.

26 James Clifford, "Traveling Cultures," *Cultural Studies*, ed. Lawrence Grossberg, Cary Nelson, and Paula Triechler (New York: Routledge, 1992), 96–112.

27 Stevenson, "Globalization, National Cultures and Cultural Citizenship."

28 Brennan, *At Home in the World*.

29 Barbieri, *Ethics of Citizenship*, 105–9.

30 Caren Kaplan, *Questions of Travel*.

31 Fabian, *Time and the Other*.

32 Robbins, "Introduction Part I," 3.

33 Clifford, "Traveling Cultures."

34 Cheah, "Introduction Part II," 20–41.

35 Ibid.

36 Caren Kaplan, *Questions of Travel*.

37 Hardt and Negri, *Empire*.

38 Amitav Ghosh, "The March of the Novel through History: The Testimony of My Grandfather's Bookcase," *The Imam and the Indian: Prose Pieces* (Delhi: Ravi Dayal, 2002), 287–304.

39 Ibid.

40 Quote cited in Moretti, "Conjectures on World Literature."

41 Dharwadkar, "The Internationalization of Literature."

42 Prendergast, "Negotiating World Literature."

43 Amitav Ghosh, *The Shadow Lines*; Amitav Ghosh, *The Glass Palace*.

44 Stuart Hall, "The Local and the Global"; Stuart Hall, "Cultural Identity and Diaspora"; Said, "Reflections on Exile"; Said, *Reflections on Exile and Other Essays* (Cambridge: Harvard University Press, 2000).

45 Stuart Hall, "Cultural Identity and Diaspora," 51–58.

46 Lisa Lowe, *Immigrant Acts*, 60–83.

47 Gilroy, "Diaspora and the Detours of Identity."

48 Safran, "Diasporas in Modern Societies."

49 Lisa Lowe, *Immigrant Acts*, 60–83.

50 Gilroy, *The Black Atlantic*.

51 My use of "worlding" comes from Gayatri Spivak's important essay, where she discusses the "worlding" of the "third world woman" within British literature: Spivak, "Three Women's Texts and a Critique of Imperialism."

52 Rée, "Internationality."

53 Vinay Lal, "Review-Article on Amitav Ghosh, *In an Antique Land*," http://www .sscnet.ucla.edu/southasia/History/British/Amitav_Ghosh.html.

54 Hardt and Negri, *Empire*.

55 Biddick, "Translating the Foreskin."

56 Goitein, *A Mediterranean Society.*

57 Lal, "Review-Article on Amitav Ghosh, *In an Antique Land.*"

58 Spivak, "Three Women's Texts and a Critique of Imperialism."

59 Jayawardena, *Feminism and Nationalism in the Third World.*

60 Inderpal Grewal, *Home and Harem.*

61 Grewal and Kaplan, "Warrior Marks."

62 Inderpal Grewal, *Home and Harem.*

63 Lisa Lowe, *Immigrant Acts.*

64 Rosaldo, "Cultural Citizenship and Educational Democracy."

65 Whereas the "canon" of Asian-American studies focused heavily on events such as the Chinese Exclusion Act of 1882, the construction of the "Asiatic Barred Zone" within the Immigration Acts of 1917 and 1924, and the internment and incarceration of entire Japanese communities during the Second World War, new migrations have changed this heavily East Asian focus. In recent years, there has been more of an interest in other immigrant groups from Southeast Asia. For the most part, however, in the United States, Asia is defined in very limited terms, with south, west, and central Asia virtually absent and many communities of southeast Asia similarly ignored.

66 Leonard, *Making Ethnic Choices.*

67 United States v. Bhagat Singh Thind, 261 U.S. 204 (1923).

68 Rachel C. Lee, *The Americas of Asian American Literature.*

69 Takaki, *Strangers from a Different Shore.*

70 Mukerji, *Caste and Outcast.*

71 Mukherjee's first novel published in the United States was *The Tiger's Daughter* (1972), followed by *Wife* (1975).

72 Asian Women United of California, *Making Waves.*

73 Also visible in Mira Nair's films, such as *Mississippi Masala* or even *Kama Sutra.*

74 Bulosan, *America Is in the Heart.*

75 Caren Kaplan, *Questions of Travel.*

76 Espin, *Women Crossing Boundaries.*

77 Tan, *The Joy Luck Club.*

78 Jen, *Typical American.*

79 See for instance essays in *positions: east asia cultures critique* 7, no. 3 (winter 1999) (special issue on Asian Transnationalities).

80 Kingston, *The Woman Warrior.*

81 Mukherjee, *Jasmine.*

82 Brewster, "A Critique of Bharati Mukherjee's Neo-Nationalism."

83 http://www.motherjones.com/commentary/columns/1997/01/mukherjee .html (visited 28 March 2004).

84 Gurleen Grewal, "Born Again American."

85 Mukherjee, "American Dreamer."

86 "An Interview with Bharati Mukherjee," *Mosaic* (spring 1994).

87 Mukherjee, "American Dreamer."

88 Carey, "Breaking the Rules," 1.

89 Mukherjee, "American Dreamer."

90 Carey, "Breaking the Rules."

91 Mukherjee, "American Dreamer."

92 Ibid.

93 Ibid.

94 Mukherjee, *Jasmine*.

95 Mukherjee, *The Middleman and Other Stories*.

96 On the Amazon.com website, by the week of 20 August 2002 she had twenty-eight reviews from the general public, far more than for any other of her works. Her latest book, *Desirable Daughters*, ranks 3,338 in sales, a very high number for a nonwhite author. Although Amazon's ranks do not tell us about worldwide or U.S. sales, the comparison with her other works can tell us something about the popularity of *Jasmine*.

97 http://www.amazon.com/exec/obidos/tg/stores/detail/-/books/0802136303/customer-reviews/1 . . . (visited 20 August 2002).

98 Ibid.

99 Brewster, "A Critique of Bharati Mukherjee's Neo-Nationalism."

100 Nityanandam, "Yasmine Gooneratne's 'A Change of Skies' and Bharati Mukherjee's *Jasmine*: The Immigrant Experience in Australia and the USA."

101 Bose, "A Question of Identity."

102 Bharvani, "*Jasmine*: An Immigrant Experience?"

103 Roy, "The Aesthetics of an (Un)willing Immigrant."

104 Knippling, "Toward an Investigation of the Subaltern in Bharati Mukherjee's *The Middleman and Other Stories* and *Jasmine*," 143–60.

105 Gurleen Grewal, "Born Again American," 181–96.

106 Alexander, *Faultlines*.

107 Divakaruni, *The Mistress of Spices*.

108 For more on the construction of authenticity and tradition in Indian cuisine within the diaspora in the West, see Parama Roy's unpublished essay, "Reading Communities and Culinary Communities: The Gastropoetics of the South Asian Diaspora."

109 At least one other story of spices emerged on a bestseller list: Giles Milton, *Nathaniel's Nutmeg, or, The True and Incredible Adventures of the Spice Trader Who Changed the Course of History* (New York: Farrar, Straus and Giroux, 1999). Written in the genre of the tale of adventure and travel, so that it ignores the lives and histories of any non-Europeans, the book can be read against its intent to reveal the violence of the trade in spices in seventeenth-century Europe.

110 Chitra Bannerjee Divakaruni, *Arranged Marriage* (New York: Anchor, 1996).

111 Ong, *Flexible Citizenship*.

CHAPTER 2: TRAVELING BARBIE: INDIAN TRANSNATIONALITIES
AND THE GLOBAL CONSUMER

1 See for instance the discussion in Hardt and Negri, *Empire*.

2 This is the term used for the white Barbie in the Mattel Corporation annual report, 1991.

3 Chakravarty, "Labour Market under Trade Liberalization in India."

4 Dev, "Economic Liberalization and Employment in South Asia."

5 Mattelart, *Advertising International.*

6 Marchand, *Advertising and the American Dream.*

7 See for instance Mark Rufino, John Caputo, and Robin Wynyard, eds., *McDonaldization Revisited: Critical Essays on Consumer Culture* (Westport, Conn.: Praeger, 1998); Perry Johansson, *Chinese Women and Consumer Culture* (Stockholm: Stockholm Universitet, 1998); David Howes, *Cross-cultural Consumption: Global Markets, Local Realities* (London: Routledge, 1996); Miller, ed., *Modernity.*

8 Fukuyama, *The End of History and the Last Man.*

9 Ohmae, *The Borderless World.*

10 Robert D. Kaplan, *The Ends of the Earth.*

11 Warde, "Consumers, Identity and Belonging."

12 Appadurai, *Modernity at Large.*

13 See for instance Rand, *Barbie's Queer Accessories*; and Ducille, "Dyes and Dolls."

14 Kang, *Compositional Subjects.*

15 Appadurai, *Modernity at Large.*

16 Oza, "Showcasing India."

17 Panini, "Trends in Cultural Globalization."

18 See the chapter "Fashion Fables of an Urban Village," in Tarlo, *Clothing Matters.*

19 Arvind Rajagopal, "Hindu Nationalism in the U.S.: Changing Configurations of Political Practice," *Ethnic and Racial Studies* 23, no. 3 (May 2000): 68–96.

20 "Removing the Hurdles," *India Today*, 15 August 1995.

21 Here I do not want to claim that multinationals have been uniformly welcomed or that they have had easy access to Indian markets. The example of Enron in India is a fascinating narrative of the political and economic issues of state policies at the level of the central and state government, corporate strategies and mistakes, and the ways in which policies and practices often conflict at many different levels of government. See Antoinette D'Sa, K. V. Narasimha Murthy, and K. N. Reddy, "India's Power Sector Liberalization: An Overview," *Economic and Political Weekly* 34, no. 23 (2 June 1999): 1427–34.

22 Gilroy, *"There Ain't No Black in the Union Jack."*

23 Stuart Hall, "The Spectacle of the 'Other.' "

24 Mankekar, "Brides Who Travel."

25 Rouse, "Mexican Migration and the Social Space of Postmodernism."

26 A parallel issue of the role of cultural studies and the intersection of diaspora studies, feminist studies, and area studies in a transnational perspective is raised by my choice of topic: Barbie.

27 Gordon and Newfield, eds., *Mapping Multiculturalism.*

28 *Business World*, 1–14 November 1995.

29 Ibid.

30 I am defining the "quality" of the product through the responses of children who told me, for instance, that Barbie's hair could be played with much more readily than the hair of other dolls. Of course, Mattel uses such characteristics to suggest ways in which its product is superior.

31 Sklair, *Sociology of the Global System.*

32 Ewen, *Captains of Consciousness.*

33 Dreifus, *Radical Lifestyles.*

34 de Mooij, *Global Marketing and Advertising.*

35 Donald Lowe, *The Body in Late-Capitalist USA.*

36 Bocock, *Consumption.*

37 Leiss, Kline, and Jhally, *Social Communication in Advertising.*

38 Donald Lowe, *The Body in Late-Capitalist USA,* 62.

39 Ibid., 62–64.

40 *Asian Wall Street Journal,* 6 October 1985.

41 *Asian Wall Street Journal,* 1 January 1988.

42 *Los Angeles Times,* 22 September 1996.

43 Lee, *Gender and the South China Miracle*; Wolf, *Factory Daughters*; Aihwa Ong, *Spirits of Resistance and Capitalist Disciplining in Malaysia* (Albany: State University of New York Press, 1987).

44 Mattel Corporation annual report, 1989.

45 See Eric Smoodin's *Disney Discourse* and *Animating Culture* (New Brunswick: Rutgers University Press, 1993) for the connections between U.S. nationalism, imperialism, and the cold war.

46 Mattel Corporation annual report, 1992.

47 Mattel Corporation annual report, 1990.

48 Mattel Corporation annual report, 1991.

49 Mohanty, "Under Western Eyes."

50 See Rand for more on this topic.

51 Appadurai, *Modernity at Large,* 54–55.

52 Hannerz, *Cultural Complexity.*

53 Berlant, *The Queen of America Goes to Washington City,* 158.

54 Rand, *Barbie's Queer Accessories,* 28–29.

55 My thanks to Eric Smoodin and Caren Kaplan for pointing out this important connection. For more on this see Bryman, *Disney and His Worlds.*

56 Rand, *Barbie's Queer Accessories,* 28–29.

57 Ibid., 87.

58 See for instance Ebersole and Peabody, eds., *Mondo Barbie.*

59 Schein, "The Consumption of Color and the Politics of White Skin in Post-Mao China."

60 Ong, *Spirits of Resistance and Capitalist Disciplining in Malaysia*; Freeman, *High Tech and High Heels in the Global Economy.*

61 Schein, "The Consumption of Color and the Politics of White Skin in Post-Mao China."

62 Ducille, "Dyes and Dolls."

63 Urla and Swedlund, "The Anthropometry of Barbie."

64 Ducille, "Dyes and Dolls," 52.

65 Ducille, "Dyes and Dolls."

66 Mattel Corporation annual report, 1986.

67 Cohen, Wilk, and Stoeltje, eds., *Beauty Queens on the Global Stage.*

68 Arvind Rajagopal, "Advertising, Politics, and the Sentimental Education of the Indian Consumer," *Visual Anthropology Review* 14, no. 2 (1998–99): 14–31.

69 *Business World*, 16 September–1 October 1996, 74–76.

70 *Business World*, 11–24 March 1996, 131–32.

71 Conversation with Bharat Ponga, a former toy manufacturer, Ludhiana, January 1997.

72 I am making this point in defiance of all those with whom I spoke in India, industry experts and parents, who assured me that there was gender parity in how income was spent on boys and girls. Much feminist research indicates otherwise.

73 "A Lot of Gloss and Gumption," *Business World*, 27 November–10 December 1996.

74 "A Lot of Gloss and Gumption," *Business World*, 25 December–7 January 1997, 128–29.

75 *Business World*, 27 November–10 December 1996, 130–37.

76 "The Indian Vanity Fair," *Business World*, 27 November–10 December 1996.

77 It is worthy of note that the Miss World contest, sponsored by the Indian consumer good manufacturer Godrej, and the movie star Amitabh Bachchan's new corporation, ABCL, used an image from the Ajanta caves in its publicity campaign.

78 Mankekar, "Brides Who Travel."

79 Khan, "Asian Women's Dress."

80 Ibid.

81 Schein, "The Consumption of Color and the Politics of White Skin in Post-Mao China," 141–64.

82 Caren Kaplan, "A World without Boundaries."

83 Quotes from the advertisement and other information from *India Today*, 15 October 1994, North American special section.

84 See for instance Nilita Vachani's terrific film about migrant domestic workers, *When Mother Comes Home for Christmas* (Film Sixteen Production for ZDF and the Greek Film Centre, Germany/Greece, 1996).

85 Stuart Hall, "The Local and the Global."

86 Ewen, *All Consuming Images*, 271.

87 Halter, *Shopping for Identity*.

88 Bauman, *Legislators and Interpreters*.

89 Giddens, *Modernity and Self-Identity*.

90 Featherstone, *Consumer Culture and Postmodernism*.

91 Warde, "Consumers, Identity and Belonging," 58–74.

92 Alan Tomlinson, Introduction, *Consumption, Identity and Style*.

CHAPTER 3: "WOMEN'S RIGHTS AS HUMAN RIGHTS":
THE TRANSNATIONAL PRODUCTION OF GLOBAL FEMINIST SUBJECTS

1 Kiss, "Is Nationalism Compatible with Human Rights?"

2 Rajni Kothari, "Globalization and 'New World Order.'"

3 Gayatri Chakravorty Spivak, "Righting Wrongs," *Human Rights, Human Wrongs: The Oxford Amnesty Lectures 2001*, ed. Nicholas Owen (Oxford: Oxford University Press, 2002), 164–227.

4 See for instance Pannikar, "Is the Notion of Human Rights a Western Concept?" 201–9.

5 *Our Global Neighborhood: The Report of the Commission on Global Governance* (New York: Oxford University Press, 1995).

6 Burgerman, "Mobilizing Principles."

7 Rittich, "Feminism after the State."

8 See the documents collected in Marin and Lansang–De Mesa, eds., *Women on the Move.*

9 Rose, *Powers of Freedom.*

10 James, "Challenging Patriarchal Privilege though the Development of International Human Rights."

11 Ibid.

12 Steiner and Alston, eds., *International Human Rights in Context,* 691.

13 See for instance the works by Charlotte Bunch: "Transforming Human Rights from a Feminist Perspective"; "Women's Rights as Human Rights"; Charlotte Bunch and Niamh Reilly, *Demanding Accountability*; Charlotte Bunch and Susanna Fried, "Beijing '95." Also see Agosín, Introduction, *Women, Gender, and Human Rights,* 1–11; Cook, "Women's International Human Rights Law"; Keck and Sikkink, *Activists beyond Borders.*

14 Bunch, "Transforming Human Rights from a Feminist Perspective," 11–17.

15 Elizabeth Friedman, "Women's Human Rights."

16 Ibid.

17 Iyer, Introduction, *The Struggle to Be Human.*

18 Ibid.

19 James, "Challenging Patriarchal Privilege though the Development of International Human Rights," 563–78.

20 Ilumoka, "African Women's Economic, Social and Cultural Rights."

21 John, "Gender and Development in India, 1970s–1990s."

22 Coomaraswamy, "To Bellow Like a Cow."

23 Kirti Singh, "Obstacles to Women's Rights in India."

24 Agosín, Introduction, *Women, Gender, and Human Rights,* 1.

25 Ibid., 1–11.

26 Sen and Grown, eds., *Development, Crises, and Alternative Visions.*

27 Momsen, *Women and Development in the Third World.*

28 Gupta, *Postcolonial Developments.*

29 Escobar, "Power and Visibility."

30 Michel Foucault, *Résumé des cours, 1970–1982,* Paris 1989, 113, cited in Burchell, "Peculiar Interests."

31 Alston, *Development and the Rule of Law.*

32 Ibid., 63.

33 Ibid., 64.

34 UNESCO Doc ss.78 Conf. 630/12 6 1978.

35 Alston, *Development and the Rule of Law,* 118–19.

36 Ibid., 119.

37 Chandler, "The Road to Military Humanitarianism."

38 Charlesworth, Chinkin, and Wright, "Feminist Approaches to International Law."

39 Jan Goodwin, "Afghan Women Are Free of the Taliban."

40 Bell, Nathan, and Peleg, eds., *Negotiating Cultures and Human Rights*.

41 Cheah, "Introduction Part II."

42 Edward Friedman, "Asia as a Fount of Universal Human Rights."

43 Koshy, "From Cold War to Trade War."

44 Rajni Kothari, "Human Rights"; Kothari and Sethi, "On Categories and Interventions."

45 Rajni Kothari, "Human Rights."

46 Howard, "Dignity, Community, and Human Rights."

47 Kothari and Sethi, "On Categories and Interventions."

48 Anaya, *Indigenous Peoples in International Law*.

49 Merry, "Women, Violence and the Human Rights System."

50 Howard, "Dignity, Community, and Human Rights."

51 Patricia J. Williams, *The Alchemy of Race and Rights*.

52 Rajan, "Multiculturalism, Group Rights and Identity Politics."

53 Norma Alarcón, "The Theoretical Subject(s) of *This Bridge Called My Back* and Anglo-American Feminism," *Making Face, Making Soul: Haciendo Caras*, ed. Gloria Anzaldúa (San Francisco: Aunt Lute Foundation, 1990), 356–69.

54 Agosín, Introduction, *Women, Gender and Human Rights*, 1–11.

55 Ilumoka, "African Women's Economic, Social and Cultural Rights."

56 Nivedita Menon, "State/Gender/Community."

57 Koshy, "The Fiction of Asian American Studies."

58 Charlesworth, "What Are 'Women's International Human Rights'?"

59 Keck and Sikkink, Preface, *Activists beyond Borders*.

60 Merry, "Women, Violence, and the Human Rights System."

61 Geske and Bourque, "Grassroots Organizations and Women's Human Rights."

62 Basu, "Globalization of the Local/Localization of the Global."

63 Fakhro, "Civil Society and Non-Governmental Organization in the Middle East."

64 James Petras, "NGOs: In the Service of Imperialism," *Journal of Contemporary Asia* 29, no. 4 (1999): 429–41.

65 Lopez, Smith, and Pagnucco, "The Global Tide."

66 Krishnaraj, "Women and the Public Domain."

67 For an excellent analysis of this phenomenon, see Honor Ford Smith, "Ring Ding in a Tight Corner: Sistren, Collective Democracy, and the Organization of Cultural Production," *Feminist Genealogies, Colonial Legacies, Democratic Futures*, ed. M. Jacqui Alexander and Chandra Talpade Mohanty (New York: Routledge, 1997), 213–58.

68 Maria Guadalupe, Garcia Hernandez, and Manuel Diaz Montejo, "Mama Maquin: Guatemalan Refugee Women's Participation and Organization," *Women on the Move*, ed. Marin and Lansang–De Mesa, 7–10.

69 Hagland, "International Theory and LGBT Politics."

70 In Beijing, the use of English, the protests about substandard accommodations by many groups from the United States, the continued focus on Chinese women as victims of their government and on Chinese censorship, as well as the em-

phasis on human rights as governing agenda are some indications of the clout of North American (and European) women's groups in the NGO forum. Yet women's groups from other parts of the world are also using these frameworks, partly because they come from non-subaltern groups in their nations and partly because nothing else seems to advance their particular and diverse goals. Thus "global" feminism is being used by a wide range of women globally, albeit in vastly different ways.

71 Grewal and Kaplan, "Introduction: Transnational Feminist Practices and Questions of Postmodernity."

72 Robbins, "Sad Stories in the International Public Sphere."

73 Ibid.

74 Marin and Lansang–De Mesa, eds., *Women on the Move*, appendices.

75 "Building on Indigenous Conceptions of Women's Human Rights," *Al-Raida* 13, nos. 74–75 (summer–fall 1996): 13–18.

76 See website: www.sigi.org/Programs/index.htm.

77 Hartmann, *The Other Feminists*, 132–75.

78 *Al-Raida* 13, nos. 74–75 (summer–fall 1996): 2.

79 http://www.columbia.edu/cu/humanrights/training/training.htm (visited 12 May 2004).

80 Rajni Kothari, "Globalization and 'New World Order.'"

81 See Rajni Kothari's analysis of the UN, for instance, in "Globalization and 'New World Order.'"

82 Edward Friedman, "Asia as a Fount of Universal Human Rights," 56–79.

83 Among white militia organizations, it is believed that army helicopters and all-terrain vehicles painted black or white constitute a UN invasion force, and the UN is seen as representing third world nations as well as a multinational, often supposedly Jewish-dominated, global economy. It is revealing of the complicity between some elements of the state and such racist national imaginary that according to the *New York Times* the military attaché of the U.S. mission to the UN had to write to the leader of the Michigan Militia to assure him that the UN was not taking over a Michigan camp for training its troops (25 June 1995). Such courtesy as writing to reassure the Militia reveals the importance of a racist white constituency to politicians in Washington.

84 Amity Shlaes, "The Rights Stuff," *Wall Street Journal*, 19 May 1993, § A, p. 14.

85 Ibid.

86 Sen and Grown, *Development, Crises, and Alternative Visions*.

87 Rajni Kothari, "Globalization and 'New World Order.'"

88 Ibid.

89 Howard and Donelly, "Human Rights in World Politics."

90 Byrnes, "Toward a More Effective Enforcement of Women's Human Rights."

91 Kothari and Sethi, "On Categories and Interventions."

92 Malkki, "Citizens of Humanity."

93 Rée, "Internationality."

94 Malkki, "Citizens of Humanity."

95 Henkin, "Human Rights Conditionality for U.S. Security and Development Assistance," 818–21.

96   Huntington, "American Ideals versus American Institutions."

97   Rey Chow, *The Protestant Ethnic and the Spirit of Capitalism*, 19–49.

98   Pachauri, *Women and Human Rights*.

99   Vadackumchery, *Human Rights Friendly Police*.

100   Subramanian, *Human Rights Training*.

101   Dutta, "From Subject to Citizen."

102   Pritam Singh, "Sectarian and Human Rights Discourse."

103   See the publications of this group for more information: Center for Women's Global Leadership, Douglass College, Rutgers University, *International Campaign for Women's Human Rights, 1992–1993 Report: Women, Violence and Human Rights* (1993), *From Vienna to Beijing: The Cairo Hearing on Reproductive Health and Human Rights* (1995).

104   Center for Women's Global Leadership, *International Campaign for Women's Human Rights, 1992–1993 Report*.

105   Morgan, *Sisterhood Is Global*.

106   Groups such as W.E.A.P. (the Women's Economic Agenda Project), based in Oakland, California, to address the needs of poor women in the United States are much less in the news than groups working on domestic violence or rape or abortion rights such as NARAL, B.A.W.A.R. (Bay Area Women against Rape), etc. The focus on SAPS (Structural Adjustment Programs) worldwide was raised by women from developing countries at the NGO forum at Huairou.

107   Keck and Sikkink, *Activists beyond Borders*, 166.

108   Thomas and Beasley, "Domestic Violence as a Human Rights Issue."

109   Even though such a search for "common" ground is a problem everywhere, women's groups in India, even if they are formed by middle-class women, tend to focus on economic issues much more than dominant women's groups in the United States do.

110   Keck and Sikkink, *Activists beyond Borders*, 166.

111   Basu, "Globalization of the Local/Localization of the Global," 68–84.

112   Karlekar, "Domestic Violence."

113   Ibid.

114   Rose, *Inventing Our Selves*, 31, 58.

115   Agosín, Introduction, *Women, Gender and Human Rights*, 1–11.

116   Crenshaw, "Mapping the Margins."

117   For instance, the Asian Women's Shelter in San Francisco has had an important impact and provides specialized services for certain groups of women.

118   My thanks to Jayne Lee for making this important point, among many others.

119   Jayne Lee, "Constructing Battered Women Who Kill."

120   Gupta, *Postcolonial Developments*, 317–21.

CHAPTER 4: GENDERING REFUGEES:
NEW NATIONAL/TRANSNATIONAL SUBJECTS

1   Amnesty International annual report, 1997.

2   My critique here is indebted to Ann Stoler's work examining why Foucault is

both important and problematic in his erasure of European colonialism as a major context for the formation of modernity: Stoler, *Race and the Education of Desire*.

3 See for instance the work of Cécile Dubernet on the "international" reaction to "Internally Displaced People" in Eastern Europe: Dubernet, *The International Containment of Displaced Persons*.

4 Senate Judiciary Committee, Refugee Act of 1980, S. Rep. No. 256, 96th Cong., 2nd Sess. (23 July 1979), 1.

5 Helton, *The Price of Indifference*.

6 Malkki, *Purity and Exile*, 9.

7 One such title is revealing of the ways in which the "problem" is one of controlling populations as "masses" and thus a problem of governmentality: Bimal Ghosh, *Huddled Masses and Uncertain Shores*.

8 UN High Commissioner for Refugees, *The State of the World's Refugees 1995*.

9 Ibid., 187.

10 Ervolina, "Fatin v. INS."

11 Jacqueline Bhabha, "Embodied Rights."

12 Ó Tuathail, *Critical Geopolitics*, 18.

13 Hyndman, *Managing Displacement*, xviii.

14 Crisp, "Policy Challenges," 1–8.

15 "Rights: Rethinking Theory and Practice," introduction to special section, *Economic and Political Weekly* 33, no. 5 (31 February 1998): PE-2.

16 Subramanian, *Human Rights Training*.

17 Dusenbery, "Introduction: A Century of Sikhs beyond Punjab."

18 Demetrios Papademetrious, "Migration," *Foreign Policy* 109 (1997): 18.

19 Pandey, *The Construction of Communalism in Colonial North India*.

20 James Clifford, "Traveling Cultures," *Cultural Studies*, ed. Lawrence Grossberg, Cary Nelson, and Paula Triechler, 96–112.

21 Schein, "Importing Miao Brethren to Hmong America."

22 Caren Kaplan, *Questions of Travel*.

23 Jackman, "Well-Founded Fear of Persecution and Other Standards of Decision-Making."

24 Richmond, *Global Apartheid*, xv.

25 Tuitt, *False Images*, 13.

26 Arulanantham, "Restructuring Safe Havens."

27 Tuitt, *False Images*, 25.

28 Ibid.

29 Malkki, *Purity and Exile*, 9.

30 Martin, *Refugee Women*.

31 Razack, *Looking White People in the Eye*, 88.

32 Razack, "What Is to Be Gained by Looking White People in the Eye?"

33 For more on this topic, see Sima Shakhsari, "Diasporic Sexualities: Discursive Formation of Iranian Queer Subjects in Diaspora" (MA thesis, Women's Studies, San Francisco State University, 2001).

34 Eve Hall, "Vocational Training for Women Refugees in Africa."

35 Espin, *Women Crossing Boundaries.*

36 Macklin, "Refugee Women and the Imperative of Categories."

37 Refugee Act, Pub. L. No. 96-212, 201(a)(42), 94 Stat. 102, 102 (1980) (codified at 8 U.S.C. 1158(a)(42)(A) (1985)).

38 Steven Lee, "The Refugee's Burden of Proof for Asylum."

39 Hathaway, *The Law of Refugee Status,* 102.

40 Goodwin-Gill, *The Refugee in International Law,* 67.

41 Bureau of Population, Refugees and Migration, July 1998, at www.state.gov/wow/global/arm/refugee-protect-9807.html.

42 Gilroy, *Against Race.*

43 Bureau of Population, Refugees and Migration, Office of Admissions, U.S. Refugee Admissions Program for Fiscal Year 1998, Department of State Publication 10559, April 1998.

44 Maureen Mulligan, "Obtaining Political Asylum."

45 The connection to cultural feminism in the United States is both obvious and implicit. It can be glimpsed, for instance, in Emily Love's claim that women's refugee claims are essentially different to men's. She says about one refugee asylum case that "a judge who had been more aware of these possible distinctions between men's and women's roles and moralities might have better understood Maria's story and found it more credible." She states that women are more caring than men, quoting Carol Gilligan's comment in her book *In a Different Voice* (1982) that for "many women, morality focuses on caring, rather than on the rights and rules emphasized by men." Love, "Equality in Political Asylum Law."

46 Kelly, "Guidelines for Women's Asylum Claims."

47 I have mentioned a number of these essays in this chapter. To that list can be added: Bower, "Recognizing Violence against Women as Persecution on the Basis of Membership in a Particular Social Group"; and Ervolina, "Fatin v. INS."

48 Levy, *Asylum Based on Sexual Orientation.*

49 See Vienna Declaration and Programme of Action (1993), para. 28, UN doc A/CONF. 157/23; Beijing Declaration (1995), paras. 29–30.

50 Kelley, "Report on the International Consultation on Refugee Women."

51 UNHCR, "Gender-Related Persecution: An Analysis of Recent Trends," UNHCR Symposium on Gender-Based Persecution, Geneva, 1996, *International Journal of Refugee Law,* autumn 1997 (special issue), 79–113.

52 Connors, "Legal Aspects of Women as a Particular Social Group."

53 Ibid.

54 Goldberg, "Anyplace but Home"; Marin and Lansang-De Mesa, eds., *Women on the Move.*

55 Ervolina, "Fatin v. INS," 61–83.

56 Mulligan, "Obtaining Political Asylum," 355–80.

57 Kelly, "Gender-Related Persecution," 625–74.

58 Bissland and Lawand, "Report of the UNHCR Symposium on Gender-Based Persecution."

59 Anker, Kelly, and Willshire-Carrera, "The BIA's New Asylum Jurisprudence and Its Relevance for Women's Claims."

60   http://www.amnestyusa.org/women/asylum/ (May 12, 2004).

61   Greatbatch, "The Gender Difference."

62   In her very useful and perceptive work *Entry Denied*, Eithne Luibhéid sees all border crossers in this light, although she notes that the refugee asylum guidelines in recent years have changed the construction of the refugee.

63   UNHCR, "Gender-Related Persecution: An Analysis of Recent Trends."

64   Lutton, "Fleeing Their Culture."

65   Statement released by the Bureau of Population, Refugees and Migration, July 1998, found at www.state.gov/www/global/prm/refugee-protect-9807.html.

66   Scialabba, "The Immigration and Naturalization Service Considerations for Asylum Officers Adjudicating Asylum Claims from Women."

67   Macklin, "Refugee Women and the Imperative of Categories."

68   Ervolina, "Fatin v. INS."

69   Gayatri Chakravorty Spivak, "Explanation and Culture: Marginalia," *The Spivak Reader*, ed. D. Landry and G. Maclean (New York: Routledge, 1996), 53–74.

70   Pollitt, "Women's Rights, Human Rights."

71   See for instance *New York Times*, 15 April 1996, § A, p. 12. The first paragraph states: "Fauziya Kasinga says she fled her homeland of Togo at age 17 to avoid the tribal rite of female genital mutilation and an arranged marriage as the fourth wife of a man nearly three times her age." Here the words "tribal" and the mention of an arranged marriage of a young woman to an older man are meant to convey the backwardness and oppression of this culture.

72   See for instance Gunning, "Arrogant Perception, World-Travelling and Multicultural Feminism"; Grewal and Kaplan, "Warrior Marks"; Abusharaf, "Unmasking Tradition"; Pederson, "National Bodies, Unspeakable Acts."

73   News Release, U.S. Department of Justice, Bureau of Citizenship and Immigration Services, 7 December 2000. Available at http://www.immigration.gov/graphics/publicaffairs/newsrels/Gender.htm.

74   The signatories to the Scialabba INS report were all women.

75   Razack, "What Is to Be Gained by Looking White People in the Eye?"

76   Macklin, "Refugee Women and the Imperative of Categories," 213–77.

77   Danielsen and Engle, eds., *After Identity*, 210–28.

78   Spijkerboer, *Gender and Refugee Status*.

79   Moallem, "Universalization of Particulars."

80   From a Country Presentation on the U.S.A. by Paula Lynch, Department of State, and Lori Scialabba, Immigration and Naturalization Service, at the Symposium on Gender-Based Persecution, Geneva, Feb 1996. In *International Journal of Refugee Law*, autumn 1997 (special issue), 73–75.

81   Ibid.

82   Jackman, "Well-Founded Fear of Persecution and Other Standards of Decision-Making," 37–70.

83   Ibid.

84   Luibhéid, *Entry Denied*, 113.

85   U.S. Department of State, Bureau of Democracy, Human Rights and Labor, "India: Comments on Country Conditions and Asylum Claims" (June 1996).

86 U.S. Department of State, Bureau of Population, Refugees and Migration, Office of Admissions, *Refugee Admissions Program for Fiscal Year 1998*, Department of State Publication 10559 (April 1998).

87 See for instance *Oppression in Punjab* (New Delhi, 1986; Columbus, Ohio: Sikh Religious and Educational Trust, 1985), a Citizens for Democracy report.

88 U.S. Dept of State, Bureau of Democracy, Human Rights and Labor, "India: Comments on Country Conditions and Asylum Claims" (June 1996).

89 Ibid.

90 My thanks to Jagdeep Singh Sekhon for making this point.

91 Kelly, "Guidelines for Women's Asylum Claims."

92 This was my experience in trying to get pro bono legal assistance from a supposedly progressive nonprofit legal organization.

93 I served as a consultant to the INS since this was one way to learn about what asylum officers believed. The meeting in San Francisco in early 1998 was instructive. The questions sent to me for my comment were the following:

–If a woman is in custody, is it assumed that she has been sexually violated? If so, does this affect her chances of marriage?
–Can a single woman or widowed woman relocate in India?
–If a woman has been sexually violated in police custody, would she reveal this to her family and friends?
–Would the police target a woman merely because her husband is a political activist?
–What kinds of discrimination do women face in India?
–Are there differences between the ways Sikhism regards women's role in society and that of Hinduism?
–What percentage of women are never married in Punjab?
–What is the average age of women when they marry?
–Are "dowry deaths" a problem in the Sikh community?

94 Human Rights Watch/Asia and Physicians for Human Rights, *Dead Silence: The Legacy of Abuses in Punjab* (Human Rights Watch/Asia, 1994).

95 Ibid., 23–25.

96 *Oppression in Punjab*, 41.

97 Menon and Bhasin, *Borders and Boundaries*; Butalia, *The Other Side of Silence*.

98 Das, "National Honor and Practical Kinship."

99 Chowdhry, "Contesting Claims and Counter Claims," 65.

CHAPTER 5: TRANSNATIONAL AMERICA

1 Mitchell, *Colonizing Egypt*; Stoler, *Race and the Education of Desire*; Stoler, *Carnal Knowledge and Imperial Rule*.

2 Rose, *Powers of Freedom*.

3 Mbembe, "Necropolitics."

4 Mbembe's use of the occupation of Palestine and the biopolitical, disciplinary necropolitical aspects of rule over Palestinians leaves out the transnational and

national contexts of sovereignty as freedom that keep the Intifada alive. The news media, NGOS, and Palestinians in diaspora play a big part in the everyday practices of the Palestinians. Mbembe, Wellek Lectures, University of California, Irvine, 19 October 2004.

5 Inderpal Grewal, *Home and Harem.*

6 Dipesh Chakrabarty, "The Difference-Deferral of (a) Colonial Modernity."

7 Stoler, *Race and the Education of Desire.*

8 Ibid., 46.

9 Stoler, *Race and the Education of Desire.*

10 Rosaldo, "Cultural Citizenship and Educational Democracy."

11 Gloria Anzaldúa, *Borderlands/La Frontera: The New Mestiza* (San Francisco: Aunt Lute, 1987).

12 Ewald, "Insurance and Risk."

13 Colin Gordon, "Governmental Rationality."

14 Donald Rumsfeld, "A New Kind of War," *New York Times,* 27 September 2001.

15 Raymond Williams, *Culture and Society.*

16 Gilroy, *"There Ain't No Black in the Union Jack."*

17 Bodnar, *Blue Collar Hollywood*; Susman, *Culture as History.*

18 See Eric Smoodin's forthcoming book on Frank Capra and Hollywood audiences, *Regarding Frank Capra: Audience, Celebrity, and American Film Studies, 1930–1960* (Durham: Duke University Press, 2004).

19 *Le Monde,* 13 September 2001, 1.

20 *New York Times,* 16 September 2001, 45.

21 For instance, Shiv Visvanathan, from the Center for the Study of Developing Societies in New Delhi, stated in a letter posted in the Professors for Peace weblist that he felt "sheer horror" in seeing the World Trade Center collapse and went on to say, "There is an American in all of us and we join in the rituals of grief and mourning." Though his letter was a strong critique of what he called George W. Bush's fundamentalism, Visvanathan's letter was an act of solidarity as well as a critique of American foreign policy.

22 Aaron McGruder, "The Boondocks," *San Francisco Chronicle,* 9 November 2001, § D,p. 19.

23 Moallem, "Whose Fundamentalism?"

24 Klein, *Cold War Orientalism.*

25 Marchetti, *Romance and the "Yellow Peril"*; Shohat, "Gender and Culture of Empire."

26 Michael Mello, "Man on Train Not Linked to Assaults," *Contra Costa Times,* 13 September 2001, § A, p.16.

27 Mark Constantini, "Joginder Singh, a Sikh from San Jose, Attended a Memorial Service," *San Francisco Chronicle,* 18 September 2001, § A p. 13.

28 Gregory Rodriguez, "Identify Yourself," *New York Times,* 23 September 2001, 1, 4.

29 Scott Stantis, "Before/After September 11, 2001," *Contra Costa Times,* 22 September 2001, § A p. 21.

30 *West County Times,* 17 September 2001, § A p. 6.

31 Carlos Avila Gonzalez, *San Francisco Chronicle*, 19 September 2001, § A p. 1.

32 *West County Times*, 20 September 2001, § A p. 1. Photograph from Associated Press.

33 *San Francisco Chronicle*, 20 September 2001, § A p. 1.

34 *New York Times*, 23 September 2001, § A p. 3.

35 *New York Times*, 16 September 2001, § A p. 31.

36 *San Francisco Chronicle*, 20 September 2001, § D p. 1.

37 Barbalet, *Citizenship*, 72.

bibliography

★

Abusharaf, Rogaia. "Unmasking Tradition." *Sciences*, March–April 1998, 23–77.

Agnes, Flavia. "Economic Rights of Women in Islamic Law." *Economic and Political Weekly* 31, nos. 41–42 (12–19 October 1996): 2832–38.

Agosín, Marjorie, ed. *Women, Gender, and Human Rights: A Global Perspective*. New Brunswick: Rutgers University Press, 2001.

Al-Ali, Nadje. "Trans- or a-National? Bosnian Refugees in the UK and the Netherlands." *New Approaches to Migration? Transnational Communities and the Transformation of Home*. Ed. Nadje Al-Ali and Khalid Koser, 96–117. New York: Routledge, 2002.

Al-Ali, Nadje, and Khalid Koser, eds. *New Approaches to Migration? Transnational Communities and the Transformation of Home*. New York: Routledge, 2002.

Alexander, Meena. *Faultlines*. New York: Feminist Press, 1993.

Al-Hibri, Azizah Y. "Is Western Patriarchal Feminism Good for Third World Women?" *Is Multiculturalism Bad for Women?* Ed. Joshua Cohen, Matthew Howard, and Martha C. Nussbaum, 41–46. Princeton: Princeton University Press, 1999.

Alston, Philip. *Development and the Rule of Law: Prevention versus Cure as a Human Rights Strategy*. Conference on Development and the Rule of Law. International Commission of Jurists. The Hague, 1981.

Amnesty International. *Amnesty International Report 1991*. London: Amnesty International Publications, 1991.

——. *Amnesty International Report 1994*. London: Amnesty International Publications, 1994.

——. *Amnesty International Report 1995*. London: Amnesty International Publications, 1995.

——. *Amnesty International Report 1999*. London: Amnesty International Publications, 1999.

Anaya, S. James. *Indigenous Peoples in International Law*. New York: Oxford University Press, 1996.

Anderson, Benedict. *Imagined Communities: Reflections on the Origin and Spread of Nationalisms*. London: Verso, 1983.

Ang, Ian. *Watching Dallas: Soap Opera and the Melodramatic Imagination*. London: Methuen, 1991.

Anker, Deborah, Nancy Kelly, and John Willshire-Carrera. "The BIA's New Asylum Jurisprudence and Its Relevance for Women's Claims." *Interpreter Releases* 73, no. 34 (9 September 1996): 1173–84.

An-Na'im, Abdullahi Ahmed, ed. *Human Rights in Cross-Cultural Perspectives: A Quest for Consensus*. Philadelphia: University of Pennsylvania Press, 1992.

Anveshi Law Committee. "Is Gender Justice Only a Legal Issue? Political Stakes in the UCC Debate." *Economic and Political Weekly* 32, nos. 9–10 (1–8 March 1997): 453–58.

Appadurai, Arjun. "Patriotism and Its Future." *Public Culture* 5 (1993): 412–13, 420.

——. *Modernity at Large: Cultural Dimensions of Globalization*. Minneapolis: University of Minnesota Press, 1996.

Arulanantham, Ahilan T. "Restructuring Safe Havens: A Proposal for Reform of the Refugee Protection System." *Human Rights Quarterly* 22 (February 2000): 1–56.

Asian Women United of California. *Making Waves: An Anthology of Writings by and about Asian American Women*. Boston: Beacon, 1989.

Axel, Brian Keith. *The Nation's Tortured Body: Violence, Representation, and the Formation of the Sikh "Diaspora."* Durham: Duke University Press, 2001.

Bacchetta, Paola. "Militant Hindu Nationalist Women Reimagine Themselves: Notes on Mechanisms of Expansion/Adjustment." *Journal of Women's History* 10, no. 4 (winter 1999): 125–47.

Bachu, Parminder. "The East African Sikh Diaspora." *The Sikh Diaspora: Migration and Experience beyond Punjab*. Ed. N. Gerald Barrier and Verne A. Dusenbery, 235–60. Delhi: Chanakya, 1989.

Bahri, Deepika. *Bharati Mukherjee*. Postcolonial Studies at Emory. www.emory.edu/ENGLISH/Bahri/Mukherjee.html.

Balibar, Étienne, and Immanuel Wallerstein. *Race, Nation, Class: Ambiguous Identities*. London: Verso, 1991.

Ballard, Roger. "Differentiation and Disjunction amongst the Sikhs in Britain." *The Sikh Diaspora: Migration and Experience beyond Punjab*. Ed. N. Gerald Barrier and Verne A. Dusenbery, 200–34. Delhi: Chanakya, 1989.

Bannerjee, Sumanta. *In the Wake of Naxalbari: A History of the Naxalite Movement in India*. Calcutta: Subarnarekha, 1980.

Barbalet, J. M. *Citizenship: Rights, Struggle, and Class Inequality*. Minneapolis: University of Minnesota Press, 1988.

Barbieri, William. *Ethics of Citizenship: Immigration and Group Rights in Germany*. Durham: Duke University Press, 1998.

Barns, Ian. "Technology and Citizenship." *Poststructuralism, Citizenship and Social Policy*. Ed. Alan Peterson, Ian Barns, Janice Dudley, and Patricia Harris, 154–98. London: Routledge, 1999.

Barrier, N. Gerald. "Sikh Emigrants and Their Homeland." *The Sikh Diaspora: Migration and Experience beyond Punjab*. Ed. N. Gerald Barrier and Verne A. Dusenbery, 49–89. Delhi: Chanakya, 1989.

Barry, Andrew, Thomas Osborne, and Nikolas Rose, eds. *Foucault and Political Rea-son: Liberalism, Neo-Liberalism and Rationalities of Government.* Chicago: University of Chicago Press, 1996.

Basch, Linda, Nina Glick Schiller, and Cristina Szanton Blanc. *Nations Unbound: Transnational Projects, Postcolonial Predicaments, and Deterritorialized Nation-States.* Amsterdam: Gordon and Breach, 1994.

Basu, Amrita. "Women's Activism and the Vicissitudes of Hindu Nationalism." *Journal of Women's History* 10, no. 4 (winter 1999): 105–24.

——. "Globalization of the Local / Localization of the Global: Mapping Transnational Women's Movements." *Meridians: Feminism, Race, Transnationalism* 1, no. 1 (autumn 2000): 68–84.

Baudrillard, Jean. *Selected Writings.* London: Polity, 1988.

Bauman, Zygmunt. *Legislators and Interpreters: On Modernity, Postmodernity and Intellectuals.* Cambridge: Polity, 1987.

——. *Globalization: The Human Consequences.* New York: Columbia University Press, 1998.

Baxi, Upendra. "From Human Rights to the Right to Be Human: Some Heresies." *Rethinking Human Rights.* Ed. Smitu Kothari and Harsh Sethi, 151–67. Delhi: Lokayan, 1991.

Bayefsky, Anne F., and Joan Fitzpatrick, eds. *Human Rights and Forced Displacement.* Boston: Martinus Nijhoff, 2000.

Bell, Lynda S., Andrew J. Nathan, and Ilan Peleg, eds. *Negotiating Cultures and Human Rights.* New York: Columbia University Press, 2001.

Beneria, Lourdes. *Women and Development: The Sexual Division of Labor in Rural Societies.* New York: Praeger/ILO, 1982.

Berlant, Lauren. *The Queen of America Goes to Washington City: Essays on Sex and Citizenship.* Durham: Duke University Press, 1997.

Berman, Marshall. *All That Is Solid Melts into Air: The Experience of Modernity.* Harmondsworth: Penguin, 1988.

Bhabha, Homi, ed. *Nation and Narration.* New York: Routledge, 1990.

——. *The Location of Culture.* New York: Routledge, 1994.

Bhabha, Jacqueline. "Embodied Rights: Gender Persecution, State Sovereignty, and Refugees." *Public Culture* 9, no. 1 (fall 1996): 3–32.

Bharvani, Shakuntala. "*Jasmine*: An Immigrant Experience?" *The Fiction of Bharati Mukherjee.* Ed. R. K. Dhawan, 178–81. New Delhi: Prestige, 1996.

Bhattacharjee, Anannya. "The Habit of Ex-Nomination: Nation, Woman, and the Indian Immigrant Bourgeoisie." *Emerging Voices: South Asian Women Redefine Self, Family, and Community.* Ed. Sangeeta R. Gupta, 232–36. Walnut Creek: Alta Mira, 1999.

Biddick, Kathleen. *The Shock of Medievalism.* Durham: Duke University Press, 1998.

——. "Translating the Foreskin." *Queering the Middle Ages.* Ed. Glenn Burger and Steven Kruger, 193–212. Minneapolis: University of Minnesota Press, 2002.

Bissland, Julie, and Kathleen Lawand. "Report of the UNHCR Symposium on Gender-Based Persecution." *International Journal of Refugee Studies,* autumn 1997, 13–31. Special issue: UNHCR Symposium on Gender-Based Persecution, Geneva, 22–23 February 1996.

Blum, Carolyn P. "Refugee Status Based on Membership in a Particular Social Group: A North American Perspective." *Asylum Law and Practice in Europe and North America*. Ed. Jacqueline Bhabha and Geoffrey Coll, 82–100. Washington: Federal Publications, 1992.

Bocock, Robert. *Consumption*. London: Routledge, 1993.

Bodnar, John. *Blue Collar Hollywood: Liberalism, Democracy and Working People in American Film*. Baltimore: Johns Hopkins University Press, 2003.

Bose, Brinda. "A Question of Identity: Where Gender, Race, and America Meet in Bharati Mukherjee." *Bharati Mukherjee: Critical Perspectives*. Ed. Emmanuel Nelson, 47–63. New York: Garland, 1993.

Bourne, Randolph. *History of a Literary Radical and Other Essays*. New York: B. W. Huebsch, 1920.

Bower, Karen. "Recognizing Violence against Women as Persecution on the Basis of Membership in a Particular Social Group." *Georgetown Immigration Law Journal* 7 (1993): 173–83.

Brah, Avtar. *Cartographies of Diaspora: Contesting Identities*. London: Routledge, 1996.

Bremen, Jan. "The Civilization of Racism: Colonial and Post-Colonial Development Policies." *Imperial Monkey Business: Racial Supremacy in Social Darwinist Theory and Colonial Practice*. Ed. Jan Breman, 123–52. Amsterdam: VU University Press, 1990.

Brennan, Timothy. *At Home in the World*. Cambridge: Harvard University Press, 1997.

Brewster, Anne. "A Critique of Bharati Mukherjee's Neo-Nationalism." *SPAN: Journal of the South Pacific Association for Commonwealth Literature and Language Studies* 34–35 (1993): 1–8.

Brown, Chris. "Universal Human Rights: A Critique." *Human Rights in Global Politics*. Ed. Tim Dunne and Nicholas J. Wheeler, 103–27. Cambridge: Cambridge University Press, 1999.

Brown, Widney. "Human Rights Watch: An Overview." *NGOs and Human Rights: Promise and Performance*. Ed. Claude E. Welsh, 72–84. Philadelphia: University of Pennsylvania Press, 2001.

Bryman, Alan. *Disney and His Worlds*. New York: Routledge, 1995.

Bulosan, Carlos. *America Is in the Heart*. Seattle: University of Washington Press, 1990.

Bunch, Charlotte. "Women's Rights as Human Rights: Toward a Revision of Human Rights." *Human Rights Quarterly* 12 (November 1990): 486–98.

——. "Transforming Human Rights from a Feminist Perspective." *Women's Rights, Human Rights: International Feminist Perspectives*. Ed. Julie Peters and Andrea Wolper, 11–17. New York: Routledge, 1995.

Bunch, Charlotte, and Niamh Reilly. *Demanding Accountability: The Global Campaign and Vienna Tribunal for Women's Human Rights*. New Brunswick: Center for Women's Global Leadership, 1994.

Bunch, Charlotte, and Susanna Fried. "Beijing '95: Moving Women's Rights from Margin to Center." *Signs* 22, no. 1 (autumn 1996): 200–204.

Burchell, Graham. "Peculiar Interests: Civil Society and Governing 'the System of

Natural Liberty.'" *The Foucault Effect: Studies in Governmentality.* Ed. Graham Burchell, Colin Gordon, and Peter Miller, 119–50. Chicago: University of Chicago Press, 1991.

Burchell, Graham, Colin Gordon, and Peter Miller. *The Foucault Effect: Studies in Governmentality.* Chicago: University of Chicago Press, 1991.

Burgerman, Susan D. "Mobilizing Principles: The Role of Transnational Activists in Promoting Human Rights Principles." *Human Rights Quarterly* 20 (November 1998): 905–23.

Burke, Timothy. *Lifebuoy Men, Lux Women: Commodification, Consumption, and Cleanliness in Modern Zimbabwe.* Durham: Duke University Press, 1996.

Burton, Antoinette. *Burdens of History : British Feminists, Indian Women, and Imperial Culture, 1865–1915.* Chapel Hill: University of North Carolina Press, 1994.

Bush, Diane Mitsch. "Women's Movements and State Policy Reform Aimed at Domestic Violence against Women: A Comparison of the Consequences of Movement Mobilization in the US and India." *Gender and Society* 6 (December 1992): 587–608.

Busia, Albena P. A. "On Cultures of Communication: Reflections on Beijing." *Signs: Journal of Women in Culture and Society* 22, no. 1 (autumn 1996): 204–10.

Butalia, Urvashi. *The Other Side of Silence: Voices from the Partition of India.* New Delhi: Penguin, 1998.

Byrnes, Andrew. "Toward a More Effective Enforcement of Women's Human Rights through the Use of International Human Rights Law and Procedures." *Human Rights of Women: National and International Perspectives.* Ed. Rebecca J. Cook, 189–227. Philadelphia: University of Pennsylvania Press, 1994.

Carey, Lynn. "Breaking the Rules." *Contra Costa Times*, 25 May 1999, § E, pp. 1–2.

Carmichael, William D. "The Role of the Ford Foundation." *NGOs and Human Rights: Promise and Performance.* Ed. Claude E. Welsh, 248–60. Philadelphia: University of Pennsylvania Press, 2001.

Castells, Manuel. *The Rise of Network Society.* Cambridge: Basil Blackwell, 1996.

——. *The Power of Identity: Economy, Society and Culture.* Oxford: Basil Blackwell, 1997.

Center for Women's Global Leadership. *1991 Women's Leadership Institute Report: Women, Violence and Human Rights.* New Brunswick: Center for Women's Global Leadership, 1992.

——. *International Campaign for Women's Human Rights, 1992–1993 Report.* New Brunswick: Center for Women's Global Leadership, 1993.

——. *From Vienna to Beijing: The Cairo Hearing on Reproductive Health and Human Rights.* New Brunswick: Center for Women's Global Leadership, 1995.

Chadney, James G. "The Formation of Ethnic Communities: Lessons from the Vancouver Sikhs." *The Sikh Diaspora: Migration and Experience beyond Punjab.* Ed. N. Gerald Barrier and Verne A. Dusenbery, 185–99. Delhi: Chanakya, 1989.

Chakrabarty, Dipesh. "The Difference-Deferral of (a) Colonial Modernity: Public Debates on Domesticity in British Bengal." *History Workshop Journal* 36 (1993): 1–33.

——. *Provincializing Europe: Postcolonial Thought and Historical Difference.* Princeton: Princeton University Press, 2000.

Chakravarty, Deepita. "Labour Market under Trade Liberalization in India." *Economic and Political Weekly* 34, no. 48 (27 November 1999): M163–68.

Chandler, David. "The Road to Military Humanitarianism: How the Human Rights NGOS Shaped a New Humanitarian Agenda." *Human Rights Quarterly* 23 (August 2001): 678–700.

Charlesworth, Hilary. "What Are 'Women's International Human Rights'?" *Human Rights of Women: International and National Perspectives*. Ed. Rebecca J. Cook, 58–84. Philadelphia: University of Pennsylvania Press, 1994.

Charlesworth, Hilary, Christine Chinkin, and Shelley Wright. "Feminist Approaches to International Law." *American Journal of International Law* 85 (1991): 613–45.

Chatterjee, Partha. *The Nation and Its Fragments*. Princeton: Princeton University Press, 1993.

Cheah, Pheng. "Posit(ion)ing Human Rights in the Current Global Conjuncture." *Public Culture* 9, no. 2 (winter 1997): 233–66.

——. "Introduction Part II: The Cosmopolitical Today." *Cosmopolitics: Thinking and Feeling beyond the Nation*. Ed. Pheng Cheah and Bruce Robbins, 20–43. Minneapolis: University of Minnesota Press, 1998.

Cheah, Pheng, and Bruce Robbins, eds. *Cosmopolitics: Thinking and Feeling beyond the Nation*. Minneapolis: University of Minnesota Press, 1998.

Chen, Martha Alter. "Engendering World Conferences: The International Women's Movement and the UN." *NGOS, the UN, and Global Governance*. Ed. Thomas G. Weiss and Leon Gordenker, 139–55. Boulder: Lynne Rienner, 1996.

Cheung, King-Kok. "Reviewing Asian American Literary Studies." *An Interethnic Companion to Asian American Literature*. Ed. King-Kok Cheung, 1–20. Cambridge: Cambridge University Press, 1997.

Chimni, B. S. *International Refugee Law: A Reader*. Thousand Oaks: Sage, 2000.

Chow, Esther Ngan-ling. "Making Waves, Moving Mountains: Reflections on Beijing '95 and Beyond." *Signs* 22, no. 1 (autumn 1996): 185–92.

Chow, Rey. *The Protestant Ethnic and the Spirit of Capitalism*. New York: Columbia University Press, 2002.

Chowdhry, Prem. "Contesting Claims and Counter Claims: Questions of Inheritance and Sexuality of Widows." *Social Reform, Sexuality and the State*. Ed. Patricia Uberoi, 65–82. New Delhi: Sage, 1996.

Cisneros, Sandra. "Barbie-Q." *Woman Hollering Creek and Other Stories*, 14–16. New York: Random House, 1991.

Clark, Ann Marie, Elisabeth J. Friedman, and Katheryn Hochstetler. "The Sovereign Limits of Global Civil Society: A Comparison of NGO Participation in UN World Conferences on the Environment, Human Rights, and Women." *World Politics* 51, no. 1 (October 1998): 1–35.

Clark, Danae. "Commodity Lesbianism." *The Lesbian and Gay Studies Reader*. Ed. Henry Abelove, Michele Aina Barale, and David M. Halperin, 186–201. New York: Routledge, 1993.

Clifford, James. *Routes: Travel and Translation in the Late Twentieth Century*. Cambridge: Harvard University Press, 1997.

Cohen, Colleen Ballerino, Richard Wilk, and Beverly Stoeltje, eds. *Beauty Queens on the Global Stage: Gender, Contests, and Power*. New York: Routledge, 1996.

Conklin, Alice L. "Colonialism and Human Rights: A Contradiction in Terms? The Case of France and West Africa, 1895–1914." *American Historical Review* 103, no. 2 (April 1998): 419–42.

Connors, Jane. "Legal Aspects of Women as a Particular Social Group." *International Journal of Refugee Law*. Special issue on gender-based asylum, autumn 1997, 114–28.

Cook, Rebecca J. "Women's International Human Rights Law: The Way Forward." *Human Rights Quarterly* 15 (May 1993): 230–61.

——. "Advancing Safe Motherhood through Human Rights." *Giving Meaning to Economic, Social, and Cultural Rights*. Ed. Isfahan Merali and Valerie Osterveld, 109–23. Philadelphia: University of Pennsylvania Press, 2001.

Coomaraswamy, Radhika. "To Bellow Like a Cow: Women, Ethnicity, and the Discourse of Rights." *Human Rights of Women: National and International Perspectives*. Ed. Rebecca Cook, 39–57. Philadelphia: University of Pennsylvania Press, 1994.

Crenshaw, Kimberle. "Mapping the Margins: Intersectionality, Identity Politics, and Violence against Women of Color." *After Identity: A Reader in Law and Culture*. Ed. Dan Danielsen and Karen Engle, 332–54. New York: Routledge, 1995.

Crisp, Jeff. "Policy Challenges." *Policy Challenges of the New Diasporas: Migrant Networks and Their Impact on Asylum Flows and Regimes*. UNHCR Working Papers. Geneva: UNHCR, 1999.

Danielsen, Dan, and Karen Engle, eds. *After Identity: A Reader in Law and Culture*. New York: Routledge, 1995.

Das, Veena. "National Honor and Practical Kinship: Of Unwanted Women and Children." *Critical Events: An Anthropological Perspective on Contemporary India*, 55–84. New Delhi: Oxford University Press, 1995.

Dauer, Sheila. "Indivisible or Invisible: Women's Human Rights in the Public and Private Sphere." *Women, Gender, and Human Rights: A Global Perspective*. Ed. Marjorie Agosín, 65–82. New Brunswick: Rutgers University Press, 2001.

de Mooij, Marieke. *Global Marketing and Advertising: Understanding Cultural Paradoxes*. London: Sage, 1998.

Dev, S. Mahendra. "Economic Liberalization and Employment in South Asia." *Economic and Political Weekly* 35, nos. 1–2 (8–14 January 2000): 40–51.

Devakaruni, Chitra. "Yuba City School." *Our Feet Walk the Sky: Women of the South Asian Diaspora*, ed. Women of South Asian Descent Collective, 120–21. San Francisco: Aunt Lute, 1993.

Dharwadkar, Vinay. "The Internationalization of Literature." *New National and Postcolonial Literatures*. Ed. Bruce King, 59–77. Oxford: Clarendon, 1996.

——. "Print Culture and Literary Markets in Colonial India." *Language Machines: Technologies of Literary and Cultural Production*. Ed. Jeffrey Masten, Peter Stallybrass, and Nancy Vickers, 108–33. New York: Routledge, 1997.

Dicklitch, Susan. "Action for Development in Uganda." *NGOs and Human Rights: Promise and Performance*. Ed. Claude E. Welsh, 182–203. Philadelphia: University of Pennsylvania Press, 2001.

Digeser, Peter. "The Fourth Face of Power." *Journal of Politics* 54, no. 4 (November 1992): 997–1007.

Dillon, Michael. "The Security of Governance." Unpublished paper, 2004.

Dirks, Nicholas. "In Near Ruins: Cultural Theory at the End of the Century." *In Near Ruins: Cultural Theory at the End of the Century.* Ed. Nicholas Dirks, 1–18. Minneapolis: University of Minnesota Press, 1998.

———. *Castes of Mind: Colonialism and the Making of Modern India.* Princeton: Princeton University Press, 2001.

Divakaruni, Chitra Banerjee. *The Mistress of Spices.* New York: Anchor, 1997.

Dreifus, Claudia. *Radical Lifestyles.* New York: Lancer, 1971.

Dubernet, Cécile. *The International Containment of Displaced Persons: Humanitarian Spaces without Exit.* Burlington, Vt.: Ashgate, 2001.

Ducille, Ann. "Dyes and Dolls: Multicultural Barbie and the Merchandising of Difference." *Differences* 6, no. 1 (spring 1994): 46–68.

Dusenbery, Verne A. "Introduction: A Century of Sikhs beyond Punjab." *The Sikh Diaspora: Migration and Experience beyond Punjab.* Ed. N. Gerald Barrier and Verne A. Dusenbery, 1–28. Delhi: Chanakya, 1989.

Dutt, Mallika. *Women's Human Rights in the United States.* New Brunswick: Center for Women's Global Leadership, 1994.

Dutta, Nilanjan. "From Subject to Citizen: Toward a History of the Civil Rights Movement." *Changing Concepts of Rights and Justice in South Asia.* Ed. Michael R. Anderson and Sumit Guha, 275–88. New Delhi: Oxford University Press, 2000.

Ebersole, Lucinda and Richard Peabody, eds. *Mondo Barbie.* New York: St. Martin's, 1993.

Ensted, Nan. *Ladies of Labor, Girls of Adventure.* New York: Columbia University Press, 1999.

Ervolina, Anna J. "Fatin v. INS: Gender-Based Persecution under United States Asylum Law." *New York International Law Review* 8, no. 1 (winter 1995): 61–81.

Escobar, Arturo. "Power and Visibility: Development and the Invention and Management of the Third World." *Cultural Anthropology* 3, no. 4 (November 1988): 428–43.

———. *Encountering Development: The Making and Unmaking of the Third World.* Princeton Studies in Culture/Power/History. Princeton: Princeton University Press, 1995.

Espin, Olivia. *Women Crossing Boundaries: A Psychology of Immigration and Transformations of Sexuality.* New York: Routledge, 1999.

Ewald, François. "Insurance and Risk." *The Foucault Effect: Studies in Governmentality.* Ed. Graham Burchell, Colin Gordon, and Peter Miller, 197–210. Chicago: University of Chicago Press, 1991.

Ewen, Stuart. *Captains of Consciousness: Advertising and the Social Roots of Consumer Culture.* New York: McGraw-Hill, 1976.

———. *All Consuming Images: The Politics of Style in Contemporary Culture.* New York: Basic Books, 1988.

Fabian, Johannes. *Time and the Other: How Anthropology Makes Its Object.* New York: Columbia University Press, 1983.

Fakhro, Munira A. "Civil Society and Non-Governmental Organization in the Middle East: Reflections on the Gulf." *Middle East Women's Studies: The Review* 51, no. 4 (January 1997): 1–3.

Featherstone, Mike. *Consumer Culture and Postmodernism.* London: Sage, 1991.

Featherstone, Mike, Scott Lash, and Roland Robertson, eds. *Global Modernities*. London: Sage, 1995.

Fellmeth, Aaron Xavier. "Feminism and International Law: Theory, Methodology, and Substantive Reform." *Human Rights Quarterly* 22 (August 2000): 658–733.

Finnegan, Margaret. *Selling Suffrage: Consumer Culture and Votes for Women*. New York: Columbia University Press, 1999.

Fisher, Julie. *Non-Governments: NGOs and the Political Development of the Third World*. West Hartford: Kumarian, 1998.

Foucault, Michel. "About the Beginning of the Hermeneutics of the Self: Two Lectures at Dartmouth." *Political Theory* 21, no. 2 (May 1993): 198–227.

———. "The Birth of Biopolitics." *Essential Works of Foucault*, vol. 1, *Ethics: Subjectivity and Truth*. Ed. Paul Rabinow, 73–80. New York: New Press, 1994.

Fraser, Arvonne S. "The Origins and Development of Women's Human Rights." *Women, Gender, and Human Rights: A Global Perspective*. Ed. Marjorie Agosín, 15–64. New Brunswick: Rutgers University Press, 2001.

Freeden, Michael. *Rights*. Minneapolis: University of Minnesota Press, 1991.

Freeman, Carla. *High Tech and High Heels in the Global Economy*. Durham: Duke University Press, 2000.

Friedman, Edward. "Asia as a Fount of Universal Human Rights." *Debating Human Rights*. Ed. Peter Van Ness, 56–79. New York: Routledge, 1998.

Friedman, Elisabeth. "Women's Human Rights: The Emergence of a Movement." *Women's Rights, Human Rights, International Feminist Perspectives*. Ed. Julie Peters and Andrea Wolper, 18–35. New York: Routledge, 1995.

Fukuyama, Francis. *The End of History and the Last Man*. New York: Free Press, 1992.

Gaer, Felice D. "Mainstreaming a Concern for the Human Rights of Women: Beyond Theory." *Women, Gender, and Human Rights: A Global Perspective*. Ed. Marjorie Agosín, 98–122. New Brunswick: Rutgers University Press, 2001.

Gallagher, Nancy. "Human Rights Education for Women in Muslim Societies: A Test Run at MESA." *Middle East Women's Studies: The Review* 51, no. 4 (January 1997): 4.

Gallin, Rita, Marilyn Aronoff, and Anne Ferguson, eds. *The Women and International Development Manual*, vol. 1. Boulder: Westview, 1989.

George, Rosemary Marongoly. "From Expatriate Aristocrat to Immigrant Nobody: South Asian Racial Strategies in the Southern California Context." *Diaspora* 6, no. 1 (1997): 31–60.

Geske, Mary, and Susan C. Bourque. "Grassroots Organizations and Women's Human Rights: Meeting the Challenge of the Local-Global Link." *Women, Gender, and Human Rights: A Global Perspective*. Ed. Marjorie Agosín, 246–64. New Brunswick: Rutgers University Press, 2001.

Ghosh, Amitav. *The Shadow Lines*. Delhi: R. Dayal, 1988; New York: Viking, 1989.

———. *In an Antique Land: History in the Guise of a Traveler's Tale*. New York: Vintage Departures, 1992.

———. *The Glass Palace*. Delhi: R. Dayal, 2000; New York: Random House, 2001.

———. *The Imam and the Indian*. Delhi: Ravi Dayal, 2002.

Ghosh, Bimal. *Huddled Masses and Uncertain Shores: Insights into Irregular Migration*. The Hague: Martinus Nijhoff, 1998.

Gibson, Margaret A. "Punjabi Orchard Farmers: An Immigrant Enclave in Rural California." *International Migration Review* 22, no. 1 (spring 1988): 28–50.

Gibson-Graham, J. K. *The End of Capitalism (as We Knew It)*. Oxford: Basil Blackwell, 1996.

Giddens, Anthony. *Modernity and Self-Identity*. Cambridge: Polity, 1991.

Gilroy, Paul. *"There Ain't No Black in the Union Jack": The Cultural Politics of Race and Nation*. Chicago: University of Chicago Press, 1991.

——. *The Black Atlantic: Double Consciousness and Modernity*. Cambridge: Harvard University Press, 1993.

——. "Diaspora and the Detours of Identity." *Identity and Difference*. Ed. Kathryn Woodward, 301–46. London: Sage, 1997.

——. *Against Race: Imagining Political Culture beyond the Color Line*. Cambridge: Harvard University Press, 2000.

Goitein, S. D. *A Mediterranean Society: The Jewish Society of the Arab World as Portrayed in the Documents of the Cairo Geniza*. Berkeley: University of California Press, 1967.

Goldberg, Pamela. "Refugee and Migrant Women around the Globe." *Women on the Move: Proceedings of the Workshop on Human Rights Abuses against Immigrant and Refugee Women*. Ed. Leni Marin and Blandina Lansang–De Mesa, 1–4. San Francisco: Family Violence Prevention Fund, 1993.

——. "Anyplace but Home: Asylum in the United States for Women Fleeing Intimate Violence." *Cornell International Law Journal* 26, no. 3 (1994): 565–603.

Goodwin, Jan. "Afghan Women Are Free of the Taliban, but Liberation Is Still a Distant Dream." *Nation*, 29 April 2002, 20.

Goodwin, Neva, Frank Ackerman, and David Kiron. *The Consumer Society*. Washington: Island, 1997.

Goodwin-Gill, Guy S. *The Refugee in International Law*. 2d ed. Oxford: Clarendon, 1996.

Gordon, Avery, and Christopher Newfield, eds. *Mapping Multiculturalism*. Minneapolis: University of Minnesota Press, 1996.

Gordon, Colin. "Governmental Rationality: An Introduction." *The Foucault Effect: Studies in Governmentality*. Ed. Graham Burchell, Colin Gordon, and Peter Miller, 1–51. Chicago: University of Chicago Press, 1991.

Greatbatch, Jacqueline. "The Gender Difference: Feminist Critiques of Refugee Discourse." *International Journal of Refugee Law* 1, no. 4 (October 1989): 518–27.

Grewal, Gurleen. "Born Again American: The Immigrant Consciousness in *Jasmine*." *Bharati Mukherjee: Critical Perspectives*. Ed. Emmanuel Nelson, 181–96. New York: Garland, 1993.

Grewal, Inderpal. "Reading and Writing the South Asian Diaspora." *Our Feet Walk the Sky*. Ed. Women of South Asian Descent Collective, 226–36. San Francisco: Aunt Lute, 1993.

——. "The Postcolonial, Ethnic Studies, and the Diaspora: The Contexts of Ethnic Immigrant/Migrant Cultural Studies in the U.S." *Socialist Review* 24, no. 4 (1994): 45–74.

——. *Home and Harem: Nation, Gender, Empire, and the Cultures of Travel*. Durham: Duke University Press, 1996.

———. "On the New Global Feminism and the Family of Nations: Dilemmas of Transnational Feminist Practice." *Talking Visions: Multicultural Feminism in a Transnational Age*. Ed. Ella Shohat, 501–32. Cambridge: MIT Press, 1998.

Grewal, Inderpal, Akhil Gupta, and Aihwa Ong, eds. *positions: east asia cultures critique* 7, no. 3 (winter 1999). Special issue: Asian Transnationalities.

Grewal, Inderpal, and Caren Kaplan. "Introduction: Transnational Feminist Practices and Questions of Postmodernity." *Scattered Hegemonies: Postmodernity and Transnational Feminist Practices*. Ed. Inderpal Grewal and Caren Kaplan, 1–33. Minneapolis: University of Minnesota Press, 1994.

———. "Warrior Marks: Global Womanism's Neo-Colonial Discourse in a Multicultural Context." *Camera Obscura* 39 (September 1996): 5–33.

———. "Transnational Practices and Interdisciplinary Feminist Scholarship: Refiguring Women and Gender Studies." *Locating Feminism: The Politics of Women's Studies*, 66–81. Ed. Robyn Wiegman. Durham: Duke University Press, 2002.

Grossberg, Lawrence, Cary Nelson, and Paula Triechler, eds. *Cultural Studies*. New York: Routledge, 1992.

Gunning, Isabelle. "Arrogant Perception, World-Travelling and Multicultural Feminism: The Case of Female Genital Surgeries." *Columbia Human Rights Law Review* 23 (1992): 189–248.

Gupta, Akhil. "Beyond 'Culture': Space, Identity, and the Politics of Difference." *Cultural Anthropology* 7, no. 1 (February 1992): 6–24.

———. "The Song of the Nonaligned World: Transnational Identities and the Reinscription of Space in Late Capitalism." *Cultural Anthropology* 7, no. 1 (February 1992): 63–79.

———. "Blurred Boundaries: The Discourse of Corruption, the Culture of Politics, and the Imagined State." *American Ethnologist* 22, no. 2 (May 1995): 375–402.

———. *Postcolonial Developments: Agriculture in the Making of Modern India*. Durham: Duke University Press, 1998.

Hagland, Paul EeNam Park. "International Theory and LGBT Politics: Testing the Limits of a Human Rights-Based Strategy." *GLQ* 3, no. 4 (1997): 357–84.

Hall, Eve. "Vocational Training for Women Refugees in Africa." *International Labour Review* 129, no. 1 (1990): 91–107.

Hall, Stuart. "The Toad in the Garden: Thatcherism among the Theorists." *Marxism and the Interpretation of Culture*. Ed. Cary Nelson and Lawrence Grossberg, 35–73. Urbana: University of Illinois Press, 1988.

———. "Cultural Identity and Diaspora." *Identity and Difference*. Ed. Kathryn Woodward, 51–58. London: Sage, 1997.

———. "The Local and the Global: Globalization and Ethnicity." *Dangerous Liaisons: Gender, Nation and Postcolonial Perspectives*. Ed. Anne McClintock, Aamir Mufti, and Ella Shohat, 173–87. Minneapolis: University of Minnesota Press, 1997.

———. "The Spectacle of the 'Other.'" *Representation: Cultural Representations and Signifying Practices*. Ed. Stuart Hall, 223–79. London: Sage, 1997.

Hall, Stuart, and Paul DuGay, eds. *Questions of Cultural Identity*. London: Sage, 1996.

Halter, Marilyn. *Shopping for Identity: The Marketing of Ethnicity*. New York: Schocken, 2000.

Hanawa, Yukiko. "Inciting Sites of Political Interventions: Queer 'n' Asian." *positions: east asia cultures critique* 4, no. 3 (winter 1996): 459–90.

Hannerz, Ulf. *Cultural Complexity: Studies in the Social Organization of Meaning.* New York: Columbia University Press, 1992.

——. *Transnational Connections: Culture, People, Places.* London: Routledge, 1996.

Hardt, Michael, and Antonio Negri. *Empire.* Cambridge: Harvard University Press, 2000.

Hartmann, Susan M. *The Other Feminists: Activists in the Liberal Establishment.* New Haven: Yale University Press, 1998.

Harvey, David. *The Condition of Postmodernity.* Cambridge: Basil Blackwell, 1990.

Hathaway, James C. *The Law of Refugee Status.* Toronto: Butterworths, 1991.

Heater, Derek. *World Citizenship and Government: Cosmopolitan Ideas in the History of Political Thought.* London: Macmillan, 1996.

Held, David. *Democracy and the Social Order: From the Modern State to Cosmopolitan Governance.* Cambridge: Polity, 1995.

Helton, Arthur C. *The Price of Indifference: Refugees and Humanitarian Action in the New Century.* New York: Oxford University Press, 2002.

Helwig, Arthur. *An Immigrant Success Story: East Indians in America.* Philadelphia: University of Pennsylvania Press, 1990.

——. "Punjabi Identity: A Structural/Symbolic Analysis." *Punjabi Identity in a Global Context.* Ed. Pritam Singh and Shinder Singh Thandi, 358. New Delhi: Oxford University Press, 1999.

Hendrickson, Hildi, ed. *Clothing and Difference: Embodied Identities in Colonial and Post-Colonial Africa.* Durham: Duke University Press, 1996.

Henkin, Louis. "Human Rights Conditionality for U.S. Security and Development Assistance." *International Human Rights in Context: Law, Politics, Morals.* Ed. Henry J. Steiner and Philip Alston. Oxford: Clarendon, 1996.

Hennessy, Rosemary. *Pleasure and Profit: Sexual Identities in Late Capitalism.* New York: Routledge, 2000.

Herman, Andrew, and Thomas Swiss, eds. *The World Wide Web and Contemporary Cultural Theory.* New York: Routledge, 2000.

Hobsbawm, Eric. *Nations and Nationalisms since 1798.* Cambridge: Cambridge University Press, 1990.

Howard, Rhoda E. "Dignity, Community, and Human Rights." *Human Rights in Cross-Cultural Perspectives: A Quest for Consensus.* Ed. Abdullahi Ahmed An-Na'im, 81–102. Philadelphia: University of Pennsylvania Press, 1992.

——. "Gay Rights and the Right to a Family: Conflicts between Liberal and Illiberal Belief Systems." *Human Rights Quarterly* 23 (February 2001): 73–95.

Howard, Rhoda, and Jack Donelly. "Human Rights in World Politics." *International Politics: Enduring Concepts and Contemporary Issues.* Ed. Robert Art and Robert Jervis, 505–24. New York: Harper, 1992.

Human Rights Watch/Asia and Physicians for Human Rights. *Dead Silence: The Legacy of Abuses in Punjab.* New York: Human Rights Watch/Asia, 1994.

Human Rights Watch Women's Rights Division. *Seeking Protection: Addressing Sexual and Domestic Violence in Tanzania's Refugee Camps.* New York: Human Rights Watch, 2000.

Human Rights Watch Women's Rights Project. *The Human Rights Watch Global Report on Women's Human Rights.* New York: Human Rights Watch, 1995.

Huntington, Samuel. "American Ideals versus American Institutions." *International Human Rights in Context: Law, Politics, Morals.* Ed. Henry J. Steiner and Philip Alston, 815–17. Oxford: Clarendon, 1996.

Hutchings, Kimberley, and Roland Dannreuther, eds. *Cosmopolitan Citizenship.* New York: St. Martin's, 1999.

Hyndman, Jennifer. *Managing Displacement: Refugees and the Politics of Humanitarianism.* Minneapolis: University of Minnesota Press, 2000.

Ilumoka, Adetoun O. "African Women's Economic, Social and Cultural Rights: Towards a Relevant Theory and Practice." *Human Rights of Women: National and International Perspectives.* Ed. Rebecca Cook, 307–25. Philadelphia: University of Pennsylvania Press, 1994.

"An Interview with Bharati Mukherjee." *Mosaic,* spring 1994.

Isin, Engin, and Patricia Wood. *Citizenship and Identity.* London: Sage, 1999.

Iyer, Saroj. *The Struggle to Be Human: Women's Human Rights.* Bangalore: Books for Change, 1999.

Jackman, Barbara. "Well-Founded Fear of Persecution and Other Standards of Decision-Making: A North American Perspective." *Asylum Law and Practice in Europe and North America.* Ed. Jacqueline Bhabha and Geoffrey Coll, 37–70. Washington: Federal Publications, 1992.

James, Stanlie M. "Challenging Patriarchal Privilege through the Development of International Human Rights." *Women's Studies International Forum* 17, no. 6 (1994): 563–78.

Jayawardena, Kumari. *Feminism and Nationalism in the Third World.* London: Zed, 1986.

Jen, Gish. *Typical American.* Boston: Houghton Mifflin, 1991.

John, Mary. "Gender and Development in India, 1970s–1990s: Some Reflections on the Constitutive Role of Contexts." *Economic and Political Weekly,* 23 November 1996, 3071–77.

Johnsson, Anders B. "The International Protection of Women Refugees: A Summary of Principal Problems and Issues." *International Journal of Refugee Law* 1, no. 2 (April 1989): 221–31.

Jones, Charles. *Global Justices: Defending Cosmopolitanism.* New York: Oxford University Press, 1999.

Kandiyoti, Deniz. *Women, Islam and the State.* Philadelphia: Temple University Press, 1991.

Kang, Laura. *Compositional Subjects: Enfiguring Asian American Women.* Durham: Duke University Press, 2002.

Kant, Immanuel. "Idea for a Universal History from a Cosmo-political Point of View." Ed. and with an introduction by Lewis White Beck. Trans. Lewis White Beck, Robert E. Anchor, and Emil L. Fackenheim. Indianapolis: Bobbs-Merrill, 1963.

Kaplan, Amy, and Donald E. Pease, eds. *Cultures of United States Imperialism.* Durham: Duke University Press, 1993.

Kaplan, Caren. " 'Getting to Know You': Travel, Gender, and the Politics of Representation in *Anna and The King of Siam* and *The King and I.*" *Late Imperial Culture.*

Ed. Roman de la Campa, E. Ann Kaplan, and Michael Sprinker, 33–52. London: Verso, 1995.

———. "A World without Boundaries: The Body Shop's Trans/National Geographics." *Social Text* 13, no. 2 (fall 1995): 45–66.

———. *Questions of Travel: Postmodern Discourses of Displacement*. Durham: Duke University Press, 1996.

Kaplan, Caren, Norma Alarcón, and Minoo Moallem, eds. *Between Woman and Nation: Nationalisms, Transnational Feminisms, and the State*. Durham: Duke University Press, 1999.

Kaplan, Robert D. *The Ends of the Earth*. New York: Random House, 1996.

Kaplan, Temma. "Women's Rights as Human Rights: Women as Agents of Social Change." *Women, Gender, and Human Rights: A Global Perspective*. Ed. Marjorie Agosín, 191–204. New Brunswick: Rutgers University Press, 2001.

Karlekar, Malavika. "Domestic Violence." *Economic and Political Weekly* 33, no. 27 (4–10 July 1998): 1741–51.

Kartar Dhillon. "The Parrot's Beak." *Making Waves: An Anthology of Writings by and about Asian American Women*. Ed. Asian Women United of California. Boston: Beacon, 1989.

Keck, Margaret E., and Kathryn Sikkink. *Activists beyond Borders: Advocacy Networks in International Politics*. Ithaca: Cornell University Press, 1998.

Kelley, Ninette. "Report on the International Consultation on Refugee Women, Geneva, 15–19 November 1988, with Particular Reference to Protection Problems." *International Journal of Refugee Law* 1, no. 2 (April 1989): 231–41.

Kelly, Nancy. "Gender-Related Persecution: Assessing the Asylum Claims of Women." *Cornell International Law Journal* 26 (1993): 625–74.

———. "Guidelines for Women's Asylum Claims." *Interpreter Releases*, 27 June 1994, 813–28.

Khan, Naseem. "Asian Women's Dress: From Burqah to Bloggs: Changing Clothes for Changing Times." *Chic Thrills: A Fashion Reader*. Ed. Juliet Ash and Elizabeth Wilson, 61–75. Berkeley: University of California Press, 1993.

Kingston, Maxine Hong. *The Woman Warrior*. New York: Vintage, 1976.

Kishwar, Madhu. "Breaking the Stalemate: Uniform Civil Code vs. Personal Law." *Manushi* 77 (July–August 1993): 2–5.

Kiss, Elizabeth. "Is Nationalism Compatible with Human Rights? Reflections on East-Central Europe." *Identities, Politics, and Rights*. Ed. Austin Sarat and Thomas R. Kearns, 367–402. Ann Arbor: University of Michigan Press, 1995.

Klein, Christina. *Cold War Orientalism: Asia in the Middlebrow Imagination, 1945–1961*. Berkeley: University of California Press, 2003.

Knippling, Alpana Sharma. "Toward an Investigation of the Subaltern in Bharati Mukherjee's *The Middleman and Other Stories* and *Jasmine*." *Bharati Mukherjee: Critical Perspectives*. Ed. Emmanuel Nelson, 143–60. New York: Garland, 1993.

Koser, Khalid. "From Refugees to Transnational Communities?" *New Approaches to Migration? Transnational Communities and the Transformation of Home*. Ed. Nadje Al-Ali and Khalid Koser, 138–52. New York: Routledge, 2002.

Koshy, Susan. "The Fiction of Asian American Studies." *Yale Journal of Criticism* 9, no. 2 (fall 1996): 315–46.

——. "From Cold War to Trade War: Neocolonialism and Human Rights." *Social Text* 17, no. 1 (spring 1999): 1–32.

Kothari, Rajni. "Human Rights: A Movement in Search of a Theory." *Rethinking Human Rights*. Ed. Smitu Kothari and Harsh Sethi, 19–29. Delhi: Lokayan, 1991.

——. "Globalization and 'New World Order': What Future for the United Nations?" *Economic and Political Weekly*, 7 October 1995, 2513–17.

Kothari, Smith, and Harsh Sethi. "On Categories and Interventions." *Rethinking Human Rights*. Ed. Smith Kothari and Harsh Sethi, 1–17. Delhi: Lokayan, 1991.

Krishna, Srinivas. *Masala*. Prod. Camelia Friedberg. New York: Divani Films, 1993.

Krishnaraj, Maitreyi. "Women and the Public Domain: Critical Issues for Women Studies." *Economic and Political Weekly*, 21–27 February 1998, 391–95.

Kymlicka, Will. *Multicultural Citizenship: A Liberal Theory of Minority Rights*. Oxford: Oxford University Press, 1995.

La Brack, Bruce. "The New Patrons: Sikhs Overseas." *The Sikh Diaspora: Migration and Experience beyond Punjab*. Ed. N. Gerald Barrier and Verne A. Dusenbery, 260–304. Delhi: Chanakya, 1989.

Laguerre, Michel S. *Diasporic Citizenship: Haitian Americans in Transnational America*. New York: St. Martin's, 1998.

Lammers, Ellen. *Refugees, Gender, and Human Security: A Theoretical Introduction and Annotated Bibliography*. Utrecht: International, 1999.

Larner, Wendy. "Neo-Liberalism: Policy, Ideology, Governmentality." *Studies in Political Economy* 63 (2000): 5–25.

Lash, Scott, and John Urry. *Economies of Signs and Space*. London: Sage, 1994.

Lee, Ching Kwan. *Gender and the South China Miracle: Two Worlds of Factory Women*. Berkeley: University of California Press, 1998.

Lee, Jayne. "Constructing Battered Women Who Kill: The Interaction of Feminism, Psychiatry and the Law." Unpublished paper.

Lee, Martyn J. *Consumer Culture Reborn*. London: Routledge, 1993.

Lee, Rachel C. *The Americas of Asian American Literature*. Princeton: Princeton University Press, 1999.

Lee, Steven. "The Refugee's Burden of Proof for Asylum: Why Two Standards Are Better Than One." *Florida International Law Journal* 2 (1986–87): 227–48.

Leiss, William, Stephen Kline, and Sut Jhally. *Social Communication in Advertising: Persons, Products and Images of Well-Being*. New York: Methuen, 1986.

Leonard, Karen. *Making Ethnic Choices: California's Punjabi Mexican Americans*. Philadelphia: Temple University Press, 1992.

——. "Historical Constructions of Ethnicity: Research on Punjabi Immigrants in California." *Journal of American Ethnic History* 12, no. 4 (summer 1993): 4.

Levison, Julie H., and Sandra P. Levison. "Women's Health and Human Rights." *Women, Gender, and Human Rights: A Global Perspective*. Ed. Marjorie Agosín, 125–51. New Brunswick: Rutgers University Press, 2001.

Levy, Simon. *Asylum Based on Sexual Orientation: A Resource Guide*. San Francisco: International Gay and Lesbian Human Rights Commission and Lambda Legal Defense and Education Fund, 1996.

Lewis, Hope. "Between *Irua* and 'Female Genital Mutilation': Feminist Human

Rights Discourse and the Cultural Divide." *Harvard Human Rights Journal* 8 (spring 1995): 1–55.

Lim, Shirley Geok-lin. "Immigration and Diaspora." *An Interethnic Companion to Asian American Literature*. Ed. King-Kok Cheung, 289–311. Cambridge: Cambridge University Press, 1997.

Lopez, George, Jackie G. Smith, and Ron Pagnucco. "The Global Tide." *Bulletin of the Atomic Scientists* 51, no. 4 (July–August 1995): 33–39.

Love, Emily. "Equality in Political Asylum Law: For a Legislative Recognition of Gender-Based Persecution." *Harvard Women's Law Journal* 17 (spring 1994): 133–55.

Lowe, Donald. *The Body in Late-Capitalist USA*. Durham: Duke University Press, 1995.

Lowe, Lisa. *Immigrant Acts: On Asian American Cultural Politics*. Durham: Duke University Press, 1996.

Luibhéid, Eithne. *Entry Denied: Controlling Sexuality at the Border*. Minneapolis: University of Minnesota Press, 2002.

Lutton, Wayne. "Fleeing Their Culture: Extending Asylum to Women." *Social Contract*, summer 1997.

Lutz, Catherine, and Jane L. Collins. *Reading National Geographic*. Chicago: University of Chicago Press, 1993.

Macaulay, Thomas Babington. "Minute on Education of India." *Literature and Nation: Britain and India, 1800–1990*. Ed. Harish Trivedi and Richard Allen, 204–5. London: Routledge, 2000.

Macklin, Audrey. "Refugee Women and the Imperative of Categories." *Human Rights Quarterly* 17 (May 1995): 213–77.

Malkki, Liisa. "National Geographic: The Rooting of Peoples and the Territorialization of National Identity among Scholars and Refugees." *Cultural Anthropology* 7, no. 1 (February 1992): 24–44.

——. "Citizens of Humanity: Internationalism and the Imagined Community of Nations." *Disapora* 3, no. 1 (spring 1994): 41–68.

——. *Purity and Exile: Violence, Memory, and National Cosmology among Hutu Refugees in Tanzania*. Chicago: University of Chicago Press, 1995.

Mamdani, Mahmood. "Africa: Democratic Theory and Democratic Struggles." *Economic and Political Weekly*, 10 October 1992, 2228–32.

Mani, Lata. "Gender, Class and Cultural Conflict: Indu Krishnan's Knowing Her Place." *Our Feet Walk the Sky*. Ed. Women of South Asian Descent Collective, 32–36. San Francisco: Aunt Lute, 1993.

Mankekar, Purnima. "Brides Who Travel: Gender, Transnationalism, and Nationalism in Hindi Film." *positions: east asia cultures critique* 7, no. 3 (winter 1999): 731–61.

Marchand, Roland. *Advertising and the American Dream: Making Way for Modernity, 1920–1940*. Berkeley: University of California Press, 1985.

Marchetti, Gina. *Romance and the "Yellow Peril": Race, Gender and Discursive Strategies in Hollywood Fiction*. Berkeley: University of California Press, 1993.

Marin, Leni and Blandina Lansang-De Mesa, eds. *Women on the Move: Proceedings of the Workshop on Human Rights Abuses against Immigrant and Refugee Women*. San Francisco: Family Violence Prevention Fund, 1993.

Marshall, Thomas Humphrey. "Citizenship and Social Class." *Citizenship and Social Development*. Ed. T. H. Marshall, 71–134. New York: Anchor, 1967.

Martin, Susan Forbes. *Refugee Women*. London: Zed, 1992.

Mattelart, Armand. *Advertising International: The Globalization of Consumer Culture*. Trans. Michael Chanan. New York: Routledge, 1991.

Maurer, Bill. "On Divine Markets and the Problem of Justice: Empire as Theodicy." *Empire's New Clothes*. Ed. Paul Passavant and Jodi Dean. New York: Routledge, forthcoming.

Mawani, Nurjehan. "Women Refugee Claimants Fearing Gender-Related Persecution: The Canadian Experience." *Women on the Move: Proceedings of the Workshop on Human Rights Abuses against Immigrant and Refugee Women*. Ed. Leni Marin and Blandina Lansang–De Mesa, 1–4. San Francisco: Family Violence Prevention Fund, 1993.

Mbembe, Achille. "Prosaics of Servitude and Authoritarian Civilities." *Public Culture* 5, no. 1 (fall 1992): 123–48.

——. "Necropolitics." *Public Culture* 15, no. 1 (winter 2003): 11–40.

Melwani, Lavina. "Living the Dark Side of the Moon." *India Today*, 31 January 1994, 60c–60f.

Menon, Nivedita. "The Impossibility of Justice: Female Foeticide and Feminist Discourse on Abortion." *Social Reform, Sexuality and the State*. Ed. Patricia Uberoi, 369–92. New Delhi: Sage, 1996.

——. "State/Gender/Community: Citizenship in Contemporary India." *Economic and Political Weekly*, 31 January 1998, PE 3–10.

Menon, Ritu, and Kamla Bhasin. *Borders and Boundaries: Women in India's Partition*. New Delhi: Kali for Women, 1998.

Merali, Isfahan, and Valerie Osterveld, eds. *Giving Meaning to Economic, Social, and Cultural Rights*. Philadelphia: University of Pennsylvania Press, 2001.

Mercer, Kobena. "Diaspora Culture and the Dialogic Imagination." *Blackframes: Celebration of Black Cinema*. Ed. Mbye Cham and Claire Andrade-Watkins, 50–61. Cambridge: MIT Press, 1988.

Merry, Sally Engle. "Women, Violence and the Human Rights System." *Women, Gender, and Human Rights: A Global Perspective*. Ed. Marjorie Agosín, 83–97. New Brunswick: Rutgers University Press, 2001.

Mertus, Julie A., and Judy A. Benjamin. *War's Offensive on Women: The Humanitarian Challenge in Bosnia, Kosovo, and Afghanistan*. Bloomfield, Conn.: Kumarian, 2000.

Miles, Steven. *Consumerism as a Way of Life*. London: Sage, 1998.

Mill, James. *The History of British India*. Ed. John Clive. Chicago: University of Chicago Press, 1975 [1817].

Miller, Daniel, ed. *Modernity: An Ethnographic Approach: Dualism and Mass Consumption in Trinidad*. Providence, R.I.: Berg, 1994.

——. *Worlds Apart: Modernity through the Prism of the Local*. London: Routledge, 1995.

——, ed. *Material Cultures*. London: University College London Press, 1997.

Mitchell, Arnold. *The Nine American Lifestyles: Who We Are and Where We're Going.* New York: Macmillan, 1983.

Mitchell, Timothy. *Colonizing Egypt.* New York: Cambridge University Press, 1988.

Mitra, Indrani. " 'Luminous Brahmin Children Must Be Saved': Imperialist Ideologies, 'Postcolonial' Histories in Bharati Mukherjee's *The Tiger's Daughter.*" *Between the Lines: South Asians and Postcoloniality.* Ed. Deepika Bahri and Mary Vasudeva, 284–97. Philadelphia: Temple University Press, 1996.

Miyoshi, Masao. "A Borderless World? From Colonialism to Transnationalism and the Decline of the Nation-State." *Global/Local: Cultural Production and the Transnational Imaginary.* Ed. Rob Wilson and Wimal Dissanayake, 78–106. Durham: Duke University Press, 1996.

Moallem, Minoo. "Universalization of Particulars: The Civic Body and Gendered Citizenship in Iran." *Citizenship Studies* 3, no. 3 (November 1999): 319–36.

——. "Whose Fundamentalism?" *Meridians: Feminism, Race, Transnationalism* 2, no. 2 (2002): 298–301.

Mohanty, Chandra. "Under Western Eyes: Feminist Scholarship and Colonial Discourses." *Boundary* 12, no. 3 (spring–fall 1984): 333–58. Repr. in *Third World Women and the Politics of Feminism.* Ed. Chandra Mohanty, Ann Russo, and Lourdes Torres, 51–80. Bloomington: Indiana University Press, 1991.

Mohanty, Chandra, Ann Russo, and Lourdes Torres, eds. *Third World Women and the Politics of Feminism.* Bloomington: Indiana University Press, 1991.

Momsen, Janet. *Women and Development in the Third World.* London: Routledge, 1991.

Monshipuri, Mahmood, and Claude E. Welsh. "The Search for International Human Rights and Justice: Coming to Terms with the New Global Realities." *Human Rights Quarterly* 23, no. 2 (May 2001): 370–401.

Moretti, Franco. "Conjectures on World Literature." *New Left Review* 1 (January–February 2000): 54–68.

Morgan, Robin. *Sisterhood Is Global: The International Women's Movement.* New York: Anchor, 1984.

Morley, David, and Kevin Robins. *Spaces of Identity: Global Media, Electronic Landscapes and Cultural Boundaries.* London: Routledge, 1995.

Mosco, Vincent. "Webs of Myth and Power: Connectivity and the New Computer Technopolis." *The World Wide Web and Contemporary Cultural Theory.* Ed. Andrew Herman and Thomas Swiss, 37–60. New York: Routledge, 2000.

Moser, Caroline O. N., and Fiona Clark. *Victims, Perpetrators, or Actors? Gender, Armed Conflict, and Political Violence.* New York: Zed, 2001.

Mouffe, Chantal. "Democratic Citizenship and the Political Community." *Dimensions of Radical Democracy: Pluralism, Citizenship, Community.* Ed. Chantal Mouffe, 225–39. London: Verso, 1992.

——. "Democratic Politics and the Question of Identity." *The Identity in Question.* Ed. John Rajchman, 33–45. New York: Routledge, 1995.

Moyers, Bill. *Conquering America with Bharati Mukherjee.* Videotape recording, 1990.

Mukerji, Dhan Gopal. *Caste and Outcast.* Presented and ed. Gordon H. Chang, Purnima Mankekar, and Akhil Gupta. Stanford: Stanford University Press, 2002.

Mukherjee, Bharati. *The Tiger's Daughter.* Boston: Houghton Mifflin, 1972.

——. *The Middleman and Other Stories.* New York: Penguin, 1988.

——. *Jasmine.* New York: Fawcett Crest, 1989.

——. "American Dreamer." *Mother Jones,* January–February 1997.

Mulligan, Maureen. "Obtaining Political Asylum: Classifying Rape as a Well-Founded Fear of Persecution on Account of Political Opinion." *Boston College Third World Law Journal* 10 (1990): 355–80.

Mutua, Makau. "Human Rights International NGOs: A Critical Evaluation." *NGOs and Human Rights: Promise and Performance.* Ed. Claude E. Welsh, 151–63. Philadelphia: University of Pennsylvania Press, 2001.

Nagengast, Carole. "Women, Minorities, and Indigenous Peoples: Universalism and Cultural Relativity." *Journal of Anthropological Research* 53, no. 3 (fall 1997): 349–69.

Narayan, Uma. *Dislocating Cultures: Identities, Traditions, and Third World Feminism.* New York: Routledge, 1997.

Nguyen, Viet Thanh, and Tina Chen, eds. *Jouvert: A Journal of Postcolonial Studies* 4, no. 3 (spring–summer 2000). Special issue: Postcolonial Asian America.

Nityanandam, Indira. "Yasmine Gooneratne's 'A Change of Skies' and Bharati Mukherjee's *Jasmine*: The Immigrant Experience in Australia and the USA." *The Fiction of Bharati Mukherjee.* Ed. R. K. Dhawan, 148–52. New Delhi: Prestige, 1996.

Nussbaum, Martha. "Patriotism and Cosmopolitanism." *For Love of Country: Debating the Limits of Patriotism.* Ed. Joshua Cohen, 2–17. Boston: Beacon, 2002.

Oberoi, Harjot. *The Construction of Religious Boundaries: Culture, Identity and Diversity in the Sikh Tradition.* Chicago: University of Chicago Press, 1994.

Ohmae, Kenichi. *The Borderless World: Power and Strategy in the Interlinked Economy.* Rev. ed. New York: Harper Business, 1999.

Okin, Susan Moller. "Is Multiculturalism Bad for Women?" *Is Multiculturalism Bad for Women?* Ed. Joshua Cohen, Matthew Howard, and Martha C. Nussbaum, 9–24. Princeton: Princeton University Press, 1999.

Ong, Aihwa. "On the Edge of Empires: Flexible Citizenship among Chinese in Diaspora." *positions: east asia cultures critique* 1, no. 3 (winter 1993): 745–78.

——. "Cultural Citizenship as Subject-Making: Immigrants Negotiate Racial and Cultural Boundaries in the United States." *Current Anthropology* 37, no. 5 (December 1996): 737–62. Repr. in *Race, Identity, and Citizenship: A Reader.* Ed. Rodolfo D. Torres, Louis F. Miron, and Jonathan Xavier Inda, 262–93. Malden, Mass.: Basil Blackwell, 1999.

——. *Flexible Citizenship: The Cultural Logics of Transnationality.* Durham: Duke University Press, 1999.

Otta, Dianne. "Defending Women's Economic and Social Rights: Some Thoughts on Indivisibility and a New Standard of Equality." *Giving Meaning to Economic, Social, and Cultural Rights.* Ed. Isfahan Merali and Valerie Osterveld, 52–67. Philadelphia: University of Pennsylvania Press, 2001.

Ó Tuathail, Gearóid. *Critical Geopolitics.* Minneapolis: University of Minnesota Press, 1996.

Oza, Rupal. "Showcasing India: Gender, Geography and Globalization." *Signs: Journal of Women in Culture and Society* 26, no. 4 (summer 2001): 1067–96.

Pachauri, S. K. *Women and Human Rights*. New Delhi: A.P.H., 1999.

Palumbo-Liu, David. *Asian/American: Historical Crossings of a Racial Frontier*. Stanford: Stanford University Press, 1999.

Pandey, Gyanendra. *The Construction of Communalism in Colonial North India*. Delhi: Oxford University Press, 1990.

——. "The Culture of History." *In Near Ruins: Cultural Theory at the End of the Century*. Ed. Nicholas Dirks, 19–37. Minneapolis: University of Minnesota Press, 1998.

Panini, M. N. "Trends in Cultural Globalization: From Agriculture to Agribusiness in Karnataka." *Economic and Political Weekly*, 31 August 1999, 2168–73.

Pannikar, Raimundo. "Is the Notion of Human Rights a Western Concept?" *International Human Rights in Context: Law, Politics, Morals*. Ed. Henry J. Steiner and Philip Alston, 201–9. Oxford: Clarendon, 1996.

Pappu, Rekha. "Rethinking Legal Justice for Women." *Economic and Political Weekly*, 10 May 1997, 1048–52.

Parker, Andrew, Mary Russo, Doris Sommer, and Patricia Yaeger, eds. *Nationalisms and Sexualities*. New York: Routledge, 1992.

Pederson, Susan. "National Bodies, Unspeakable Acts: The Sexual Politics of Colonial Policy-Making." *Journal of Modern History* 63 (1991): 647–80.

Peters, Julie, and Andrea Wolper, eds. *Women's Rights, Human Rights: International Feminist Perspectives*. New York: Routledge, 1995.

Peterson, Alan, Ian Barns, Janice Dudley, and Patricia Harris. *Poststructuralism, Citizenship and Social Policy*. London: Routledge, 1999.

Phillips, Anne. *Democracy and Difference*. University Park: Pennsylvania State University Press, 1993.

Pollitt, Katha. "Women's Rights, Human Rights." *Nation*, 13 May 1997.

Pollock, Sheldon. "Cosmopolitanisms." *Public Culture* 12, no. 3 (2000): 591–626.

Potts, Lydia, and Terry Bond, trans. *The World Labor Market: A History of Migration*. Atlantic Highlands, N.J.: Zed, 1990.

Povrzanovic Frykman, Maja. "Homeland Lost and Gained: Croatian Diaspora and Refugees in Sweden." *New Approaches to Migration? Transnational Communities and the Transformation of Home*. Ed. Nadje Al-Ali and Khalid Koser, 118–37. New York: Routledge, 2002.

Prashad, Vijay. *The Karma of Brown Folk*. Minneapolis: University of Minnesota Press, 2001.

Pratt, Mary Louise. *Imperial Eyes: Travel Writing and Transculturation*. New York: Routledge, 1992.

Prendergast, Christopher. "Negotiating World Literature." *New Left Review* 8 (2001): 100–121.

Rajagopal, Arvind. "Advertising, Politics and the Sentimental Education of the Indian Consumer." *Visual Anthropology Review* 14, no. 2 (1998–99): 14–31.

——. "Hindu Nationalism in the US: Changing Configurations of Political Practice." *Ethnic and Racial Studies* 23, no. 3 (May 2000): 468–96.

Rajan, Nalini. "Multiculturalism, Group Rights and Identity Politics." *Economic and Political Weekly*, 7 April 1998, 1699–1701.

Rand, Erica. *Barbie's Queer Accessories*. Durham: Duke University Press, 1995.

Rawls, John. *A Theory of Justice*. Cambridge: Harvard University Press, 1971.

Razack, Sherene. "What Is to Be Gained by Looking White People in the Eye? Culture, Race, and Gender in Cases of Sexual Violence." *Signs: Journal of Women in Culture and Society* 19, no. 4 (summer 1994): 894–923.

——. *Looking White People in the Eye: Gender, Race and Culture in Classrooms and Courtrooms*. Toronto: University of Toronto Press, 1998.

——. "Looking for Race in Gender: A Race Critique of How Domestic Violence as Gender Persecution Is Adjudicated." *Canadian Journal of Women and the Law* (forthcoming).

Rée, Jonathan. "Internationality." *Radical Philosophy* 60 (spring 1992): 3–11.

"Refugees Face Barriers to Political Asylum." *Human Rights: Opposing Viewpoints*. Ed. Mary E. Williams. San Diego: Greenhaven, 1998. Orig. pubd. in Amnesty International Report 1997.

Richmond, Anthony H. *Global Apartheid: Refugees, Racism and the New World Order*. Toronto: Oxford University Press, 1994.

Riles, Annelise. "Infinity within the Brackets." *American Ethnologist* 23, no. 3 (August 1998): 378–98.

Rittich, Kerry. "Feminism after the State: The Rise of the Market and the Future of Women's Rights." *Giving Meaning to Economic, Social, and Cultural Rights*. Ed. Isfahan Merali and Valerie Osterveld, 95–108. Philadelphia: University of Pennsylvania Press, 2001.

Ritzer, George. *The McDonaldization of Society*. Thousand Oaks: Pine Forge, 1993.

Robbins, Bruce, ed. "Sad Stories in the International Public Sphere: Richard Rorty on Culture and Human Rights." *Public Culture* 9, no. 2 (winter 1997): 209–32.

——. "Introduction Part I: Actually Existing Cosmopolitanism." *Cosmopolitics: Thinking and Feeling beyond the Nation*. Ed. Pheng Cheah and Bruce Robbins, 1–19. Minneapolis: University of Minnesota Press, 1998.

Roediger, David R. *The Wages of Whiteness: Race and the Making of the American Working Class*. New York: Verso, 1991.

Rosaldo, Renato. "Cultural Citizenship and Educational Democracy." *Cultural Anthropology* 9, no. 3 (1994): 402–11.

Rose, Nikolas. *Governing the Soul: The Shaping of the Private Self*. London: Routledge, 1990.

——. "Government, Authority and Expertise in Advanced Liberalism." *Economy and Society* 22, no. 3 (1993): 283–99.

——. "Identity, Genealogy, History." *Questions of Cultural Identity*. Ed. Stuart Hall and Paul du Gay, 128–50. Thousand Oaks: Sage, 1996.

——. *Inventing Our Selves: Psychology, Power and Personhood*. Cambridge: Cambridge University Press, 1998.

——. *Powers of Freedom: Reframing Political Thought*. New York: Cambridge University Press, 1999.

Rosenberg, Emily. *Spreading the American Dream: American Economic and Cultural Expansion, 1890–1945*. New York: Hill and Wang, 1982.

Rouse, Roger. "Mexican Migration and the Social Space of Postmodernism." *Diaspora* 1, no. 1 (spring 1991): 8–23.

——. "Thinking Through Transnationalism: Notes on the Cultural Politics of Class Relations in the Contemporary United States." *Public Culture* 7, no. 2 (winter 1995): 353–402.

Rowe, John Carlos. *Literary Culture and U.S. Imperialism: From the Revolution to World War II*. Oxford: Oxford University Press, 2000.

Roy, Anindyo. "The Aesthetics of an (Un)willing Immigrant: Bharati Mukherjee's *Days and Nights in Calcutta* and *Jasmine*." *Bharati Mukherjee: Critical Perspectives*. Ed. Emmanuel Nelson, 127–42. New York: Garland, 1993.

Ruiz, Vicki. " 'Star Struck': Acculturation, Adolescence, and Mexican American Women, 1920–1950." *Small Worlds: Children and Adolescents in America, 1850–1950*. Ed. Elliot West and Paula Petrik, 61–80. Lawrence: University Press of Kansas, 1992.

Rushdie, Salman. *Imaginary Homelands: Essays and Criticism, 1981–1991*. New York: Penguin, 1992.

——. *Midnight's Children*. New York: Penguin, 1995.

Safran, William. "Diasporas in Modern Societies: Myths of Homeland and Return." *Diaspora* 1, no. 1 (spring 1991): 83–99.

Said, Edward. *Orientalism*. New York: Vintage, 1978.

——. "Reflections on Exile." *Granta* 13 (1984): 159–72.

——. *Culture and Imperialism*. New York: Alfred A. Knopf, 1993.

Saldívar, José David. *Border Matters: Remapping American Cultural Studies*. Berkeley: University of California Press, 1997.

Sangari, Kum-Kum, and Sudesh Vaid, eds. *Recasting Women: Essays in Indian Colonial History*. New Brunswick: Rutgers University Press, 1990.

Scanlon, Jennifer. *Inarticulate Longings: The Ladies' Home Journal, Gender and the Promises of Consumer Culture*. New York: Routledge, 1995.

Schein, Louisa. "The Consumption of Color and the Politics of White Skin in Post-Mao China." *Social Text* 12, no. 4 (winter 1994): 141–64.

——. "Importing Miao Brethren to Hmong America: A Not-So-Stateless Transnationalism." *Cosmopolitics: Thinking and Feeling beyond the Nation-State*. Ed. Pheng Cheah and Bruce Robbins, 163–91. Minneapolis: University of Minnesota Press, 1998.

Scialabba, Lori. "The Immigration and Naturalization Service Considerations for Asylum Officers Adjudicating Asylum Claims from Women." *International Journal of Refugee Studies*, autumn 1997, 174–81. Special issue: UNHCR Symposium on Gender-Based Persecution, Geneva, 22–23 February 1996.

Sen, Gita, and Caren Grown, eds. *Development, Crises, and Alternative Visions: Third World Women's Perspectives*. New York: Monthly Review, 1987.

Shankar, Lavina Dhingra, and Rajini Srikanth. Introduction, *A Part, yet Apart: South Asians in Asian America*. Ed. Lavina Dhingra Shankar and Rajini Srikanth, 9. Philadelphia: Temple University Press, 1998.

Shields, Rob. "Hypertext Links: The Ethic of the Index and Its Space-Time Effects." *The World Wide Web and Contemporary Cultural Theory.* Ed. Andrew Herman and Thomas Swiss, 145–60. New York: Routledge, 2000.

Shklar, Judith N. *American Citizenship: The Quest for Inclusion.* Cambridge: Harvard University Press, 1991.

Shohat, Ella. "Gender and Culture of Empire: Toward a Feminist Ethnography of the Cinema." *Quarterly Review of Film and Video* 13, nos. 1–3 (1991): 45–84.

——. "Post-Third-Worldist Culture: Gender, Nation, and the Cinema." *Feminist Genealogies, Colonial Legacies, Democratic Futures.* Ed. M. Jacqui Alexander and Chandra T. Mohanty, 183–209. New York: Routledge, 1997.

Shohat, Ella, and Robert Stam. *Unthinking Eurocentrism: Multiculturalism and the Media.* New York: Routledge, 1994.

Sinclair, John, Elizabeth Jacka, and Stuart Cunningham, eds. *New Patterns in Global Television.* Oxford: Oxford University Press, 1996.

Singh, Kirti. "Obstacles to Women's Rights in India." *Human Rights of Women: National and International Perspectives.* Ed. Rebecca Cook, 375–96. Philadelphia: University of Pennsylvania Press, 1994.

Singh, Prakash. *The Naxalite Movement in India.* New Delhi: Rupa, 1995.

Singh, Pritam. "Sectarian and Human Rights Discourse: The Politics of Human Rights in Post-Colonial Punjab." *Changing Concepts of Rights and Justice in South Asia.* Ed. Michael R. Anderson and Sumit Guha, 239–74. New Delhi: Oxford University Press, 2000.

Sishwa, Bhapsi. *Cracking India.* Minneapolis: Milkweed, 1991.

Sklair, Leslie. *Sociology of the Global System.* Baltimore: Johns Hopkins University Press, 1991.

Slater, David, and Peter J. Taylor, eds. *The American Century: Consensus and Coercion in the Projection of American Power.* Oxford: Basil Blackwell, 1999.

Smith, Jackie, Ron Pagnucco, and George A. Lopez. "Globalizing Human Rights: The Work of Transnational Human Rights NGOs in the 1990s." *Human Rights Quarterly* 20 (May 1998): 379–412.

Smith, Neil. *American Empire: Roosevelt's Geographer and the Prelude to Globalization.* Berkeley: University of California Press, 2003.

Smoodin, Eric. *Regarding Frank Capra: Audience, Celebrity, and American Film Studies, 1930–1960.* Durham: Duke University Press, 2004.

——, ed. *Disney Discourse: Producing the Magic Kingdom.* New York: Routledge, 1994.

Soja, Edward. *Postmodern Geographies: The Reassertion of Space in Critical Social Theory.* London: Verso, 1989.

Song, Min. "Pahkar Singh's Argument with Asian America." *A Part, Yet Apart: South Asians and Asian America.* Ed. Lavina Dhingra Shankar and Rajini Srikanth, 79–101. Philadelphia: Temple University Press, 1998.

Sood, Malini. "Expatriate Nationalism and Ethnic Radicalism: The Ghadar Party in North America, 1910–1920" (diss., State University of New York, Stony Brook, 1995).

Soysal, Yasemin Nuhoglu. *Limits of Citizenship: Migrants and Postnational Membership in Europe.* Chicago: University of Chicago Press, 1994.

Spijkerboer, Thomas. *Gender and Refugee Status.* Burlington, Vt.: Ashgate, 2000.

Spivak, Gayatri Chakravorty. "Three Women's Texts and a Critique of Imperialism."
"Race," Writing and Difference. Ed. Henry Louis Gates Jr., 262–80. Chicago: University of Chicago Press, 1985.

———. *In Other Worlds: Essays in Cultural Politics.* New York: Methuen, 1987.

———. "Can the Subaltern Speak?" *Marxism and the Interpretation of Culture.* Ed. Cary Nelson and Lawrence Grossberg, 271–313. Urbana: University of Illinois Press, 1988.

———. "French Feminism in an International Frame." *In Other Worlds: Essays in Cultural Politics,* 134–53. New York: Metheun, 1987.

———. *Outside in the Teaching Machine.* New York: Routledge, 1993.

———. "Diasporas Old and New: Women in the Transnational World." *Class Issues: Pedagogy, Cultural Studies, and the Public Sphere.* Ed. Amitava Kumar, 87–116. New York: New York University Press, 1997.

———. *A Critique of Postcolonial Reason: Toward a History of the Vanishing Present.* Cambridge: Harvard University Press, 1999.

Spivak, Gayatri Chakravorty, Rashmi Bhatnagar, Lola Chatterjee, and Rajeshwari Sunder Rajan. "The Post-Colonial Critic." *The Post-Colonial Critic: Interviews, Strategies, Dialogues.* Ed. Sarah Harasym, 67–74. New York: Routledge, 1990.

Steiner, Henry J., and Philip Alston, eds. *International Human Rights in Context: Law, Politics, Morals.* Oxford: Clarendon, 1996.

Stevenson, Nick. "Globalization, National Cultures and Cultural Citizenship." *Sociological Quarterly* 38, no. 1 (winter 1997): 41–66.

Stoler, Ann. "Making Empire Respectable: The Politics of Race and Sexual Morality in 20th-Century Colonial Cultures." *Imperial Monkey Business: Racial Supremacy in Social Darwinist Theory and Colonial Practice.* Ed. Jan Breman, 35–70. Amsterdam: VU University Press, 1990.

———. *Race and the Education of Desire.* Durham: Duke University Press, 1995.

———. *Carnal Knowledge and Imperial Rule: Race and the Intimate in Colonial Rule.* Berkeley: University of California Press, 2002.

Subramanian, Dr. S. *Human Rights Training.* New Delhi: Manas, 2000.

Susman, Warren. *Culture as History: The Transformation of American Society in the Twentieth Century.* New York: Pantheon, 1984.

Takaki, Ron. *Strangers from a Different Shore.* Boston: Little, Brown, 1989.

Tan, Amy. *The Joy Luck Club.* New York: Putnam's, 1989.

Tarlo, Emma. *Clothing Matters: Dress and Identity in India.* Chicago: University of Chicago Press, 1996.

Taussig, Michael. "Culture of Terror—Space of Death: Roger Casement's Putumayo Report and the Explanation of Torture." *Colonialism and Culture.* Ed. Nicholas Dirks, 135–73. Ann Arbor: University of Michigan Press, 1992.

Thomas, Dorothy Q., and Michele E. Beasley. "Domestic Violence as a Human Rights Issue." *Human Rights Quarterly* 15 (February 1993): 36–62.

Tölöyan, Khachig. "Rethinking Diaspora(s): Stateless Power in the Transnational Moment." *Diaspora* 5, no. 1 (spring 1996): 3–36.

Tomasevski, Katarina. *Women and Human Rights.* London: Zed, 1993.

Tomlinson, Alan. Introduction. *Consumption, Identity, and Style.* Ed. Alan Tomlinson, 1–38. London: Routledge, 1990.

Tomlinson, John. *Cultural Imperialism: A Critical Introduction.* London: Pinter, 1991.

Tuitt, Patricia. *False Images: Law's Construction of the Refugee.* London: Pluto, 1996.

———. "Rethinking the Refugee Concept." *Refugee Rights and Realities: Evolving International Concepts and Regimes.* Ed. Frances Nicholson and Patrick Twomey, 106–18. New York: Cambridge University Press, 1999.

Turner, Bryan S., ed. *Citizenship and Social Theory.* London: Sage, 1993.

UN High Commissioner for Refugees. *The State of the World's Refugees 1995: In Search of Solutions.* New York: Oxford University Press, 1995.

Urla, Jacqueline, and Alan Swedlund. "The Anthropometry of Barbie: Unsettling Ideals of the Feminine Body in Popular Culture." *Deviant Bodies: Critical Perspectives on Difference in Science and Popular Culture.* Ed. Jennifer Terry and Jacqueline Urla, 277–313. Bloomington: Indiana University Press, 1995.

Vadackumchery, James. *Human Rights Friendly Police: A Myth or Reality?* New Delhi: A.P.H., 2000.

Verdirame, Guglielmo. "Testing the Effectiveness of International Norms: UN Humanitarian Assistance and Sexual Apartheid in Afghanistan." *Human Rights Quarterly* 23 (August 2001): 733–68.

Visweswaran, Kamala. "Diaspora by Design: Flexible Citizenship and South Asians in U.S. Racial Formations." *Diaspora* 6, no. 1 (1997): 5–29.

Voet, Rian. *Feminism and Citizenship.* London: Sage, 1998.

Volpp, Leti. "(Mis)identifying Culture: Asian Women and the 'Cultural Defense.'" *Harvard Women's Law Journal* 17 (spring 1994): 57–101.

Warde, Alan. "Consumers, Identity and Belonging: Reflections on Some Theses of Zygmunt Bauman." *The Authority of the Consumer.* Ed. Russell Keat, Nigel Whiteley, and Nicholas Abercrombie, 58–74. London: Routledge, 1994.

Waters, Malcolm. *Globalization.* London: Routledge, 1995.

Welsh, Claude E., ed. *NGOs and Human Rights: Promise and Performance.* Philadelphia: University of Pennsylvania Press, 2001.

Williams, Patricia J. *The Alchemy of Race and Rights.* Cambridge: Harvard University Press, 1991.

Williams, Raymond. *Culture and Society.* London: Chatto and Windus, 1958.

Winter, Bronwyn. "Women, the Law, and Cultural Relativism in France: The Case of Excision." *Rethinking the Political.* Ed. Barbara Laslett et al., 315–50. Chicago: University of Chicago Press, 1995.

Wolf, Diane. *Factory Daughters: Gender, Household Dynamics, and Rural Industrialization in Java.* Berkeley: University of California Press, 1992.

Wong, Sau-ling Cynthia. "Denationalization Reconsidered: Asian American Cultural Criticism at a Theoretical Crossroads." *Amerasia Journal* 21, nos. 1–2 (1995): 1–27.

Wright, Shelley. *International Human Rights, Decolonisation and Globalisation: Becoming Human.* London: Routledge, 2001.

index

*

Abusharaf, Rogaia, 237 n. 72
Ackerman, Frank, 224 n. 75
Advertising: of Barbie, 103–4, 108; global, 94–95; identity politics and, 95; of suffrage, 29; to women, 109. *See also* Marketing
Afghanistan, women's rights in, 133–34
Africa: diaspora from, 49; female genital mutilation in, 177, 179; refugees from, 59, 173; slave trade and, 50–52
Agosin, Marjorie, 130, 136–37, 155–56, 231 nn. 24–25, 232 n. 54, 234 n. 115
AISSF (All India Sikh Student Federation), 185, 187
Al-Raida, 144–45
Alarcon, Norma, 232 n. 53
Alexander, M. Jacquie, 223 n. 60, 232 n. 67
Alexander, Meena, 75, 227 n. 106
All India Sikh Student Federation (AISSF), 185, 187
Alonso-Zaldivar, Ricardo, 222 n. 29
Alston, Phillip, 230 n. 12, 231 nn. 31–33, 231 nn. 35–36
"America": choice represented by, 66–68, 99–100; freedom represented by, 8–9, 98–99, 170–71, 205–6; idea of, 207–8; identity in, 2, 76–78; imagin-

aries of, 9–10; meaning of, 2–3, 9–10, 196–97; national identity in, 2; after 9/11, 208–9; for prospective migrants, 6–7. *See also* United States
American, "becoming," 203; defined, 64; by purchasing Barbie, 119–20; through multiculturalism, 7, 200–202; whiteness and, 7
"American Dream," 4–14
American flag, after 9/11, 211–12, 214–18
"American lifestyle," 94–96
"Americanness," 5, 7–8, 93–94, 98–99, 214
American subjects, 1, 60–61
"American values," 149–50
"American way of life," 9, 203–4, 203–9, 205, 206
Amnesty International, 171–72
Anaya, S. James, 232 n. 48
Anker, Deborah, 236 n. 59
Anzaldua, Gloria, 232 n. 53, 239 n. 11
Appadurai, Arjun, 30, 84, 99, 223 n. 43, 224 n. 4, 224 n. 67, 224 n. 75, 228 n. 12, 228 n. 15, 229 n. 51
"Area studies," 33
Arranged Marriage (Divakaruni), 77
Arulanantham, Ahilan, 235 n. 26

"Asian-Americans," 60–63, 72, 209–10

Asian women immigrants, 59, 63–65, 170

Asylum, refugee: credibility of claims of, 186–92; encouraged testimony and, 181–82; gender-based claims, *see* Gender-based asylum claims; human rights and, 158–59, 161; laws governing, 172; sexual identity and, 170–71; sexual orientation and, 182; transnational cultural politics and, 182–84

Barad, Jill, 99–100

Barbalet, J. M., 222 n. 15, 240 n. 37

Barbie: advertising, 93–94, 103–4, 108–10; becoming American and, 119–20; black, 102; body of, 101; criticism of, 100–103; cultural and economic changes allowing, 82–83; diasporic subjects and, 89–90; dress of, 82; in ethnic dress, 102, 104, 105; identity and, 119; in India, 29, 32, 80–120; marketing of, 98–99, 104–5; nationalism and, 100–103; as role model, 102; sales of, 85–87, 111; stereotypes and, 102–3; as symbol of Americanness, 98–99; "traditional," 81; as white, 81–82, 96

Barbieri, William, 42–43, 225 n. 29

Barns, Ian, 31, 224 n. 73

Basu, Amrita, 139, 154, 232 n. 62, 234 n. 111

Bauman, Zygmunt, 119, 230 n. 88

Beasley, Michele E., 234 n. 108

Beauty pageants, 112–14. *See also* Modeling industry, in India

"Before/After September 11, 2001," 213

Beijing Declaration, 175

Beijing international women's conference, 150, 154

Bell, Lynda S., 232 n. 40

Bengal, India, 40–41

Benhabib, Seyla, 221–22 n. 13

Berlant, Lauren, 221 n. 9, 224 n. 69, 229 n. 53

Berman, Marshall, 222 n. 26

Bhabha, Homi, 48–49

Bhabha, Jacqueline, 235 n. 11

Bharvani, Shakuntala, 227 n. 102

Bhasin, Kamla, 193, 238 n. 97

Biddick, Kathleen, 55, 225 n. 55

Biopolitics, geopolitics and, 3, 17–18, 159

Bissland, Julie, 236 n. 58

Black Atlantic, The (Gilroy), 50

Bocock, Robert, 95, 229 n. 36

Bodnar, John, 206, 239 n. 17

Body shop owners, 5–6

Bombay cinema, 111–13

Bomma, story of, 56–57

Bose, Brinda, 227 n. 101

Bourque, Susan, 139, 232 n. 61

Bower, Karen, 236 n. 47

Brand-name goods, in India, 86–87, 89

Brennan, Tim, 44–45, 224 n. 13, 225 n. 28

Brewster, Anne, 73–74, 226 n. 82, 227 n. 99

Brooks, Geraldine, 237 n. 70

Bryman, Alan, 229 n. 55

Bulosan, Carlos, 63, 226 n. 74

Bunch, Charlotte, 126–27, 231 nn. 13–14

Bureau of Citizenship and Immigration Services, 14–15

Burgerman, Susan D., 231 n. 6

Burke, Timothy, 224 n. 75

Burton, Dan, 152

Bush, George W., 146, 203–4; human rights under, 133; immigration under, 15, 160; nationalism under, 206; patriotism under, 217–18

Butalia, Urvashi, 193, 238 n. 97

Butler, Judith P., 223 n. 60

Byrnes, Andrew, 148, 233 n. 90

Canada, asylum in, 67, 175, 180–81

Capitalism, 30–32, 44–45

Caputo, John, 228 n. 7

Carey, Lynn, 226 n. 88, 227 n. 90

Caribbean diaspora, 49

Castells, Manuel, 6, 23, 31, 221 n. 6, 223 n. 52, 224 n. 74

CEDAW (Convention on the Elimination of All Forms of Discrimination Against Women), 126–28, 147, 175

Chakrabarty, Dipesh, 199, 225 n. 22, 239 n. 6

Chandler, David, 133, 231 n. 37

Charlesworth, Hilary, 133, 137, 232 n. 38, 232 n. 58

Chatterjee, Lola, 222 n. 28, 225 n. 20, 225 n. 22

Cheah, Pheng, 43, 134, 225 nn. 34–35, 232 n. 41

Chicago, immigrants in, 6–7

Children, as consumers, 85–86, 106–8

China: Beijing Declaration and, 175; Beijing international women's conference and, 150, 154; women's rights in, 134–35, 150, 179–80

Chinkin, Christine, 133, 232 n. 38

Choice: America as representing, 66–68, 99–100; arranged marriage and, 77; for Asian women immigrants, 63–65; consumer, 30–31, 119; feminists on, 28–29

Chow, Esther, 234 n. 97

Chowdhry, Prem, 194, 238 n. 99

Cisneros, Sandra, 101

Citizens: "global," 122; immigrants vs., 5; nation-state and, 147

Citizenship: "American Dream" and, 4–14; consumer, 81, 217–20; definitions of, 10–13; democratic, 26; dual, 166; hyphenated American subject and, 60–61; migrants and, 11, 35; nationalism and, 13; nation-state and, 12; neoliberal, 1–34; rights and, 10–11, 130; as status, 12; "world," 43–45

Civil society, 2, 138–45

Claiming Our Rights (manual), 144

Clark, Danae, 95

Class: construction of, 55–56; cultural production of, 27; ideas of place and nation and, 45–46; selling Barbie and, 104

Clifford, James, 43, 55–56, 167, 225 n. 26, 225 n. 33, 235 n. 20

Clinton, Bill, 146; immigration under, 160; refugees under, 173–75; rights under, 147; Violence Against Women Act and, 156

Clinton, Hillary, 150

"Coercive family planning practices," 179–80

Cohen, Colleen Ballerino, 224 n. 75, 229 n. 67

Colonialism: analysis of, 48–49; cosmopolitanism and, 56; European, 52; in India, 40; loss of connections with past and, 53–54; modernity linked to, 25; narratives of migration and, 54–55; regimes of, 199; women under, 58

Computer industry, workers in, 4

Connection, technologies of, 47–48

Connectivities, transnational, 3, 14–26, 54–55, 163

Connectivity, 23–25, 37

Connors, Jane, 176, 236 nn. 52–53

Constantini, Mark, 239 n. 27

Consumer capitalism, American, 30

Consumer choice, 119

Consumer citizenship, 81, 217–20

Consumer culture: American flag in, 217–19; choice and, 30–31; feminism and, 29; female subjects produced by, 28; gender in, 84; governmentality of rights and, 1–34; identity production and, 27–28; nationalism produced by, 81; study of migration and, 90–91; subjectivities created by, 30; subjects of, 83–84; working-class women and, 29–30

Consumers: children as, 85–86, 106–8; fantasies of, 99–100; feminism and, 109; globalized, 83–84, 91–96; Indian, 92–94, 103–11; markets for, 16–17; nationalism and, 13; practices of, 9, 108–10, 118–19; styles of, 95–

Consumers (*continued*)
 96; transnational, 111–20; young,
 108–10
Convention on the Elimination of All
 Forms of Discrimination Against
 Women (CEDAW), 126–28, 147, 175
Coomaraswamy, Radhika, 129, 231 n. 22
"Cosmopolitan citizenship," 12
Cosmopolitanism: colonial, 56; conceptualization of, 37; feminism and, 31–
 32; historical, 57; internationalism
 and, 47; multiculturalism and, 74–78;
 nonélite, 167; postcolonial, 38, 48–58;
 representation of Europeans and, 43;
 subjects of, 37, 39, 78–79; as term,
 42–43; trade as producing, 42, 50–51;
 as "world of accommodations," 55
Cosmopolitans: late-twentieth-century,
 44; nomadism and, 43–44; non-West,
 25; postcolonial, 45, 58–65; qualifying
 as, 38; as term, 37–38; theorizing, 42–
 48; trade as producing, 58
Credibility, of asylum claims, 186–90
Crenshaw, Kimberle, 156, 234 n. 116
Crisp, Jeff, 235 n. 14
Cultural citizenship, 60–61
Cultural politics, transnational, 182–84
Cultural practices, 106–7
Cunningham, Stuart, 224 n. 75

Danielsen, Dan, 237 n. 77
Das, Veena, 193, 238 n. 98
De Mooij, Marieke, 94–95, 229 n. 34
Department of Homeland Security,
 14–15
Dev, S. Mahendra, 228 n. 4
Development, human rights and, 130–34
Development policies, feminists on,
 133–34
Development regimes, 131–33
Dharwadkar, Vinay, 47, 225 nn. 23–24,
 225 n. 41
Dhillon, Kartar, 62
Diasporas: analysis of, 48–49; in Bom-
 bay films, 112–13; culture of, 90; novel

and, 35–79; studies of, 49–50; sub-
 jects of, 37, 60–61, 87–90, 95–96,
 111–20
"Diasporic citizenship," 12
Dillon, Michael, 17, 222 n. 38
Disney toys, 97, 106–8
Displacement, 35–36, 160–61, 166–67
Divakaruni, Chitra, 38–40, 224 n. 17,
 227 n. 107, 227 n. 110. *See also Mistress
 of Spices, The*
Domestic violence: asylum claims based
 on, 179–80; "global" movement
 against, 155–57; in India, 154–55; in
 United States, 154–55
Donelly, Jack, 233 n. 89
Dreifus, Claudia, 94, 229 n. 33
D'Sa, Antoinette, 228 n. 21
Dual citizenship, 166
Dubernet, Cecile, 235 n. 3
Ducille, Ann, 101, 228 n. 13, 229 n. 62,
 229 nn. 64–65
DuGay, Paul, 221–22 n. 13, 222 n. 27
Dusenbery, Verne A., 235 n. 17
Dutt, Toru, 47
Dutta, Nilanjan, 234 n. 101

Eberhardt, Isabelle, 56
Ebersole, Lucinda, 100–101, 229 n. 58
Egypt, in spice trade, 51–53, 55
Eisenstein, Zillah, 10
Elite: For the International Indian, 114–16
Élites, postcolonial cosmopolitans as, 45
Empire (Hardt and Negri), 21–22, 55
Engle, Karen, 181, 237 n. 77
"English" education, for Indians, 40–41
Ensted, Nan, 29, 224 n. 63
Ervolina, Anna, 176, 235 n. 10, 236 n. 47,
 236 n. 55, 237 n. 68
Escobar, Arturo, 131, 231 n. 29
Espin, Olivia M., 170–71, 226 n. 76, 236
 n. 35
Ethnic dress, Barbie in, 102, 104–5
Ethnic groups, consumer practices of,
 118–19
Ethnic identity, American, 76–78

Eurocentrism, human rights as, 135
Europe: colonialism and, 52; cosmopolitanism and, 51; as haven for refugees, 168–69; powers of, 22; reaction to 9/11 in, 206–7; women in, 58
Europeans, as "world citizens," 43
Ewald, Françoise, 201, 239 n. 12
Ewen, Stuart, 224 n. 66, 229 n. 32, 230 n. 86

Fabian, Johannes, 43, 225 n. 31
Fakhro, Munira A., 232 n. 62
Fantasies, of consumers, 99–100
Fashion industry, in India, 110–11
Fault Lines (Alexander), 75
Featherstone, Mike, 119, 230 n. 90
Female genital mutilation, 177, 179
Female subject: consumer culture as producing, 28; in human rights, 136–37; refugee, 32, 163, 168, 170, 183–84; "third world," 59–60
Feminism: activism and, 145–46; choice as concept in, 28–29; consumerism and, 29, 109; development policies and, 133–34; domestic violence and, 156; exoticism and, 77; human rights and, 124–25, 128, 130, 152–57; in India, 31–32; neoliberalism and, 26–34; as political opinion, 178–79; sexual abuse and, 163; "third world" female subject and, 59–60; transnational connectivities and, 3–4, 147–48; universalism and, 137–38; in West, 63–65
Feminist agency, 30–31
Feminist cosmopolitans, postcolonial, 58–65
Fernandez, Bob, 221 n. 5
Fieldwork, on Mattel, 84–85
Film stars, in Bombay, 111–12
Finnegan, Margaret, 29, 223 nn. 61–62
Flag, American, 211–12, 214–19
Ford Foundation, 144–45
Foucault, Michel, 16–18, 129–32, 159, 199, 202, 222 n. 36, 223 n. 41, 231 n. 30, 234–35 n. 2

Freedom, America as representing, 8–9, 98–99, 170–71, 205–6. *See also* Choice
Freeman, Carla, 99
Fried, Susanna, 231 n. 13
Friedman, Edward, 232 n. 42, 233 n. 81
Friedman, Elizabeth, 127, 146, 231 nn. 15–16
Fukuyama, Francis, 83, 228 n. 8

Gandhi, Indira, 88, 151
Gandhi, Rajiv, 88
Gender: construction of, 55–56; cultural production of, 27; governmentality and, 197–98; transnationalism and, 1, 84; visibility and, 209–17. *See also* Gender-based asylum claims
Gender-based asylum claims, 177–82; in Canada, 180–81; female genital mutilation and, 177, 179; in United States, 176–77, 180–81, 183–84
Gender-based violence, 175–76
Gendered consumption practices, 108–10
Gendered identity, 26
Gendered subjects: feminist action and, 27; politics and, 3; refugee, 158–95; transnational, 163, 192–95
Geneva Convention, 183
Geopolitics: biopolitics and, 3, 17, 159; human rights as tool of, 149; refugee narrative and, 186–87
Geske, Mary, 139, 232 n. 61
Ghosh, Amitav, 224 n. 15, 225 nn. 38–39, 225 n. 43, 235 n. 7; as anti-colonial, 38–39; postcolonial cosmopolitanism of, 48–58; on "world" literature, 45–46
—writings of: as anti-colonial, 49; class in, 55–56; cosmopolitanism in, 39, 41–42; gender in, 55–56; mobility in, 39; the nonwestern in, 75–76; publishers of, 48; story of Bomma in, 56–57; transnational trade in, 57–58; in United States, 48
Gibson-Graham, J. K., 223 n. 60

Giddens, Anthony, 119, 230 n. 89

Gill, K. P. S., 185

Gilligan, Carol, 236 n. 45

Gilroy, Paul, 50, 173, 225 n. 47, 225 n. 50, 228 n. 22, 236 n. 42, 239 n. 16

Global advertising, 94–95

Global citizenship, 44–45, 122, 130

Global community, 23–24

Global consumer, 80–120

Global feminism, 59–60, 124–25, 143, 152–57

Globalization: of publishing industry, 41; relevance of nation-state in, 80; as term, 22–23, 124

Globalized consumer subjects, 83–84, 91–96

Global marketing, 90–91, 98–99

Global Marketing and Advertising (De Mooij), 94–95

"Global" movement, against domestic violence, 155–57

"Global sisterhood," 152–53

Goethe, Johann Wolfgang von, 46–47

Goitein, S. D., 226 n. 56

Goldberg, Pamela, 176, 236 n. 54

Gonzalez, Carlos Avila, 216, 240 n. 31

Goodwin, Neva, 224 n. 75

Goodwin-Gill, Guy S., 236 n. 40

Gordon, Avery, 228 n. 27, 239 n. 13

Gordon, Colin, 202

Governance: human rights and, 122, 125; of populations, 17–18

Governmentality, 16–18; consumer culture and, 1–34; gender and, 197–198; human rights and, 123–24, 134–38, 157; nationalism produced by, 199; race and, 197–98; risk as form of, 201–3; the state and, 20, 198; of women's welfare, 141–42

Greatbatch, Jacqueline, 177, 237 n. 61

Grewal, Gurleen, 74, 227 n. 105

Grewal, Inderpal, 222 n. 37, 223 n. 60, 224 n. 76, 226 nn. 60–62, 226 n. 84, 233 n. 71, 237 n. 72, 239 n. 5

Grossberg, Lawrence, 225 n. 26, 235 n. 20

Grown, Karen, 131, 147, 231 n. 26, 233 n. 86

Guadalupe, Maria, 232 n. 68

Gunning, Isabelle, 237 n. 72

Gupta, Akhil, 131, 157, 231 n. 28, 234 n. 120

H-1B visa holders, 4–5, 14

Hagland, Paul EeNam Park, 142, 232 n. 69

Hall, Stuart, 13, 49, 90, 118, 221–22 n. 13, 222 n. 27, 222 n. 34, 225 nn. 44–45, 228 n. 23, 230 n. 85

Halter, Marilyn, 118, 221 n. 8, 230 n. 87

Hannerz, Ulf, 22, 23, 99, 223 n. 51, 229 n. 52

Harasym, Sarah, 222 n. 28

Hardt, Michael, 223 nn. 47–48, 223 n. 59, 225 n. 37, 225 n. 54, 227 n. 1

Hartmann, Susan M., 233 n. 77

Hasbro toys, 106, 108

Hathaway, James C., 236 n. 39

Helton, Arthur C., 235 n. 5

Helwig, 225 n. 25

Hendrickson, Hildi, 224 n. 75

Henkin, Louis, 149, 233 n. 95

Hernandez, Garcia, 232 n. 68

Hoosein, Mehnaz, 110

Howard, Rhoda, 135, 232 n. 46, 232 n. 50, 233 n. 89

Howes, David, 228 n. 7

Human rights: citizenship and, 11; cosmopolitan nature of, 143–44; development and, 130–34; as Eurocentric, 135; female subject in, 136–37; global citizenship and, 122, 130; global feminism and, 124–25, 152–57; governmentalization of, 123–24, 158–59; management of refugees and, 158–59; neoliberalism and, 124; as political platform, 122–23; refugee asylum and, 161; as sign of good governance, 125; social movements and, 173–74; as tool

of geopolitics, 149; transnationalization by, 142–43; universal applicability
of, 134–37, 143–44; as "white man's
burden," 123; women's rights as, 29,
32, 121–57
Human Rights Advocates Training Pro-
gram, 145
Human rights discourse: emergence of,
121–23; Indian nationalism and, 164;
knowledge produced by, 129–30; refu-
gees and, 161, 167–68; refugee subject
created by, 171–72
Human rights governmentality, 134–38
Human rights laws, 128–29
Human rights organizations, 151–52
Human rights violations, 175–76,
183–84
Human Rights Watch, 171–72
*Human Rights Watch Global Report on
Women's Human Rights*, 150
Huntington, Samuel, 149–50, 234 n. 96
"Hybridity," 36, 74–75, 113
Hyndman, Jennifer, 162, 235 n. 13
Hyphenation, 37, 60–61, 69–72

Identity: ability to change, 70; American
ethnic, 76–78; Barbie in India and,
119; citizenship and, 10–13; discourse
on, 36; formation of, 13–14, 28–29;
gendered, 26; hyphenated, 69–72; of
migrants, 11; national, 2; politics of,
95; production of, 27–28, 36–37
Ilumoka, Adetoun O., 128, 231 n. 20, 232
n. 55
Immigrants: America's meaning to, 2–3;
beauty pageants for, 113–14; choices
for, 63–65, 67; citizens vs., 5; fashion
of, 113–14; impoverished, 117–18; novels by, 62–63 (*see also* Literature); professional, 117–18; tech workers as, 5;
women, 62–65, 64. *See also* Migrants
Immigration, in United States, 14–15,
159–61
Immigration and Naturalization Service, 14

In an Antique Land (Ghosh), 39, 40, 49,
50–51
India: Barbie in, *see* Barbie; brand-name
goods in, 89; capitalism in, 31–32;
children as consumers in, 85–86,
106–8; consumers in, 31, 84–86, 92–
94, 103–11; domestic violence in, 154–
55; economic changes in, 82–83;
"English" education in, 40–41; fashion industry in, 110–11; feminism in,
31–32; foreign capital in, 88; human
rights in, 128–29, 150–51, 165, 192–
93; literature and, 40, 46, 61–62;
multinationals in, 86–87; nationalism
in, 77–78, 164; nation-state in, 80;
Non Resident Indians and, 87–89;
production of subjects in, 1; refugees
and, 166–67; resistance to Sikhs in,
185 (*see also* Sikhs); spice trade and,
52–53, 55; toy industry in, 105–6;
United States chosen over, 69–70;
women's rights in, 128; work oppor-
tunities in, 114–15
India Today, 114–17
Indian dress, Barbie in, 82, 96, 104
Indian immigrants, in United States, 5–7
Indians, "international," 115–16, 117
Information technology, 23–24
*In Our Own Words: A Guide for Human
Rights Education Facilitators*, 144
Institute for Women's Studies in Arab
World, 144–45
International Bill of Rights, 125–26
"International," imaginary of the,
148–49
"International" Indian, 115–16, 117
Internet, as metaphor, 24
Isin, Engin, 12, 222 nn. 17–19, 222 nn.
23–25
Islam, 178–80, 209–10. *See also* Middle
Eastern men
Itwaru, Arnold Harrichand, 73
"It Was Time to Play Ball Again at Pac-
Bell Park," 216
Iyer, Saroj, 127–28, 231 nn. 17–18

Jacka, Elizabeth, 224 n. 75

Jackman, Barbara, 235 n. 23, 237 nn. 82–83

James, Stanlie, 128, 231 n. 11, 231 n. 19

Jasmine (Mukherjee), 29; America in, 66–68, 69–70; as "Asian-American" literature, 72; colonialism in, 40; criticism of, 73–74; history of spices in, 76; India in, 66; migration in, 70–71, 72; national subject in, 39; readership of, 72–73; story of, 65–66; trope of Asian women and, 62. *See also* Mukherjee, Bharati

Jayawardena, Kumari, 226 n. 59

Jen, Gish, 64, 226 n. 78

Jhally, Sut, 229 n. 37

Jilani, Hina, 127

Johansson, Perry, 228 n. 7

John, Mary, 128, 231 n. 21

Joy Luck Club, The (Tan), 65

Kang, Laura, 228 n. 14

Kant, Immanuel, 42–43

Kaplan, Caren, 17, 32–33, 43–44, 143, 221 n. 9, 222 n. 37, 222 n. 40, 223 n. 60, 224 nn. 6–8, 224 n. 12, 224 n. 76, 225 n. 30, 225 n. 36, 226 n. 75, 229 n. 55, 230 n. 82, 233 n. 71, 235 n. 22, 237 n. 72

Kaplan, Robert, 83

Karlekar, 234 nn. 112–13

Karzai, Hamid, 133

Kasinga, Fauzia, 179

Keck, Margaret, 138, 154, 231 n. 13, 232 n. 59, 234 n. 107, 234 n. 110

Kelly, Nancy, 174, 188, 236 n. 46, 236 n. 50, 237 n. 57, 237 n. 59, 238 n. 91

Khan, Naseem, 113, 230 nn. 79–80

Kingston, Maxine Hong, 65, 226 n. 80

Kipling, Rudyard, 199

Kiron, David, 224 n. 75

Kiss, Elizabeth, 230 n. 1

Klein, Christina, 239 n. 24

Kline, Stephen, 229 n. 37

Knippling, Alpana Sharma, 227 n. 104

Knowledge production: the "global" created by, 22–23; human rights discourse and, 129–30; identity created by, 1, 28–29; Indian nationalism and, 164; literature's role in, 41–42; refugee subjects created by, 162; transnational subjects created by, 161

Koshy, Susan, 135, 137, 232 n. 43, 232 n. 57

Kosta, Marla, 215

Kothari, Rajni, 121, 135, 147, 148, 230 n. 2, 232 n. 44, 232 n. 45, 233 n. 80, 233 n. 81, 233 nn. 87–88

Kothari, Smitu, 135

Krishnaraj, Maitreyi, 140, 232 n. 66

Kymlicka, Will, 221–22 n. 13, 222 n. 20

Laden, Osama bin, 210

Laguerre, Michel S., 222 n. 21

Lal, Vinay, 54, 57, 225 n. 53, 226 n. 57

Landry, D., 237 n. 69

Lansang–De Mesa, Blandina, 231 n. 8, 232 n. 68, 233 n. 74

Larner, Wendy, 19, 223 n. 42

Lash, Scott, 31

Lawand, Kathleen, 236 n. 58

Lee, Ching Kwan, 229 n. 43

Lee, Jayne, 156, 234 nn. 117–19

Lee, Rachel C., 226 n. 68

Lee, Steven, 236 n. 38

Leiss, William, 229 n. 37

Leonard, Karen, 61, 226 n. 66

Lesbians, in Islamic states, 180

Levy, Simon, 236 n. 48

Literature: hybridity in, 74–75; Indian-American, 61–62; transnational connectivities in, 41; "world," 45–47. *See also individual works*

Lopez, George, 232 n. 65

Love, Emily, 236 n. 45

Lowe, Donald, 95, 229 n. 35, 229 nn. 38–39

Luibhéid, Eithne, 184, 237 n. 84

Lutton, Wayne, 237 n. 64

Macaulay, Thomas, 40, 224 n. 19

Macklin, Audrey, 178, 180–81, 236 n. 36, 237 n. 67, 237 n. 76

Maclean, G., 237 n. 69

Main Houn Mehnaz (Hoosein), 110

Making Waves (anthology), 62

Malini, Hema, 110

Malkki, Liisa, 149, 169–70, 174, 233 n. 92, 233 n. 94, 235 n. 6, 235 n. 29

Mankekar, Purnima, 112, 224 n. 5, 228 n. 24, 230 n. 78

Marchand, Roland, 221 n. 7, 224 n. 68, 228 n. 6

Marchetti, Gina, 239 n. 25

Marin, Leni, 231 n. 8, 232 n. 68, 233 n. 74

Marketing: of "American lifestyle," 94–96; of Barbie, 98–99, 106, 108; to consumer fantasies, 99–100; global, 90–92. *See also* Advertising

Marriage, arranged, 77

Marshall, T. H., 10, 27, 221 n. 12

Martin, Susan Forbes, 235 n. 30

Marx, Karl, 42–43

Master of the Universe toys, 107

Mattel: consumers created by, 89; corporate practices of, 96–100; Disney and, 97; fieldwork on, 84–85; international Barbies of, 94, 96–97; marketing strategies of, 99–100. *See also* Barbie, in India

Mbembe, Achille, 25, 198, 223 n. 45, 223 n. 57, 238 n. 3; 238–39 n. 4

McGruder, Aaron, 209, 239 n. 22

Mediterranean Society, A (Goitein), 55

Mehta, Zubin, 114–15

Mello, Michael, 239 n. 26

Menon, Nivedita, 137, 232 n. 56, 238 n. 97

Menon, Ritu, 193

Merry, Sally Engle, 138, 232 n. 49, 232 n. 60

Mexican-American women, 30

Middle East, feminism in, 177–78

Middle Eastern men: Bush administration on, 160; images after 9/11 of, 208–12; racism against, 212–13; security in United States and, 204–5; as social group, 197; as "terrorists," 203, 209

Middleman and Other Stories, The (Mukherjee), 72

Migrants: allegiances of, 8; America for, 2–14; citizenship and, 11, 35; cosmopolitanism of, 57; identity of, 11; "managing," 161; production of, 36; study of, 90–91. *See also* Immigrants

Migration, 49–50, 54–55. *See also* Immigration, in United States

Mill, James, 17, 222 n. 39

Miller, Daniel, 224 n. 75, 228 n. 7

Milton, Giles, 227 n. 109

Miss India (Hoosein), 110

Mistress of Spices, The (Divakaruni), 29, 39; colonialism in, 40; ethnic identity in, 78; modern and traditional in, 76–77; multiculturalism in, 74–78; nationalism in, 77–78; readership of, 76; story of, 75–76; trope of Asian women and, 62

Mitchell, Tim, 197, 238 n. 1

Moallem, Minoo, 237 n. 79, 239 n. 23

Mobility, 56; capitalism and, 44–45; nationalism and, 35; subjects of, 35–37

Modeling industry, in India, 110. *See also* Beauty pageants

Modernity: concept of choice in, 28; forms of selfhood in, 199–200; link with colonialism, 25; tradition and, 75–77, 79

Mohanty, Chandra, 223 n. 60, 232 n. 67

Moller, Susan, 10

Momsen, Janet, 131, 231 n. 27

Monde, Le, 206–7

Mondo Barbie (Ebersole, Peabody), 100–101

Montejo, Manual Diaz, 232 n. 68

Moretti, Franco, 225 n. 40

Morgan, Robin, 153, 234 n. 105

Mosco, Vincent, 24, 223 n. 55

Mother Jones, 71

Mouffe, Chantal, 221–22 n. 13, 222 n. 16, 223 n. 60

Mukherjee, Bharati, 224 n. 14, 224 n. 16, 226 nn. 70–71, 226 n. 81, 226 n. 85, 226 n. 87, 226 n. 89, 227 nn. 91–95; as American, 69; on hyphenation, 69–72; on India, 70; on "Indian-American" label, 39; as nationalist, 38–39, 65–74; success of, 62; as writer, 62

Mulligan, Maureen, 176, 236 n. 44, 236 n. 56

Multiculturalism: in America, 7, 77–78, 200–202; consumer citizenship and, 219–20; cosmopolitan, 74–78; global marketing practices and, 90–91

Murthy, K. V. Narasimha, 228 n. 21

Music, hybridity in, 113

Muslim males, surveillance of, 15. *See also* Middle Eastern men

Naidu, Sarojini, 47

Naipaul, V. S., 62

Nair, Mira, 226 n. 73

Nanda, Neeru, 109–10

Narayan, R. K., 62

Narratives, refugee asylum, 170–71, 186–87, 189–90

Nathan, Andrew J., 232 n. 40

Nation, ideas of, 45–46

Nation-states: citizenship and, 12, 147, 166; diasporic subjects in, 87–88; globalization and, 80; hyphenated subjects in, 60–61; the "international" for, 149; management of refugees in, 158–59; power of, 80; refugees and, 166, 169–70; statelessness and, 165–68

National Book Award Critics Circle Award, 72

National Human Rights Commission, 151

Nationalism: American, 8, 196–220; consumer culture as producing, 13, 27,

81; cosmopolitanism and, 43–44; in global economy, 118; governmentality producing, 199; Indian, 77–78, 164; as mobile, 35; refugees and, 166; the state and, 145–52

National subjects, 8, 37, 39, 158–95

Negri, Antonio, 223 nn. 47–48, 223 n. 59, 225 n. 37, 225 n. 54, 227 n. 1

Nelson, Cary, 225 n. 26, 235 n. 20

Neoliberalism: America as regulatory apparatus of, 26; as array of social movements, 16–17; feminism and, 26–34; governmentality and, 16–17; human rights' claims in context of, 124; nature of state and, 19–20; problem for critique of, 19

New Jersey, Indian communities in, 5–7

Newfield, Christopher, 228 n. 27

NGOS (nongovernmental organizations): activism and theory in, 141; civil society and, 138–45; global feminism and, 143; as grassroots organizations, 140–41; human rights and, 133, 142–43; as lobbying organizations, 139–40; nonwestern, 144; power of state protested by, 151–52; professionalizing work of, 141–42; refugees and, 171–72; role of, 138–39; UN and, 138; welfare work of, 142; on women's rights, 126–27; working with women, 194–95

9/11: America and "Americans" after, 196–97, 207–9; American flag after, 211–12, 214–16; "American way of life" after, 203–9; economy and, 218; Europe and, 206–7; images of, 207–8; Middle Eastern men and, 208–11; nationalism created by, 206–7; race and gender and, 32, 196–220

Nityanadam, Indira, 227 n. 100

Nobel, Alfred, 47

Nobel Prize, 45–47

Nomadism, 43–44

Nongovernmental organizations. *See* NGOS

Non Resident Indian (NRI), 87–90, 114–17

Non-West, 25, 31, 50, 129–30, 143–44. *See also* West

Novels: diaspora and, 35–79; immigrant, 46, 62–65. *See also* Literature

NRI (Non Resident Indian), 87–90, 114–17

Ohmae, Kenichi, 83, 228 n. 9

Ong, Aihwa, 12, 222 n. 22, 227 n. 111, 229 n. 43, 229 n. 60

Oomen, T. K., 221–22 n. 13

O'Tuathail, Geroid, 18–19, 162, 235 n. 12

Oza, Rupal, 228 n. 16

Pachauri, S. K., 234 n. 98

Pagnucco, Ron, 232 n. 65

Pandey, Gyanendra, 235 n. 19

Panini, M. N., 228 n. 17

Pannikar, Raimundo, 231 n. 4

Papademetrious, Demetrios, 235 n. 18

Pateman, Carole, 10, 221–22 n. 13

Peabody, Richard, 100–101, 229 n. 58

Pease, Donald E., 221 n. 9

Pederson, Susan, 237 n. 72

Peleg, Ilan, 232 n. 40

Petras, James, 139, 232 n. 63

Phillips, Alan, 221–22 n. 13, 222 n. 14

Place, ideas of, 35–36, 45–46

Pollack, Sheldon, 224 n. 3, 224 nn. 10–11

Pollitt, Katha, 237 n. 70

Populations, 17–18, 130–34

Postcolonial cosmopolitanism, 38, 45, 48–65

Power: feminist action as form of, 27; information technology and, 24; nature of United States', 21–22; new assemblages of, 25–26; theories of, 21–22

Prendergast, Christopher, 47, 225 n. 42

Professionals, Indian, 114–17

Publishing industry, 41

Punjab, women from, 193–94. *See also* Sikhs

Race: governmentality and, 197–98; after 9/11, 196–220; as product of culture, 27; social movements based on, 60; subjects of, 3, 32; visibility and, 209–17

Racism, against Middle Eastern men, 212–13

"Raising the Flag at Iwo Jima," 215

Rajagopal, Arvind, 104, 228 n. 19, 229 n. 68

Rajan, Rajeshwari Sunder, 222 n. 28, 232 n. 52

Rand, Erica, 84, 99–101, 228 n. 13, 229 n. 50, 229 n. 54, 229 nn. 56–57

Rawls, John, 10, 221 n. 12

Razack, Sherene, 170, 180, 235 nn. 31–32, 237 n. 75

Reagan, Ronald, 15

Recovery Operation, 193

Reddy, K. N., 228 n. 21

Rée, Jonathan, 51, 149, 225 n. 52, 233 n. 93

Refugee Act of 1980, 159–60, 172

Refugee asylum: encouraged testimony against homeland and, 181–82; gender-based, *see* Gender-based asylum claims; human rights discourse and, 161; laws governing, 172; transnational cultural politics and, 182–84

Refugee discourse, 168–71

Refugee Women (Malkki), 170

Refugees: defining, 169–70, 172; encouraged testimony of, 181–82; female, 163, 168, 170; gendering, 158–95, 171–77; havens for, 168–69; human rights discourse and, 167–68, 171–72; male, 170; management of, 158–59; as non-élite cosmopolitans, 167; number of, 165–66; in United States, 166–67. *See also* Sikhs

Reilly, Niamh, 231 n. 13

Religious nationalism, 52–54

Rescue, of "third world" subjects, 58–59, 152–54

Richmond, Anthony H., 168, 235 n. 24

Risk, as form of governmentality, 201–3
Rittich, Kerry, 231 n. 7
Ritzer, George, 30, 224 n. 70
Robbins, Bruce, 43, 143, 225 n. 32, 233
    nn. 72–73
Rodriguez, Gregory, 239 n. 28
Roosevelt, Franklin Delano, 218
Rosaldo, Renato, 226 n. 64, 239 n. 10
Rose, Nikolas, 15–16, 155, 198, 222 n. 35,
    223 n. 58, 231 n. 9, 234 n. 114, 238 n. 2
Rosenthal, Joe, 215
Rouse, Roger, 228 n. 25
Rousseau, Jean Jacques, 42–43
Roy, Anindyo, 227 n. 103
Roy, Parama, 227 n. 108
Rufino, Mark, 228 n. 7
Ruiz, Vicki, 30, 224 n. 64
Rumsfeld, Donald, 203–4, 239 n. 14
Rushdie, Salman, 40, 62, 225 n. 21
Russo, Anne, 223 n. 60
Rutgers Center for Women's Global
    Leadership, 153–54

Safran, William, 225 n. 48
Said, Edward, 48–49, 224 n. 2, 225
    n. 44
Salwar kameez, 113
Scanlon, Jennifer, 224 n. 72
Schein, Louisa, 101, 167, 229 n. 59, 229
    n. 61, 230 n. 81, 235 n. 21
Scialabba, Lori, 178–80, 237 n. 66, 237
    n. 80
Security, after 9/11, 160, 202–9
Selective immigration, 159–60
Selling Suffrage (Finnegan), 29
Sen, Gita, 131, 147, 231 n. 26, 233 n. 86
Sethi, Harsh, 135, 232 n. 47, 233 n. 91
Sexual abuse, 163
"Sexual citizenship," 12
Sexual identity, 170–71
Sexual orientation, 182
Shakhsari, Sima, 235 n. 33
Shales, Amity, 233 nn. 84–85
Shields, Rob, 24, 223 n. 56
Shohat, Ella, 239 n. 25

Shopping, as patriotic act, 217–19
Shopping for Identity: The Marketing of
    Ethnicity (Halter), 118
Sikhs: female, 161, 163–64, 184–95;
    male, 210–12
Sikkink, Kathryn, 138, 154, 231 n. 13, 232
    n. 59, 234 n. 107, 234 n. 110
Silicon Valley, 6–7
Sinclair, John, 224 n. 75
Singh, Pritam, 234 n. 102
Singh, Kirti, 129, 231 n. 23
Sklair, Leslie, 94, 228 n. 31
Slater, David, 221 n. 10
Slave trade, 50–52
Smith, Honor Ford, 232 n. 66
Smith, Jackie G., 232 n. 65
Smith, Neil, 222 n. 33
Smoodin, Eric, 206, 229 n. 45, 229 n. 55,
    239 n. 18
Social groups: asylum seekers as part of,
    174–75; Middle Eastern men as, 197;
    women as, 179
Social movements, human rights and,
    173–74
Spice trade, 50–54
Spijkerboer, Thomas, 181, 237 n. 78
Spivak, Gayatri, 34, 79, 123, 179, 222 n.
    28, 225 n. 51, 226 n. 58, 230 n. 3, 237
    n. 69
Stantis, Scott, 213, 239 n. 29
State, nationalism and, 145–52
State, nature of, 19–20
State of the World's Refugees, The, 160
State power, 20–21
Steiner, Henry J., 231 n. 12
Stevenson, Nick, 225 n. 27
Stoeltje, Beverly, 224 n. 75, 229 n. 67
Stoler, Ann, 197, 199, 223 n. 44, 234–35
    n. 2, 239 nn. 7–9
Subramanian, S., 151, 234 n. 100, 235 n.
    16
Suffrage, advertising, 29
Surveillance, of Muslim males, 15
Sussman, Warren, 206
Swedlund, Alan, 101, 229 n. 63

Tagore, Rabindranath, 45–47
Takaki, Ron, 61, 226 n. 69
Tan, Amy, 64, 226 n. 77
Tarlo, Emma, 224 n. 75, 228 n. 18
Taylor, Peter J., 221 n. 10
"Terrorism": "American way of life" and, 204–5; credibility of asylum claims and, 186–88; fear of, 213–14; idea of America and, 207; immigration and, 160; Middle Eastern men and, 203, 209
Thatcher, Margaret, 15
Thind, Bhagat Singh, 61
"Third world" female subject, 58–60, 78–79, 152
Thomas, Dorothy Q., 234 n. 108
Tomlinson, Alan, 230 n. 92
Torres, Lourdes, 223 n. 60
Trade: first cosmopolitans created by, 58; of slaves, 50–52; of spices, 50–51; transnational, 57–58
Tradition: Asian immigrant woman and, 64; in Divakaruni's writings, 39–40; "group rights" and, 135–36; modernity and, 75–77, 79
"Traditional" dress, for diasporic women, 113
Transnational connectivities, 3, 23; feminism and, 3–4; gendered subjects and, 163; the "global" and, 14–26; identity production and, 36–37; literature and, 41; logics of rule and, 25–26; U.S. feminists and, 147–48
Transnational consumers, 111–20
Transnational culture, 94–95
Transnational discourse, 168
"Transnational feminist cultural studies," 33
Transnational gendered subject, 192–95
Transnationalities, Indian, 80–120
Transnationalization, of human rights, 142–43
Transnational social movement organizations (TSMOS), 139
Transnational subjects, 158–95

Triechler, Paula, 225 n. 26, 235 n. 20
Trujillo, Carla, 222 n. 28
TSMOS (Transnational social movement organizations), 139
Tuitt, Patricia, 169, 174, 235 n. 25, 235 nn. 27–28
Tutt, Cordula, 221 n. 1
Typical American (Jen), 64

UN (United Nations), 138, 146–49; Commission on Human Rights, 132; High Commissioner for Refugees, 160, 172–73, 175
United Kingdom, immigrant communities in, 113–14
United Nations. *See* UN
United States: asylum seekers in, 165–67, 172–73, 186–88; consumer capitalism in, 30; domestic violence in, 152, 154, 155; freedom represented by, 170–71; as global power, 22; multiculturalism in, 77–78, 200–201; nationalism in, 2, 8, 69–70, 196–220; national subject in, 8; neoliberalism and, 26; question of empire and, 20–21; security in, 202–3; trope of women in, 62. *See also* "America"
Universal Declaration of Human Rights, 125–26
"Universal rights," 11
Urla, Jackie, 101, 229 n. 63
Urry, John, 31
"U.S. ethnic studies," 33

Vachani, Nilita, 230 n. 84
Vadackumchery, James, 234 n. 99
Vienna Declaration, 175
Violence, gender-based, 175–76, 179–80, 183–84
Violence Against Women Act, 156
Visibility, 209–17, 216–17
Visweswaran, Kamala, 224 n. 18

Waney, Arjun, 114–16
Warde, Alan, 119, 228 n. 11, 230 n. 91

Waters, Malcolm, 30, 224 n. 65, 224 n. 71

Welfare work, 139, 142, 148

West: depiction of women in, 59; human rights in, 129–30; non-West vs., 25. *See also* Non-West

"White man's burden," 123, 199

Wilk, Richard, 224 n. 75, 229 n. 67

Williams, Patricia J., 232 n. 51, 239 n. 15

Williams, Raymond, 205

Willshire-Carrera, John, 236 n. 59

Woman Warrior, The (Kingston), 65

Women: America for, 98–99, 171; as category, 136, 137; depiction of, 59; in development regimes, 131; as population, 129–30, 130–34; as social group, 179; "status of," 17; in United States, 62; working-class, 29–30; "worlding" of, 79

Women, Gender, and Human Rights (Agosin), 130

Women's novel, 62–65

Women's rights: in Asia, 127–28; under Bush administration, 133; as human rights, 29, 32, 121–57; in India, 128; in United States, 62

Women's welfare, 141–42

Wood, Patricia, 12, 222 nn. 17–19, 222 nn. 23–25

"World" citizenship, 43–44

World Conference on Human Rights, 121

"Worlding," of women, 79

"World" literature, 45–47

Wright, Shelley, 133, 232 n. 38

Wynyard, Robin, 228 n. 7

Young, Iris Marion, 221–22 n. 13

Inderpal Grewal is a professor and the director of
women's studies at the University of California, Irvine.

An earlier version of chapter 2 appeared in *positions: east
asia cultures critique* 7, no. 3 (winter 1999): 799–826, as
"Traveling Barbie: Indian Transnationality and New Consumer
Subjects." Sections of chapter 3 appeared in *Talking Visions:
Multicultural Feminism in a Transnational Age*, ed. Ella Shohat
(Cambridge: MIT Press, 1998), 501–30, as "On the New Global
Feminism and the Family of Nations," and some portions of that
chapter also were published in *Citizenship Studies* 3, no. 3 (1999):
337–54, as " 'Women's Rights as Human Rights': Feminist
Practices, Global Feminism and Human Rights Regimes in
Transnationality." An earlier version of chapter 5 appeared in
Social Identities 9, no. 4 (2003): 535–61, as "Transnational
America: Race, Gender and Citizenship after 9/11."

Library of Congress Cataloging-in-Publication Data
Grewal, Inderpal.
Transnational America : feminisms, diasporas, neoliberalisms /
Inderpal Grewal.
p. cm. — (Next wave)
Includes bibliographical references and index.
ISBN 0-8223-3532-8 (cloth : alk. paper)
ISBN 0-8223-3544-1 (pbk. : alk. paper)
1. Transnationalism. 2. Americanization. 3. East Indians—
United States. 4. Group identity. 5. National characteristics,
American. 6. Globalization—Social aspects. 7. Consumption
(Economics)—Social aspects. 8. Nationalism and feminism.
I. Title. II. Series.
HM1271.G74 2005
305.48'891411073'09049—dc22
2004028776